MW00715134

Bill McNeil Presents: Voice of the Pioneer

Bill McNeil presents

VOICE OF THE *PIONEER*

with Foreword by
Kenneth Bagnell

Doubleday Canada Limited, Toronto

Canadian Cataloguing in Publication Data

McNeil, Bill, 1924–
Bill McNeil presents Voice of the pioneer

ISBN 0-385-25195-5

1. Interview – Canada. 2. Canada – Biography.
3. Canada – History – 20th century – Biography.*
4. Voice of the Pioneer (Radio program).
I. Title. II. Title: Voice of the pioneer.

FC25.M263 1988 971.06′092′2 C88-094188-X
F1005.M263 1988

Design: The Dragon's Eye Press

Typesetting: Q Composition

Jacket photograph: Johnnie Eisen

Printed in the United States of America

Published by
Doubleday Canada Limited
105 Bond Street
Toronto, Ontario
M5B 1Y3

To Teresa and Gerald

Contents

Foreword

One day almost forty years ago, when I was in high school in Glace Bay, the old coal-mining town in Nova Scotia where I grew up, I was sitting in the auditorium where three men from the CBC's radio station in nearby Sydney were setting up their equipment to record a student event in which I was taking part. I cannot recall the event itself—whether it was a debate, a concert, or other program—but I would always recall the day. For it was that afternoon that one of the men from the CBC, whose name was Bill McNeil, introduced himself to me. He had been a local coal miner until a few months earlier, when he'd been hired as an announcer with the CBC.

He spoke to me that day just as he has spoken to generations of Canadians since, with a quiet, casual style, and a certain genuineness, that are the true revelations of the man he is. He was, I can still recall, much more interested in me and my future than he was in himself and his role, to which we attached more importance than he did.

For the next few decades, wherever I was in Canada, and heard the natural, deep voice on "News Roundup," "Assignment," "Voice of the Pioneer" and more recently, "Fresh Air," it was not just a voice from my past, but a reminder of a thoughtful man, whose personal qualities had become for me, as much a part of the sound of Canada in my generation, as his considerable talent.

There must be tens of thousands of us who are indebted to Bill McNeil. Some have been on his programs and been struck by the genuineness of his interest in what we did or tried to say. Others, probably the majority, have never met him but almost feel that they have. I suspect we feel that way because, in the growing tumult and clamour of the media culture, we turn to a man we trust, who speaks as he always has—in a quiet, modest way, with no pretention, and with the gift that true artists always have, of finding the extraordinary within the ordinary.

The pages of his new book and the people in them, whether famous or unknown, become memorable because of Bill McNeil. Free from cynicism and tempered with gentleness, his work leaves us all grateful and better.

Kenneth Bagnell
Toronto

Introduction

It's not likely that future generations will produce the same kinds of people or experiences that you'll find in this book. These "pioneers," as I like to call them, are closing out an era that is already almost gone. They are in a way "remainders," all of them, of a much quieter much softer time. They are of a generation that experienced changes like no generation before, from the horse-and-buggy to the rocket ship and man walking on the moon. No matter what happens in the future, no one will ever again experience such massive change in one lifetime again. There is practically nothing left of the world that these people knew. The motor car was still a novelty when they were born. There was no radio or television and only birds could fly. A computer was somebody who could add a list of numbers with paper and a pencil, and long day's journey was fifty miles.

Just think of the changes, the new in their lives. It would take fifty books the length of the Bible to list them, and yet they have managed to cope, which proves that there is no machine more astounding than the one called human.

The stories in this book give a glimpse of that other time, and I thank those who took the time to talk with me. I thank Eileen who had much more of a hand in the making of this book than merely typing the manuscript. I thank John Pearce and Maggie Reeves, the publishing team at Doubleday who exceeded even themselves in meeting an almost impossible deadline, and finally my editor, Kathy Richards, who brought it all together.

I've made my story one of the fifty stories in the book, not because I think I am in any way unusual, but rather because I was very usual in an unusual time.

Bill McNeil
Toronto
May 1988

Bill McNeil

The Will to Survive

There was a great deal of misery in Canada during the Depression years, that dark decade of 1929 to 1939 when the economy of the world collapsed. Unemployment rose to dizzying heights, and for a while it seemed as though not having a job was the norm. It was different from today, as social programs such as welfare and relief were weak or non-existent. Unemployment insurance did not exist. An ocean of soup was ladled out by volunteer workers from churches and other groups to long lines of desperate and shamed men, women, and children, who couldn't understand what was happening and felt guilty themselves for the poverty that was thrust upon them.

I was five years old when it began and fifteen when it was ended by the Second World War. I was still too young to end it the way some of my slightly older school chums did by joining the army, but I was old enough during the latter half of the Depression to observe the impact on my community and my neighbours, good people for the most part who simply accepted their lot and did the best they could.

The coal mines of Cape Breton operated on a sporadic basis, sometimes one day a week sometimes two and sometimes three. The miners, most of whom were paid by the day, would therefore earn something in the area of four, eight, or twelve dollars to survive on for a week. From this pitiful sum would be deducted twenty-five cents for the doctor, the same for the church, and fifty cents rent for the Company house in which he lived. The remainder was his to support what was often a large family of from four to twelve children in those days. Smaller households than that were the exception rather than the rule.

Fortunately, the ocean was nearby and men could fish — not for sport but for survival. They could also hunt in the woods. They could wander along the railroad tracks with a sack and pick up the lumps of coal that had fallen from the trains that were pulling the product of their labours to markets out of town. Many of them would jump on these trains at night heading for God knows where, looking for a promised land that didn't exist. Young people moved in hordes across the country ever in search of jobs, and they were beaten up and thrown off the trains by railroad police.

Some, the cream of our youth, were hauled off by the government to work camps in the woods cutting down trees for National Parks for "a dollar a day and board." Even children were expected to be soldiers in this "army for survival." They dodged the "Company cops" at the mine, and pilfered bits of scrap metal, which they sold for pennies to junkmen. They gathered wood from the same source to help keep the family fires burning.

Our parish priest, Father Ronald MacDonald, wheedled farm surplus cabbages, apples, and onions, and brought them to the schools, where he dumped them on the floors of classrooms and the children scrambled to get them.

In the dead centre of Cape Breton winters these children trudged off to school with newspapers stuffed in their leaky shoes, clad only in multi-patched, thin and inadequate garments, which the parish priest managed to get from some other family that was only slightly better off. The soup kitchen at noon was the only bright spot of the day for most of these ragged little victims of the economy.

Glace Bay was a mining town built on the cheap by the companies that came in to savage Cape Breton's resources. Glace Bay was a "Company Town" created to serve the needs of the company rather than the people who would live there. There were "Company stores", "Company houses," Company-built roads, Company-influenced officials to run the local governments, Company Doctors, Company-"Unions" and "Company" just-about-everything-else, including churches and schools. There were Company police forces and in times of labour unrest, there were Company "goon-squads" to hammer submissiveness into the miners with clubs and guns. The Company's immense influence extended not only to the local governing councils but also to the provincial and federal governments as well. The Company was God and the Company store was the provider of all the necessities of life. As such, it was used as a tool to keep the miners enslaved.

The Company store provided credit to the miners who soon found that the low wages they made were never sufficient to keep them from falling behind in their accounts. This was exactly what the Company wanted. A miner in debt was a miner who couldn't quit his job and move to some other part of the country. The inter-company network blacklist of delinquent accounts looked after that. No company in the country would hire somebody who owed money to another company. It was a jolly little system of perversion invented to overcome the inconvenience of anti-slavery laws. The system was extremely successful for a long period of time, even taking into account that the period of its success was one of the most violent in Canadian labour history.

As a last act of desperation, proud fathers, family heads, would sneak out at night to the "relief" station. Nobody would stoop to accepting relief except as a very last resort. It was considered to be the bottom of the barrel — the end of the road — and when a man was finally forced to do it, he would go only at night when there was less chance of his being recognized. He would use a dark and circuitous route of back streets and alleys, and he would hide in the shadows, sometimes for hours, waiting for a moment when nobody would see him there. His reward for all this might be a bit of butter or lard, some sugar or flour, and some bread — all of which he would place in a sack before taking the same back-alley route back to his home. This system of relief came to be known as "carrying the sack." No one wanted to do it,or to admit doing it.

Many children died during the Depression in Glace Bay. Nobody said they starved to death but that was actually the reason. They were so undernourished that even the germ of a bad cold could kill them. Plagues of scarlet fever, whooping cough, and diphtheria were common all through the thirties and those pitiful little bodies couldn't resist anything. Funerals with tiny white caskets were common.

My family was luckier than most, in that my father had a minor official job with the Coal Company and he worked steadily. This is not to say that there was a lot of money coming in because there wasn't, but it was enough to survive on, given my mother's ability to make-do. I think father's salary was in the vicinity of twenty-five or thirty dollars a week: enough to feed and clothe us, but never with anything left when payday arrived on Saturday. Even so, I knew we were comparatively rich when I entered the homes of my less fortunate friends. They had what looked to me like nothing — no covering on the floors, no furniture other than a kitchen table with a few chairs and a couple of old mattresses upstairs. Newspapers took the place of curtains. The only feeling I can recall about those visits is guilt, because comparatively we had "so much."

It's difficult looking back to explain why so many of these houses were so poorly heated in a town where the product was fuel. There was coal everywhere; in huge storage banks, in the railway cars heading out of town and in seams that cropped right out at the ground surface where one would imagine that anyone should have been able to dig it.

But this was not the case. These little seams, too small to be commercially valuable to the Company, were owned by the Company under a lease that gave them rights to *all* of the coal for a period of ninety-nine years. So even though people were practically freezing to death they couldn't mine that coal for their own use and the "Company cops" made sure that they didn't—not that the miners didn't try. "Bootleg pits," as they were called, sprang up all over and they tended to operate for a couple of weeks sometimes before the authorities found them and blasted them out of existence and threw the operators in jail. The operations of new bootleg mines, however, would start up the next day.

Battling the cold of winter was a constant war for the Cape Breton coal miners, and by 1939 there wasn't a loose stick of wood anywhere in town. Picket fences disappeared almost as fast as they went up and many of the houses were stripped as clean of shingles and clapboard as a chicken being prepared for the oven. Driftwood along the Atlantic shore was hauled away almost before it hit the beach and even telephone poles disappeared in the dead of night.

It's amazing how strong is the will to survive and to have a measure of pleasure while doing it. Anybody who could do anything in the way of entertainment took part in the free concerts put on by churches and organizations all over town. Local "stars" where born in the midst of the "famine," and just about every family had a member who knew the art of making a potent home brew out of potato peelings and other kitchen scraps. Those who didn't make it could buy a quart of it for a nickel. The woods around town were alive with moonshiners constantly moving their operations to foil the Mounties who seemed to have no other tasks but to pursue them. A twenty-five cent piece could purchase a pint of this potent alcohol, and despite the poverty many quarter-dollars changed hands.

People learned to entertain themselves for practically nothing in their own homes. A comb and a piece of tissue paper served as a musical instrument, and so did a couple of spoons knocked together by a skilled self-taught percussionist. Add a violin and a guitar, and—BINGO!—a party, better known as a "kitchen racket," was in full swing and everyone was welcome. There was hardly a night that a good kitchen racket couldn't be found in Glace Bay, and in the thirties news travelled fast.

My father's official job with the company gave him a bit more security than most workers enjoyed. He could be off work sick for a short while, for example, and still get paid. It also entitled him to a better Company-owned house. "Better" is used here as a relative term. It was the same kind of house in which all the miners lived except that it had a small kitchen area added on. In fact, it wasn't really a house. It was half a house, a storey-and-a-half, with a paper-thin wall dividing us from the family who lived next door. You didn't hear what was going on in your neighbour's half only if you tried not to, which wasn't often.

The ground floor of the houses without the added-on kitchen was divided into a dining-room and living-room, which was always called the front room, and there was a small area off the dining-room about the size of a pantry, which served as a kitchen. Here was located the cook-stove, the centre of heat for the house, and a small table where most of the dining was done. Since there was room for only three chairs, eating was done in shifts in most families, except on Sundays when the action shifted to the "dining-room" where everybody could eat at the same time. The dining-room earned its title only on Sundays because during the week it was where all the living went on. The kids played there and did their homework there. It was where Mother did her sewing and patching, and it was there that somebody was always stretched out on the couch. A secondary source of heat, a small stove, was the room's main attraction and the space around it was usually occupied during most of the year by bodies and articles of clothing drying out. Above this stove there was a hole in the ceiling which provided the only heat for the upstairs portion of the house.

The other downstairs room, the "front room" was seldom used except when special visitors came. If there was any good furniture at all, it was in the front room. If there was a rug in the house that is where it would be. If a family owned anything that they were proud of it would be found in the front room, something like a gramophone or a musical instrument. This was the room that was usually wallpapered and it was where the ancestors' pictures hung on the wall. The cushions there might have knitted covers and there was actually a fireplace that might be lit once a year during the Christmas season when it also became the room with a decorated tree. Christmas was the only time of the year when the door of the front room was left open and allowed to attain the same temperature as the other downstairs rooms. The rest of the time the door was kept closed and it took on its usual atmosphere of a tomb. I suppose the reason for this was that there had to be at least one "good" room and also that those Company houses, or "shacks," as most people called them, were extremely hard to heat. They were built on the ground with no basements, no insulation and plenty of cracks where the wind could whistle through. The marauding companies of the time never built anything with permanence in mind. "Get in fast, grab the loot and get out fast" seemed to be the corporate philosophy.

So they built the town of Glace Bay as quickly and as cheaply as possible. And they built my father's house which, despite their efforts, was a happy home, thanks to a loving and good set of parents.

In their outward manner to the world my mother and father were as different as chalk and cheese. Mama, as we always called her, was demonstrably loving, always there with a laugh or a smile, a word of praise or a hug. Papa was a shy man who had great difficulty showing his affection, but we had no doubt at all that he loved us. He too would praise and hug but only when he had a few drinks of black Demerara rum, the only thing that could bring him out of his shy cocoon. The rest of the time he was usually immersed in his other great love, the books that gave him the knowledge that most miners' children were denied. He had attained grade eight by the age of fourteen, and in the mining world of Glace Bay in 1910, that was considered more than enough education for someone who was destined to labour in the bowels of the earth. So 1910 was the year that my father, Russell McNeil, began his fifty-three-year career as a Cape Breton coal miner.

When I became sensitive enough to think about such things in my teens, and as I watched this man pore over his engineering and mining books at the dining-room table, I tried to picture the agony he must have felt at the age of fourteen when the system told him he had all the education he would ever need. When I was in high school, it was this grade eight dropout who explained algebra and geometry to me when I got stuck. It was he who could toss off chemical formulas and equations, and it was he who could converse a little bit with the immigrants of many tongues who came from all over the world to work in the mines of Cape Breton. This was Russell, my Papa. He got more excited than I did when I came home with a good report card from school. That shy guy who was always reading was quite a guy. I told him that one day and I never saw anyone more embarrassed. I'm glad I did, though. At this stage of my life it gives me great satisfaction to know that I told him so while he was still alive and able to enjoy hearing it.

If Papa was shy, Mama was effusive, especially with love, affection, and praise. She praised us for everything, even for getting out of bed and dressing ourselves in the morning. She made that sound like a major accomplishment. She was always the first up, shaking the ashes out of the stove and bringing the temperature of the kitchen up to a cozy level before anyone else was allowed to appear. She always had breakfast ready and she let out a cry of delight as each of her children appeared on the scene to start a new day. "Oh ... it's Bill!" or " ... it's Teresa!", "It's Gerald!", "It's Harold!" Mama tried to make each of us feel that the very act of joining the family circle each morning was a cause for celebration.

"Are you warm enough, dear? Come over here by the stove till your blood starts to flow."

She put great store by hearty breakfasts and there was always a good one awaiting us when we got up. If there was no money for anything else, Mama made sure that there was good hearty food. In the winter there was always oatmeal porridge to begin and there were tea biscuits, fresh homemade bread, bacon and eggs and pots of good tea. Some mornings there'd even be fried potatoes and steak — "Something to stick to your ribs."

Her molasses cookies, thick and substantial, were the best I ever tasted and there were always plenty to be had. Spread with a slab of butter, they were enough to delight an angel. She made sweet tea biscuits with raisins that were a meal in themselves. Her bread was unbeatable. Mama was the cook of the world. Anything she prepared was good and I never saw her use a recipe. Her meals just happened, with an absolute minimum of fuss or bother. She just seemed to know what to do; when the oven was "right" to pop things in and when it was time to take them out. Most of the neighbourhood people, especially cousins, must have known how good a cook she was, because there were always others popping up exactly at meal time. What's more they were always accommodated too.

"No trouble at all, dear, and there's more than we can possibly eat ourselves."

Which was the truth. No matter how much was eaten or how good it was, there was always a bit left for later.

Another thing about Mama: she was never fully convinced that anyone had eaten enough. Regardless of how bursting your belly was, she was always forcing another slice of meat on you, another slice of bread or another piece of her superb pie or cake. It did no good to protest either because it would already be there in front of you and if you didn't eat it, "it will only go to waste."

Did Mama know how good a cook she was? I really don't think so. She was always talking about and envying the culinary talents of others.

"Oh my," she'd say, "how I could do with a piece of Julia Gillis' lemon meringue pie", or "Mrs. O'Brien makes such good bread. I just don't know what it is she does to make it so good."

This wasn't the insincere hyperbole of the expert either. Even though her own bread and pies were acknowledged by all to be fit for the gods, she would often buy a pie from Julia or trade something else to get a loaf of Mrs. O'Brien's bread. As far as we children were concerned, Julia and Mrs. O'Brien were okay as cooks, but they weren't in Mama's league at all.

If Mama's kitchen was the warmest spot in the house, that upstairs half-storey was certainly the coldest. Except for that little hole cut through the ceiling over the dining-room stove, there was no heat at all. Hardly any heat came through the hole anyway, because the frigid downstairs air seemed to suck up any warmth that was available.

In those long Cape Breton winters, upstairs was a place you didn't go unless you had a reason, and that reason was usually that that was where the beds were.You had to steel yourself to face the upstairs when it came time to go to sleep. To leave the warmth of the dining-room and open the door to the small hall that led to the stairs was an act of supreme courage every night. If you thought the hall was cold, it was just a small preview of what waited at the top of the stairs where your breath was expelled in white clouds. The oilcloth covering on the floors was as cold as the ice surface of an outdoor skating-rink. The windows were covered with frost so thick that it was almost impossible to melt a hole with your thumb to see through to the outdoors. The thumb would freeze first. There was frost on the walls, on the floors, and on the ceiling. Touch a damp hand to any piece of metal and your hand would stick there. The beds would be piled so thick with blankets and quilts that once you got under them, it was difficult to even turn over during the night.

To deal with all of this, we learned to waste no time when leaving the warmth of the downstairs. We raced to get up the stairs in as few strides as possible and across the cold oilcloth and under the covers still fully clothed. Once there, we waited till things warmed up a bit before removing the daytime garments and kicking them out on the floor by the side of the bed where they could be retrieved easily in the morning. Of course, by then, they too would have to be brought in under the covers, one at a time, to warm up.

Your day would start by dressing under the blankets and then racing down the same way you had come up. Anyone who hasn't experienced it can only try to imagine how lovely it was to reach the cozy warmth of Mama's kitchen. If there is such a thing as heaven, it couldn't be much better than that.

I always thought that our house was fairly big when I was small myself but I didn't realize how very small it really was until I went back many years later and had a look. I guess everybody experiences feelings akin to this. Even the distances between places that you thought were immense as a child seem to shrink to nothingness when revisited as an adult. Those miners' half-houses were really very small, obviously designed by someone who had only one thought in mind, "what is the least amount of space they can get by on?"

The upstairs had a small landing, from which three doors led off to three very small bedrooms which were big enough for a bed and maybe a piece of furniture like a dresser or a commode. There were no closets in any of the rooms so that, as you can well imagine, there were many nails driven into the walls and the doors to accommodate clothing.

There were very few places upstairs where one could stand up straight because of the slant of the roofs under which the bedrooms were located. The only exception was the landing. It had no ceiling slant but it did have a hatchway to the attic, which was simply whatever space was left under the peak of the roof. If it was cold upstairs, the attic was even colder. Nothing separated the attic from the outdoors except the boards on the walls and the clapboard or shingles that covered them. It was up there that we stored our Christmas decorations and precious little else.

To get up in the attic you needed a stepladder and the eyes of an owl. There was no light of course, so that any storing that was done was usually done no farther than you could reach from the stepladder. It was opened in winter only to pull out the box with the Christmas decorations, and it was opened once more after the holiday to shove them back in again.

The first time I was called on to do that I got the fright of my life. It was after my eyes had become accustomed to the dark. I could see all of these little white balls clinging to the boards of the roof. I thought we had been invaded by swarms of wasps or some other insects that had built their cocoons in our attic. I went down screaming for my father to come take a look. He went racing up the stairs and up the ladder, not knowing, what to expect, I guess. After sticking his head through the hatch for a few moments, he came down the ladder laughing.

"Your cocoons, Bill, are just balls of frost on the tips of the nails coming through from the shingles."

Each half-house had a yard about forty by one hundred feet and it contained two very necessary small buildings, a coal house and a privy. Inside toilets weren't installed in Glace Bay until well into the 1930s and then it was only officials of the mine who got them. The yard itself was enclosed by a picket fence kept nicely whitewashed by the miners themselves with supplies provided by the Company. It was in the Company's interest, of course, to keep their property looking good. They had a team of carpenters and painters who looked after maintenance and the miners were encouraged to report any deficiencies or damage, including broken windows or cracked plaster and things like that. Once about every two years their paint-wagon would come around and spray on a new coat of paint to the outside. The colours were always the darkest of shades in green or brown so they wouldn't show the coal dust and smoke from the mine, but the paint job sure helped to freshen things up.

In the spring just about every miner could be seen digging up the ground in front of his house for a flower garden, and in the backyard a patch for vegetables, mainly carrots and potatoes. Most of them built extra structures like workshops and garages in their backyards too, which they painted and decorated with a great deal of care. They put gates, which they also built themselves, on their driveways and they demonstrated pride and ingenuity in the design. They grassed their backyards and they planted a great number of trees. However, the greening of Glace Bay was not an easy task. Located right on the Cape Breton shoreline, the land was hardly an agriculturalist's dream. The salt Atlantic air made it difficult to grow anything and those trees that did take root were stunted and bent by the wind. Sulphurous soot from the smokestacks at the mine played havoc with any plants that survived the salt. However, and perhaps miraculously, some things managed to make it and the black of the mines was at least partially counteracted by the dahlias, nasturtiums, wild roses, and other determined species that bloomed despite it all.

The houses were built in neat rows of nine doubles on each side of eight streets, with the exception of the first street which only had one row. The streets themselves were made of clay and slag from the mine, a mixture that could be as hard as concrete when dry but a quagmire during a rainy period. Along the top of these rows was another street called West Avenue and at the bottom of the rows was a parallel street to West Avenue called Centre Avenue. The streets were never accorded the dignity of proper names so they ended up as First, Second, Third, and so on. We all lived with a conglomeration of numbers for an address. Mine was 434 3rd Street, 4th Row, Number Two (which is what my part of Glace Bay was called, being named for Number Two, the mine located in that vicinity). There was a more formal name for Number Two—it was New Aberdeen—but nobody ever called it that unless they were "putting on airs" or "trying to be snooty." Most of the time New Aberdeen was just plain old Number Two and still is.

Other sections of town which went by numbers instead of their "snooty" names were Number Four (Caledonia) and Number Eleven (Passchendaele). Then there were sections that actually had names with no numbers attached. These were Hub, Sterling, Bridgeport, and Table Head. These, too, had miners' houses, somewhat like those in Number Two, but not exactly. They were laid out in rows and streets like Number Two but again not exactly.

The little communities surrounding the borders of Glace Bay were also part of the overall company plan, but some of them had town status themselves—places like Dominion and Reserve. They were part of us, and yet somehow they weren't. Except for the men who may have worked in the same mine together, people from Glace Bay, Reserve and Dominion hardly knew each other at all. Within the borders of Glace Bay itself it was the same thing. People from Number Two didn't know and didn't bother with the people from Number Four or Number Eleven. Each of these small communities developed in its own way and after a while the people took on characteristics that made them instantly recognizable as being from another part of town. A stranger wandering around Number Two was not only recognized as a stranger; he could be spotted as somebody from "over Number Eleven" way or from Table Head or Number Four. It might be the way a boy wore his cap or a girl wore her hair, or it might be the way a stranger said a certain word that marked him or her as not belonging to our part of town. The boys from the Hub wore their caps so that the peaks pointed straight up at the sky. Those from Table Head wore them backwards with the peaks pointing out from the backs of their necks, while those from Number Two had the caps pulled far forward with the peaks pointing down to cover their eyes and nose from the sun. Little things like that were used to proudly stamp regional identification on everyone.

Even within these regions of town there were further divisions. Number Two where I lived, for example, was chock full of divisions. Those who lived down beyond the fifteen rows I've already described, down close to the Catholic church, St. John's, referred to their section as Holy Row. They had a reputation, however, of being anything but holy. One of the town's most notorious prostitutes lived there as well as two or three of the best-known bootleggers.

Another section of Number Two was called "The Shacks." The houses here were much smaller single-unit dwellings occupied mainly by non-English-speaking newcomers to Canada from Eastern Europe. Without any sense of embarrassment or discrimination, they were always referred to as Hunkies, Dagos, and Wops. Their houses were spread out along a single muddy street that ran next to the railroad line which carried the coal cars out of town. They were also so close to the surface workings of the mine that they were constantly being showered with clouds of dust from the crusher and black smoke from the stacks. Many of the occupants pursued the second career of bootlegging also.

The one element common to us all was poverty. The only difference that separated us was the degree of the poverty. Even the mine officials, like my father, were just barely making it. There wasn't a built-in margin for luxuries like sickness or even the tiniest bit of waste, but in spite of this there was always something for those who came knocking at the door: "Mama wants to know if you can lend her a cup of sugar"—flour, milk—or whatever.

I remember bringing one of my friends into our kitchen one day just as Mama was taking a pan of her molasses cookies out of the oven. She buttered two of them, one for each of us, and sent us back outside to play. A short time later after Billy had departed for home and I was back inside, there was a knock at our door. There on the step stood Billy with a kitchen plate in his hand which he thrust towards my mother: "Mama wants to know if you can lend her six molasses cookies."

He got them, of course, and I'm sure he never knew that he had repaid us a thousand times over with that often-repeated favourite family story of the Depression years.

Those were the kinds of stories that people love to remember. The rest—those of misery, hunger and despair—most of us want to bury and forget. When the car came along in 1939 and provided steady work and regular money for the first time in ten years, Cape Bretoners were just like all the rest of the Depression survivors; they couldn't wait to throw out of their houses anything that reminded them of the recent past. Out went the old brass beds, the wooden kitchen chairs, the old dressers, and the commodes. In came the Masonite and the chrome, the shiny stuff, modern junk that fell apart in less than a year. "But who cares? We'll just get more. Happy days are here again, and anyway, Saturday is payday."

All over the country and much of the world, it was the same story—men and women struggling to survive a disaster that even to this day nobody can explain satisfactorily. Why, for those ten years, was there nothing and why suddenly when war was declared was there plenty?

The Depression left a mark on all of us who went through it, a mark that can never be erased. It shows most in the way we constantly attempt to instill the virtues of thrift and security into our children, much to their everlasting boredom. It shows up in the horror we express at "the price of things today." It shows in our constant search for bargains, in our desire to get the most out of everything we pay for and our unwillingness to throw anything out. We invent uses for the garbage of the throwaway society and we try to fix everything ourselves—just as our parents did. And, oh yes, our spare cash goes into the bank.

Kate Hair

That Northern Feeling

I believe that those who live in the northern regions of the world possess a special kind of vitality. They seem less inclined to be satisfied with being like everybody else. Canada's northern residents seem to be more independent and more able to exist by themselves without a need for constant companionship. They display a greater love of the land on which they live, and even a pugilistic defensiveness towards those who would downgrade "their" home.

Everyone in the North seems to be a "character." These people are just not like the people who live on your street. They might shock a person from the south with their forthright manner and opinions, and they will more than likely make their feelings known if they don't like something or somebody. If, on the other hand, they do like something or someone, they usually express that in an equally enthusiastic way. Even the oldest among them show an almost child-like "joie de vivre".

Such was Kate Hair, a lady of ninety-eight years whom I met in Toronto. She looked to weigh not much more than a hundred pounds, and her vitality put me, forty years her junior, to shame. She didn't move about. She dashed! In and out of her chair to retrieve a book or a souvenir to show me, telling stories and laughing, plainly enjoying the experience of talking of the great life she had had, most of it in the vast expanse of Northern Ontario.

People should spend more of their time enjoying their short stay on earth. I've always tried to do that, and I still do. I played golf till I was ninety-six, and even now I like to get out with my friends, perhaps carrying a putter around the course. Maybe I can't whack the ball the way I could, but I can enjoy the walk in the outdoors and the banter with my friends. I love doing that, and I love this country.

Kate Hair

My father, the Reverend Mr. Rose, came here from Scotland as minister of a new church which was being built in Toronto before the turn of the century; but do you know, before that church was finished he died, leaving my mother with five children and very little money. She was a terrific woman who worked hard to see that we were all well-fed and well-clothed and got decent educations. Every one of us managed to get into one of the professions.

Mine was nursing, and I'm glad it was, because that's how I met my husband. He was an intern at Toronto General Hospital and it was a time when the medical profession was still doing things that many today would consider pretty primitive. It was because of one of those "primitive" practices that we got together!

I was a probationer. Brand new there in 1904. He was already a doctor, but just beginning. I was on night duty and it was two o'clock in the morning, and what do I see, but this stream of blood coming across the hallway towards me. I gave a bit of a squeal and this house surgeon poked his head out of the room where the blood was coming from and he said, "Whatever is going on out here?" I said, "I'm the one that wants to know whatever is going on—Doctor." He looked at me and laughed and said, "Don't you know what that is?" I said, "No, I do not." "Well," he said, "this man in here has had to have leeches put on his eyes to draw the blood out, and the leech you see at the head of that stream just took out more than he can carry, and he's trailing it out to the floor."

You see, they used leeches to draw off excess blood in those days. It doesn't sound very nice, but it worked. Well, it may have scared the life out of me, but it gave me an introduction to Charles Harvey Hair, the man I would eventually marry. That would be a few years down the road, though, because after his internship was over he went away up to the Noranda-Red Lake area of Northern Ontario where he began his medical practice. He loved the north, and spent his life there until the day he retired at the age of almost eighty.

So many important events were happening up there. The town of Cobalt was just getting going after the big silver discovery of 1902. Charlie was in on all of that because he went in 1904, at the very fever pitch of the new mines opening up, the new companies forming and so on. The excitement there was like the Klondike with everybody dreaming of riches. It was a real frontier town.

My Charlie was up there working by the time I was getting ready to graduate in 1907. One day he phoned me long distance, and said, "How would you like bacon and eggs for breakfast on the day you graduate in June?" "Will you be here?" says I. "Yes, I will," he said, "and I want you tell me at that time the date we'll be married."

Well, I was in heaven, I'll tell you. In June he was there for bacon and eggs as promised, and it was then that I told him we could be married in two years, in June of 1909. He went back to looking after his medical practice, while I stayed here doing my nursing stint. Of course, he'd write many letters, and come down to see me by train quite often. Also, he was buying up stock in the mines that were opening up in Cobalt. It was a form of gambling, you see. No one knew which of the mines had anything worthwhile, so buying stock was something like buying tickets in a raffle. The stock certificates were beautiful to look at, though. I remember in later years we papered the inside of one of our outhouses with certificates that hadn't worked out — so they weren't exactly worthless, were they?

When Charlie took me up there as his bride, the miners had created a fund for a hospital, by contributing a dollar a week. When the hospital was built, Charlie went in there as their doctor and had a regular salary. That was the first time he had any money really, because up to then it was just work for fees — a little bit here, and a little bit there, but now there was regular money coming in, and just in time for the beginning of our life together in the North.

I have a little piece of white quartz here. Do you know what this reminds me of? This is from one of the most famous gold mines in this country — the Dome — *before* it opened, when it was only a hope and a dream. In 1909 — or was it 1910? — Charlie and I drove north to Schumacher from Cobalt. He and a friend had plans to open a drugstore there, because by that time, other mining ventures were spreading north of Cobalt and drugstores and things like that were needed.

When we finished up that business, we were invited to see what somebody called "a dome of quartz" that some prospectors had discovered under some soil, grass, and shrubs. There just didn't seem to be any end to this quartz, so they brought in a pump and washed away all the ground cover. It was really a sight to see, just like the magnificent dome of St. Paul's Cathedral in London, which I saw many years later. When the sun hit that quartz dome, it glowed like something from out of this world. Well, that was the start of the Dome Mine, which was one of the richest gold mines ever discovered.

Everything in the North was exciting at the time and so full of promise. When the stock came on the market, Charlie and I bought whatever we could afford. Because he was the doctor for all of the mines, people expected that he should buy some just to show his support. Much of it was no good at all, but some, like the Dome, more than made up for the bad ones. Also, because we were stockholders, we were invited to the pouring of the first gold brick from the Dome mine. The furnace was underground, and that was something I'll remember all of my life.

The miners had a superstition that women underground brought bad luck. Therefore, in order to disguise me, they fitted me out just like a miner, with big trousers, sweater, mask, helmet, and jacket. So good was the disguise that I couldn't even recognize myself. Then Charlie and I went down with the president of the company and two or three other big officials. This was a ceremony they always had at a mine for "first pouring," because that was quite an event.

It was a wonderful sight to see. First of all, there was a cement box mounted on one of the ore carriers and that was pushed over in front of the metal door which sealed the furnace up. Then a couple of miners, armed with huge iron spikes banged the door until it opened. Out poured this molten gold into the box. The few splashes that went onto the floor were carefully picked up for future re-melting. After that, the whole party of us, including the president, were searched before we left. By this time, the metal had cooled and the cement box was broken away from a huge brick of gold.

What a sight that was, as it was brought over, open to view, to the railroad station platform, to wait for the next T. & O. train for Toronto. They put one man with a gun there to guard it, but nobody could've picked it up anyway. It was so heavy. Even if they could, how would they ever get it out of the North? There were no roads in those days.

I have a little box here chock full of souvenirs of those times. This, for example, is a piece of silver from Cobalt's famed silver sidewalk, which was discovered by prospector Clem Foster. He was walking along when the cleat on his heel scratched on something metallic. When he bent down to brush away the dirt cover, it was solid silver everywhere.

This little box has all sorts of things like that. Here's a splash of metal from when they poured one of the first silver ingots, and I have a small piece of gold ore from the Dome Mine in South Porcupine around the time it first opened in 1909. None of these things are valuable — except to me. No matter what it is I pull from this box, it takes me back to those wonderful northern years.

As far as I'm concerned, there are two places in the world to live. One is Edinburgh, Scotland, where I was born, and the other is Canada's northland. I can say that even bearing in mind some of the terrible fire disasters that took place while I lived there.

In 1911, there was a fire in Cobalt that just about totally destroyed the town. A forest fire swept over the town, dropping great balls of fire that set a torch to everything, and the only escape was to take to the water. I can remember sitting out the whole thing in a rowboat in Lake Temiscaming with my less-than-a-year-old baby and my case of flat silver, which was a wedding gift. We sat in that little boat for an entire day and two nights until the fire burned itself out. My husband kept his car going all that time, driving people out of the fire area.

Altogether I've been through three of those awful fires in the North. They were the bane of the settlers' existence, and even in a boat on the water, you weren't free of it at all. There was terrible heat and flying bits of lighted debris falling all around you.

I remember sitting in the boat and seeing the flames advance like a cloud and jump right over our heads, setting fire to the trees on the other side of the lake. Sure, it was frightening while it was happening, but it never made me want to leave the North. All a person wanted was to survive it and get on with life. Whatever will be will be. What's the point in crying about something you can't control?

It's like me today, for instance. I'm ninety-eight years old, and although I'd like to be younger, there's nothing I can do about my age. I had to give up my golf two years ago, and my bowling when I was ninety-two. I still make the best of it and do things to get the most out of life. And I do that by liking people, not things. You don't learn that till you're eighty. You may think at eighty that the end of your life has come, but it hasn't unless you want it to.

My dear Charlie died on the eve of our fiftieth wedding anniversary. We had all the invitations sent out when he took this stroke and died. He was eighty and I was a few years younger, and for a while I wanted to die too. But that wouldn't have done anything for me or anyone else, so I just went on the way Charlie would have wanted me to. The sadness passes after a while. You still have all of your wonderful memories, and best of all you have your friends. So here I am at ninety-eight, banging right on for one hundred and wishing I could make it to two hundred.

David Pitt

Child of an Outport Manse

The outports of Newfoundland are tiny fishing villages scattered all along the rocky coast that were accessible only by boat until well into this century. Unconnected even to the rest of the province by roads, the outport was the whole world to most of those who lived there. They were born, lived their lives, and died there, seldom if ever seeing a stranger.

The outport merchant controlled the lives of the residents, offering or withholding credit, and setting the price for the fish. The men were often away for months at sea fishing, while the women raised their families. The mainland churches established missions and schools in the communities.

Despite meagre opportunities, many of Newfoundland's finest people came from outports — men such as Ned Pratt, the famous Newfoundland poet, and David Pitt, author of a 1969 biography of Pratt and Professor Emeritus of English at Newfoundland's Memorial University. Like Pratt, Pitt was the son of a minister, whose only advantage was the books in his father's study at home.

My father was posted by his Methodist church in England to outport duty in Newfoundland early in the century by the Overseas Missionary Service. He didn't know where he was being sent. It could have been darkest Africa or darkest Newfoundland. In fact he had to dig out an atlas to see where Newfoundland was. One of his friends told him he thought it was near Australia. In any event he was sent to the outport of Musgrave and that's where I was born. We spent the usual stint of three or four years there before moving on to another, which was the practice at the time.

The minister's children didn't really become part of the outport community as did other children, because to be a true part you had to be born to an outport family. However, much depended on the individual as to how much they were accepted. In Pratt's case, his father, who was also a minister, didn't want him to mingle with the fishermen's families, who he referred to as "the world of the great unsaved." He thought that their influence on his own family wouldn't be particularly salutary.

My father, on the other hand, didn't have that attitude at all. In fact, he encouraged our mixing, which we did, but the truth is, we were still outsiders due to the different influences on our lives. My father was a university man who had plenty of books, and because of this I began reading at a very early age. There were no libraries in the outports then — and I'm talking here about the thirties, when I grew up.

They really were the hungry thirties in the outports. Nobody starved, but life was pretty rough in many ways. The minister, of course, was right in the centre of it. He would receive these huge bales of used clothing, "poor barrels," which were sent by the central headquarters of the church in Toronto. Much of my own clothing came out of those "poor barrels". I couldn't have gone to school without them. My father told us that he had first choice of these clothes sent down by the rich in Toronto and other parts of Canada. The minister received very little money there, so we were as happy as anyone else to get these castoffs.

Father would announce from the pulpit that new poor barrels had arrived and after the service the congregation would come around as he distributed the contents as equitably as possible.

I can't remember if I or any of the outport children were ever unhappy with our poverty. I guess you don't miss what you never had. In the course of a year, my father would see very little cash because fishermen were getting practically none at all and were therefore unable to pay anything for church dues. The fishermen were practically owned by the outport merchant, who outfitted them in the spring and carried them on credit during summer. In the fall they had to pay off their debts from the catch, which left them very very little cash. Then the merchant would carry them on credit over the winter months. When they came back from the seal fishery in the spring, they'd have to pay all of this back, if indeed they made enough to do that. It was hand-to-mouth and season-to-season, and as a result my father was often paid his dues with fish, potatoes, turnips, or whatever. This was all most welcome, but it also meant that we never saw luxuries of any kind.

Father got a small supplement from church headquarters, but it wasn't a lot. I think the most he ever got was eighty dollars quarterly. That was often the only cash he ever saw during the worst of the Depression, from about 1931 through to 1936.

We were then living in the outport of Wesleyville, which was north of Bonavista Bay. It was completely dependent on the fishery at a time when the bottom completely fell out of the market. The fishermen were getting a dollar-fifty a kentle, and a kentle is 112 pounds. That's only a little over a cent a pound. It really was a desperate situation for most families including ours, but I must say that those people did their best to support their minister, even under those terrible conditions.

They never talked of poverty at all, and I don't know that they even considered themselves poor. The took it all very stoically, which is very typical of the Newfoundlander. They never railed against Providence, or even against politicians, except on very rare occasions in St. John's. There was one bit of a fuss one time in Wesleyville over the dealing out of the dole, which was six cents a day—$1.80 a month. One had to be just about destitute to get on the dole in the first place. That six cents a day would buy a little flour, some molasses and fat pork and not much else, but some were forced to get by on that with whatever they could grow in small gardens. In addition, they might keep a few chickens, hunt sea birds, and catch an occasional fish. The name of the whole game was survival.

The gardens in Wesleyville weren't much. The land was extremely rocky and the soil was very shallow. Most of it had to be carted in from the outside. Even the cemeteries had to be built on solid rock with wooden restraining walls to hold the soil that was brought in from ten to twelve miles inland. When a grave was excavated, it had to be dug right down to the solid rock. There would be just enough room on top for a few inches of soil when the casket was placed in. When the heavy rains of fall came, much of the soil would go with the runoff, and some of the caskets would be exposed. That was often one of my jobs—going with my father and covering them up again.

We had our amusements too, of course. As kids we were all well aware that life was hard and there was no money, but we managed to still have fun. At school we had our recreations and plenty of indoor games. We'd fly our kites in the spring and play hopscotch and marbles. In winter we'd skate on the many ponds in the area after school and we'd go sledding. Sometimes too, we'd go for dog rides. The dog team, in fact, was the only method of transportation there, apart from boats. We had no cars and even if we had, there was nowhere to go as there were no roads.

My big pastime was reading, and trying my hand at writing. I wrote my first poem when I was twelve, and I pray now that nobody ever digs it out!

Religion was an important part of outport life, with the church itself being the centre of the social scene. Most outports had either two or three denominations, although one denomination tended to dominate in each community. There were certain sections of Newfoundland that were primarily Roman Catholic and others that were Protestant. In Wesleyville, my father's United Church was by far in the majority. There was a very small Anglican church and school, and a few Salvation Army adherents, but ninety percent belonged to the Methodist church, or the United as it later came to be called.

I think it was an interesting and exciting time to grow up, in spite of the Depression, and the isolation of the place. We children didn't realize that we were indeed isolated. When navigation closed off in November, we had no regular communication with the outside except by dog team. We got our mail by dog team once a week if we were lucky. It was a great event when that team arrived from the nearest railway point up in Gambo, about fifty or sixty miles away. The word would spread like wildfire: "The mailman's come!" We'd all flock to the post office and wait until the bags were sorted. Eaton's catalogue and the *Family Herald* were always eagerly welcomed.

Supplies for the outport always came in autumn, when the steamers came in to dock and the fishing schooners came back from Labrador. The fish would be dried and taken to the merchant headquarters in St. John's, and then they'd come back home loaded with provisions for the various outport merchants. Various government outport steamers would also bring in supplies. But after that, after November, there would be no such thing as fresh fruit and vegetables. We made do with what we had, dried apples and such.

One of the problems — hard to overcome — was the quality of education. The churches had schools, but most of the teachers were poorly trained. When I started teaching in an outpost, I had all the grades in one room, from kindergarten to grade eleven, and the only qualification I had was my own grade eleven certificate, and six weeks of teachers' training at the summer school in St. John's.

In spite of this, though, many of the children of outport fishermen went on to great things in the outside world — spurred on, maybe by a parent who took a particular interest, or a teacher or a minister. My father was responsible for many a fisherman's son or daughter going on to the professions. He often dipped his hand in his pocket to pay the necessary fee for one of these children to sign on for the public examinations. You couldn't write them without paying five dollars, which very few had. Many others like my father did that for promising students.

I don't look back with any particular nostalgia to those days, because it was such a hard life that those people had to live. Many's the time my father had to break the news to a family of a drowning or death of some kind. Tuberculosis too was one of the great scourges of the outports in those days.

Offsetting those memories, however, are many pleasant ones, but I wouldn't want to go back and do it all over again. I wouldn't want my children to go through it either, although I probably did gain value from that kind of life.

It was a good place to come from. I think I brought things from it that I wouldn't have gotten elsewhere, and that stood me in good stead later on. You can put the unpleasant happenings behind you and just relish the good times.

Bill Carter

A Special Job

Many of the families who came to Canada during the immigration years of the early twentieth century were British, people who were getting nowhere in the old country because of a class system that prevented them from advancing their station in life. These people looked to the New World for things to be different. So it was that the Carters took up the Canadian government's offer and set sail for Canada in 1911, full of hope. They didn't have much to bring with them except the clothes on their backs and their young family. Young Bill was a very young child, but he had a sharp mind, a restless personality, and the ability to observe and remember everything that happened for the rest of his life. He's eighty-two now and lives in Regina.

I had my sixth birthday on the *Megantic*, the boat that brought us to Canada. The first place I remember in the country is Quebec City, where we landed, and I recall that mostly because we sat for hours in a park there waiting for the train to take us across Canada. When we boarded we were in the poorest of the coaches, the ones with the wooden seats and a stove at each end where we cooked our own meals. We also had a three-month-old baby with us, and Mother had a terrible time trying to find milk for it. It was a helluva trip — uncomfortable.

After what seemed like forever we landed at Moosomin, Saskatchewan, where my grandparents and other relatives were already settled in so we just moved in, too, to what was really a very small house.

My folks weren't homesteaders. They simply became tired of trying to get ahead in England and they thought, "Canada can't be any worse than this. Let's give it a try." Also, we had letters from these relatives expounding on the glories of this grand new country. As rough as it was in the beginning staying in that crowded house, it was really better than what we had left.

After a while, we found a little cottage of our own, and Dad had found a job on the railroad for twenty-five cents an hour and ten hours of work a day. That was not a bad wage then, because you'd get three pounds of round beefsteak for a quarter, and our rent was just ten dollars a month. It wasn't luxury either, because I remember seeing my mother looking very distressed and talking about "hens' meat" and how hard it was. It wasn't until long afterwards that I understood what she meant; we brought a Lancashire accent with us, and she was complaining about how hard it was to make "ends meet."

None of us could believe how cold the winters were! We would all gather around the coal-and-wood stove we had there before we braved our way to the cold beds awaiting us. Temperatures of thirty and forty below zero were common, and the warmest time for us was after we got in between those cold sheets with hot water bottles and blankets piled on so high that we could hardly turn over. It took courage to crawl out of that nest and face the cold house in the mornings. But you know, I kind of enjoyed all of that after a while of getting used to it. I was a tough little kid and I seemed to be outside playing in the snowbanks more than I was in the house. It seems we got a lot more snow then than we do now.

There was nothing really unusual about my childhood except perhaps that I was really anxious to grow up and get away and avoid the life of hard labour that seemed to be all that was in store for me if I hung around home.

When I was old enough, I joined up with the South Saskatchewan Militia Regiment. This gave me a chance to take various courses that winter and qualify as a corporal. Then I was sent down to Winnipeg with the Princess Pats [Princess Patricia's Canadian Light Infantry] for more courses, leading to my sergeant's stripes which made me the senior NCO in the battalion. However, I was still based on Moosomin and I figured that if I was ever going to get away, I'd better try getting into the RCMP. I couldn't believe it when I got this letter telling me my application was approved and for me to get up to Regina for processing. Easier said than done, as I hadn't enough money to buy a rail ticket.

However, I worked for my father for a week, and he gave me ten dollars. The fare to Regina was $4.80, and the rest of the money paid for my meals until I was accepted into the force. Luckily that didn't take long.

I arrived at the recruiting office on Saturday, and before the day was out, I was in. No matter what they asked me, I was agreeable and said "Yes." "Do you ride a horse?" — "Yes." I had never ridden a horse in my life, but I learned early on that you never say you can't do something.

I learned in a hell of a hurry before anyone else was out of bed the next day, as a matter of fact. I got along fine too. In fact, I learned well enough to be part of the Musical Ride in later years.

Another time that I said I could do something that I couldn't was a few years later—also in Regina—when they needed an electrician on the staff. They asked if I had ever worked with electrical equipment. "Yes," I said. What I didn't tell them was that about all I knew was how to change a light bulb. So I became an electrician/plumber. And all I knew of plumbing in the beginning was how to turn a tap on. But one learns all those little things when you have to get along. I never had any problems. The worst part of that job for me was climbing poles to replace light bulbs. I didn't even know how to use those spurs that are worn on the feet when climbing those poles, and when I did learn, I found I was scared to death when I got up the pole and had to learn not to look down.

Around 1927, after doing just about every job there was to do in the ranks of the RCMP, I thought I'd put in for a posting to the North country. I was accepted and I was sent off to a post in Fort Providence [N.W.T.] with not much extra training except for a few law courses.

The inspector said that when I got there the NCO would tell me anything else I needed to know. That was some joke. When I arrived, the corporal, who came from southern England and spoke as if he had a potato in his mouth, came out and said something. I whispered to the other constable, "What the hell is he talking about?" I couldn't understand that English lingo at all. Anyway, he wouldn't give me a damn thing to do but cook his meals for the next two years, until I got fed up and requested a transfer.

I was given a few other postings in these out-of-the-way northern outposts until finally I had the North right up to my teeth. They let me come out and after my three months' leave, during which I spent all of my money, I was sitting in the barracks in Edmonton one day, when one of the officers said, "We've got a special job for you if you want to volunteer for it. It's kind of dangerous, though." Right off, I figured that it must be the Johnson Affair—Albert Johnson, the Mad Trapper. The newspapers were full of it, this so-called "madman of the north" who was being pursued across the snows by posses. I though this was a great chance to do some real Mountie work, and so before I knew what was happening, I was on a plane with bush pilot "Wop" May and another RCMP constable named Nicholson.

In Aklavik they got us some northern gear, and then we climbed back in the plane and flew out immediately on the hunt. We were up pretty high and I asked "Wop" to go down closer because I had a rifle ready in case we spotted him. Our orders were to shoot to kill, as Johnson had already killed one man and wounded another. "Wop" said, "No, I'm not going down any closer because if he shoots at us, one bullet could put us out of action." Anyway, we didn't see a sign of Johnson at all — maybe because we never got lower than a thousand feet from the ground. The funny part of this is that some of the dramatized stories in print that were coming out of there were saying that "Wop" May was scouring the area with his plane at bush level. That was the only time I was in an airplane for that search. The rest of the time I was on ground with a dog team — searching out different areas, but never catching a glance of him because we had lost his trail. The snow was like cement and he wasn't leaving any tracks that we could follow.

Finally, his trail was found again, and in fact that was very easy because there was a fresh snowfall. His was the only trail in the country, as everyone else was staying indoors because they were scared to death that they'd run into this "Mad Trapper." The whole story was broadcast on their radios, day and night, and the thing is that it was probably the *big* story of 1932 all over the world. At least, the big story of February 1932. It had all of the classic features of adventure: the frozen north; great expanses of snow and ice; dog teams; the RCMP; and a madman who had already murdered! Also, you must remember, in February of 1932, in the depths of the Great Depression, a lot of people didn't have much else to do except follow this story.

Anyway, the posse spotted him and he spotted them at about the same time. Johnson turned around and started to run, and as he did one of the men in the posse began firing at him. One of the bullets struck a box of shells that Johnson was carrying in his back pocket and almost shattered his hip. He started dragging himself up into the bush, but he was too badly shot up to make it. Instead of surrendering right there, he dug himself into the snow and began firing back at the posse. All of us were firing away at this one lone figure in the snow, and we must have fired hundreds of shots. Finally, there was silence. We waited at least two hours before the inspector called for him to surrender. In response, Johnson just lifted his hands above the snow and waved.

It was just bravado stuff on his part, really, because he was finished. He knew it, and so did we. After another wait and a period of silence, one of our constables made his way over and found Johnson dead. And that ended the case of the Mad Trapper. Funny thing about that entire episode. Of all the hundreds of bullets that we fired at that man, only seven had actually hit him.

Now there's a very sad aspect to that whole case that's never been properly told, and it concerns what got Johnson started in the first place. It seems there was an Indian who came to the police and reported that Johnson was stealing fur from the Indian traps. The Indian had simply made up this story because he held a grudge against Johnson. It seems that this fellow and a couple of other Indians had gone to Johnson's cabin one night and didn't get the kind of reception they expected. The practice in the north at that time was that if an Indian came to visit, you should always give him a cup of tea and some bannock or whatever you had. Well, Johnson was low on food and he was at least one hundred-and-fifty miles from any store, so he told them to get to hell out and pointed his rifle at them to show that he meant what he said. They got out all right, but they went to the police and said that Johnson had threatened to kill them. The police were obliged to investigate and they sent a couple of constables to see Johnson. They banged on his door, and he told them to go away and leave him alone. He was a bit of a loner anyway. He never bothered anybody and didn't want anybody bothering him, so when the police kept hammering at his door, he fired a shot which went right through the door and killed one of them. That's what started the whole thing. I don't think that Johnson meant to kill anyone, and I don't think he was mad—at least at the start he wasn't.

Gordon Jackson

Uniformly Colonial

Canada became a nation in 1867 but for many years afterwards the apron strings of England, the mother country, remained firmly attached. To the great dissatisfaction of most Canadians, our young nation was treated like a "wild colonial child," not to be trusted with the running of its own affairs. For example, we were well into the present century before we had a navy to call our own. In fact, all of our armed forces were looked upon as mere appendages of the British military.

When the First World War broke out there was much unhappiness with this state of affairs as young Canadians rushed off to take part in the conflict. "Over there" they were less Canadian than they were British, a small part of the larger picture. In the army, generals like Sir Arthur Currie were constantly at loggerheads with the British general staff as the Canadians fought for an independent role. Flying aces like Billy Bishop and Ray Brown had to display the insignia of the Royal Flying Corps despite the fact that they were Canadians flying machines that were often built in Canada.

It was the same with the navy. On this side of the ocean before the war, what we had was a "navy presence"—ships of the Royal Navy staffed by British officers and a complement of young Canadians who were "men of the British Navy."

Ninety-seven-year-old Gordon Jackson of Port Credit, Ontario, remembers joining the navy in Canada and not feeling very Canadian on his arrival overseas. Most Canadian volunteers felt that way—a situation that was bound to lead to trouble.

There were 1,800 of us altogether who went over, and when we got there we were drafted out here and there to different British commands. We weren't a unit. We just went as RNCVR, Royal Navy

Canadian Volunteer Reserve, and they sent us out wherever we were required, as if we were British.

Now the trouble arose because about half of those 1,800 were men who had been at sea all of their lives, merchant seamen, fishermen, and so on, and they knew more of navigation and the rules of the sea than most of the petty officers from England, who were in the Navy only because they had been called up for the war. Most of them had never been near the sea let alone a ship. They were giving orders to these *real* sailors from Canada without having any knowledge to back up these orders. You can imagine how this went down with those Canadian sea dogs.

One day I saw this notice pinned up in the minesweeping trawler I had been assigned to as an ordinary seaman. It asked for anybody who wanted to qualify for higher rating to put in an application to the regulating officer. I filled in an application before going off on a six-week tour of escort duty on the English Channel.

When I returned there was word for me to report to the regulating officer for a series of examinations. Every day for five days I was there — test after test, exam after exam — until finally I had to tell him that my ship was leaving in a half-hour and I had no desire to go AWOL. The petty officer said, "Wait here while I tell the commander."

So off he went, and in a few minutes the commander came out and said, "Jackson, what did you do in peacetime?"

"I was a lawyer, sir."

"Oh well, that explains it," he said. "I gave you an examination for Able Seaman, then Leading Seaman, Petty Officer, and Commissioned Officer. You passed all of them, and I'm going to recommend you for a commission. Have you any qualifications to show me?"

I laughed and said, "Well, not right here, sir, but I can get them by writing to Canada."

"Do that, Jackson," he said, "Then go back and join your ship and report to me when you are in port again."

I did what he asked, and when I got back to the base six weeks later, I found that I was a commissioned officer and I was sent to the Crystal Palace in London for my training course. There were seventeen thousand navy trainees of all ranks training in all the different navy skills. When I left there, I was a full-fledged gunnery officer with orders to ship out immediately to a destroyer. I was sitting on my bag, waiting for a lorry to take me down to my ship when a messenger came up to me and said, "Are you Lieutenant Jackson?" When I told him I guessed I was, he said, "Your draft is cancelled and you are to report to the Admiralty."

I asked what the heck this was all about — a court martial or something? "I don't know," he said, "but you are to go at once."

So I went up to the Edinburgh-Leith offices in Scotland. Captain Parker, the organizing director of the Auxiliary Patrol, and a couple of other officers drilled me for an entire day on what the Canadians were doing, after which the Admiral told me to come back the next day.

The following day, he said, "I think we've got you Canadians straightened out now. We're going to form a division and we're going to give you quarters at Davenport. I want you, Jackson, to go down and organize it. I'll give you a couple of petty officer instructors and I want you to go to all the bases where the Canadians have been assigned and pick out the ones who've been at sea, draft them into Davenport, and put them through qualifying courses. Then you will draft them out again into their proper ratings."

I told him that I was a gunnery officer and that I'd never done anything like that before.

"How long have you been in the navy, Jackson?"

"Two years, sir."

"Haven't you learned by now that we don't ask you what you want to do, we tell you!" The result of all of this was that I was given a crash course at the Admiralty and made a Royal Navy Officer — not a Canadian Navy Officer, but a British officer who happened to be Canadian. That was the best you could expect at the time, but it did put a lot of Canadians like me in positions of authority where we could protect the interests of Canada and fellow Canadians in the British sea forces.

Although we respected our ties with the British Empire, we wanted to be our own country and stand on our own feet. Those of us who fought in that war as part of the British forces always felt there was something demeaning about being British first, and Canadians second, especially as our record in the war was so good.

When it was all over and we returned home, we took back with us an increased sense of nationalism and independence that cried out for our own army, our own air force, and our own navy. We did get all of this, but it didn't come easy.

Part of the problem was that ordinary Canadians were tired of war. They were tired of what many thought of as useless killing and useless hardship. They only wanted to get back to the business of living their lives. Those of us in the services felt that way too, but we never lost interest in full Canadianization of the forces and in having those forces strengthened. I felt that our navy would never be as strong as it should be until it had more visibility in the country — even in peacetime. It wasn't good enough just to have a navy during a war.

Then, one day in 1922, I got a call from government authorities in Ottawa informing me that they wanted to start a Canadian Navy Reserve and they would like me to organize a branch in Toronto. A week or so later, some chaps came down to see me and I was given a commission in the Canadian Navy, which was still very young and not very strong. A couple of ships had been given on loan from England and not much else. As for the reserve force, which I was commissioned to organize, there was nothing. I was the first commissioned officer and beyond that there wasn't a thing to work with: no building, no offices, no locations, no equipment, and no men. It was a start-from-scratch situation.

My job was to whip up enthusiasm for this real Canadian Navy, unfettered by colonial bonds. They made me the first Commanding Officer of HMCS *York*, which was actually only part of a building they acquired in Toronto. Then they gave me a couple of petty officers. I organized a navy band, and we showed up in parades and exhibitions — more to let people know that we had a reserve navy of our own than any other reason. By now we were getting young people joining up for part-time activity and they were trained in gun-crew work and things like that, which we would show at the CNE and other places.

I travelled around the country making speeches. At the same time, I was made Dominion secretary of the Navy League and I went from coast to coast, talking to Rotary Clubs, church groups, and so on. My message was always the same — that here we were one of the biggest countries with one of the largest sea coasts that was practically wide open and uncontrolled, and where anybody could come in and do what they liked with our fishing, lumbering, mining, or whatever. There was nothing to stop them.

Our first "ship" for the reserve was a basement at 34 King Street West in Toronto. We met there, had a shooting gallery, taught rope splices and knots, and had our drills. That was the very small beginning, and as time went by we moved to bigger quarters at Sunnyside, where we still are. That's the way it progressed in the various locations all across the country.

When the Second World War began, we were, in a sense, ready for it. We had all of these young fellows in the reserve, and many old sailors from the First War who wanted to join up.

I had a call from Ottawa and was told that they wanted me to pursue a more active course now that the war was on. They said I would be required to instruct officers in the training course, and furthermore I would do it at my own expense. They said I would also have to scrounge the gas coupons for my own transportation — rationing was on by this time. Anyway, I accepted those terms and lectured and instructed for four years.

There was no shortage of recruits to the Royal Canadian Navy in the Second War, which may be somewhat surprising when you think that the first one had ended only twenty years before. Many recruits came from the prairies, thousands of miles from sea. Many came from both coasts and many from the areas around the Great Lakes, where sailing was familiar.

It didn't seem to matter what their backgrounds were, though. Thousands and thousands flocked in to join even though we had few actual ships at the beginning. We had the *Niobe* on the east coast and the *Rainbow* on the west coast. A few borrowed British ships and officers.

I remember that around this time I made a speech in Victoria, B.C., where I gave my usual tirade about the small size of our navy and our unprotected coastline. I was sitting with a Captain Adams of the British Navy. When the speech was reported on the front page of the Victoria paper the next day, they had all the facts right except one: they reported the speech as having come from Captain Adams. The following day in Ottawa we had members of Parliament raving about the nerve of this Brit coming over to Canada and criticizing our navy. At the same time in the British Parliament, Captain Adams was being raked over the coals for his insensitivity to the feelings of another country. Of course, he was entirely innocent. When the newspaper realized its error they apologized, but the apology was put in a tiny story on the back page, even though the original story was in front page headlines.

The RCN played a very important role in the Second World War, and always as a *Canadian* force. Although my part was on land as a member of the Reserve, I am proud of the role I played.

Ed Bennett

The Heart of a Viking

Joe Boyle was born to Irish parents in Toronto in 1867, the year that Canada became a nation. Shortly after his birth, his parents moved from the city to the rural community of Woodstock, Ontario, where young Joe grew up in the manner of most farm boys — learning the business, and daydreaming of adventure. The only difference between Joe and the others was that for him, those weren't dreams. They were plans. Before his life ended Joe Boyle would become a king. "King of the Klondike," and the queen of Romania would worship at his feet.

Ed Bennett of the Woodstock Historical Society is one of the people who helped bring Joe Boyle's remains back home where they belonged.

When Joe Boyle died in England, he was described in the newspapers there as "Canada's Greatest Hero." At one time, along with Queen Marie, he practically ran the whole country of Romania. She was the granddaughter of our own Queen Victoria, and she mourned openly when Joe died.

Joe Boyle left Woodstock the first time to go to New York state, where his father had opened a stable of racehorses. This put him into that sporting circle where he became quite successful, and it gave him the money he needed to do entrepreneurial things.

The Klondike gold rush was not yet at its height then, the kind of thing that would certainly attract someone like Joe Boyle with his adventurous spirit, so he went up there. The first thing that struck him was the slowness and the inefficiency of the "panning" for gold that miners were using. He could see that if heavy machinery were used instead, a fortune could be made. This was about a year before the gold rush hit its peak, and he had been doing some of that placer mining himself. "There's no money to be made this way," he said, as he looked across at the way the wealthy Guggenheims were doing it. They had these huge dredges scooping up tons of the bottom soil at one time. "That's for me," he said, so he used the money he made in his New York sporting activities and brought up his own dredges and other equipment and went into competition with the Guggenheims.

He soon became a millionaire and gained control of a great many Yukon businesses, including the Yukon Power and Light Company right down to the local laundry business. He reached the very top up there, and became known as "the King of the Klondike."

When the First World War broke out in 1914, Joe wanted to get into the action, but at the age of forty-seven, he was considered too old. "We'll see about that," he said, and he took some of his money and formed his own small army, which he said he would donate to Canada's war effort. It was a group of volunteers mainly recruited from the North West Mounted Police and their reserves. It consisted of fifty men picked by Boyle, and outfitted and sent overseas as a machine-gun attachment with the blessing of the government.

However, even this didn't win the government over as far as Joe Boyle himself was concerned. They told him that he was still too old for overseas action. He was, though, given a commission as an honorary colonel by Sir Sam Hughes, the Defence Minister, but even that didn't get him overseas.

In 1916, he decided to go over on his own, more or less to check up on what was happening to the machine-gun company that he had paid for. He had it in his mind, of course, that he'd be allowed to join them for real when he got over. That didn't work either, but when the Americans came into the war in 1917, he approached them and laid out all of his credentials.

The Americans must have been impressed by this honorary Canadian colonel because their company of engineers sent him to Russia to see if he could straighten out the railway supply lines there. These lines where in a terrible state of disorder, and it would take someone with the genius of a Joe Boyle to untangle the mess.

This was the year of the Bolshevik Revolution, but it still hadn't started when Joe arrived. There was a provisional government in control and Boyle found himself working under some of Karensky's ministers.

He was more than successful at that. In fact, he did such a tremendous job that the Russians couldn't understand how one man could do so much. They really appreciated his worth, and they used his talents extensively for other things.

He got to know the Bolshevik leaders, but he didn't get along with them, especially after they took over control of the government.

He was in Russia when General Dukhonin was murdered by the Bolsheviks and it was then that he turned completely against them and had nothing further to do with them. So he formed an intelligence group which had about five hundred agents operating under him, working for the British and the French. For a while, in fact, this was the only intelligence operation that Britain and France had on the Eastern front. Those were the glory days for Joe Boyle, but his *power* days were really yet to come.

After the Bolshevik Revolution, Boyle went to Romania to see if there was a way he could help them. The first opportunity he had was when the Romanian army and the people were in a position of real starvation. Through his efforts he obtained access to supplies from the Russian White armies, which he was able to divert to Romania. For that action he was referred to as the saviour of the country.

When he first arrived in Romania, he was very sympathetic to the plight of the country. Queen Marie, being the granddaughter of Victoria, was certainly pro-British even though King Ferdinand, her husband, was German. Despite this, he had kept Romania neutral during the war even though they were surrounded by all the Central Powers, Bulgaria, Austria, and Hungary. When an opportunity came for Romania to enter the war, she came in on the side of the Allies, but when the Russian offensive failed, Romania found herself in very bad straits. This was around the time that Joe Boyle arrived there.

He immediately promised Queen Marie and King Ferdinand that he would do everything in his power to help, which he certainly did. After many hair-raising episodes, he became a power in the Romanian government and certainly a great influence on the king and queen.

At one point there was hardly anything passed by the Romanian government that did not have the approval of Joe Boyle. By now, most people assumed that he was also the master of the queen's bedroom. The only thing he didn't have was residency in the palace. What prevented this, of course, was the presence of the Queen's husband, the very-much-alive Ferdinand.

Joe, however, overcame this hurdle, but not exactly in the way he wanted it to happen. At the height of his work there, he suffered a stroke. Fortunately, he survived and was brought to one of the royal palaces where Marie and her daughter personally nursed him back to good health.

Although there's no proof, most people feel that there was a romantic connection between them. There doesn't seem to be any other way to explain the close bond that existed, or the immense power he wielded in the country.

He died in England in 1923, at the age of fifty-six and was buried at Hampton Hill cemetery. One of the stones of his grave was placed by Queen Marie. The one that had been there previously was placed by Canada's Lord Beaverbrook. Marie didn't think this was a satisfactory monument to her Joe Boyle, so she arranged to bring a stone cross, a thousand-year-old one from Romania, and she also brought along an urn. She supervised the placing of these on his grave along with another stone inscribed with a line from one of Robert Service's poems, which I feel was very appropriate for this brave Canadian:

> "Man with the heart of a Viking
> and the simple faith of a child"

I am happy to say that Joe Boyle's remains now have an honoured place in his home town of Woodstock, Ontario. He truly was a Canadian hero.

Cy Strange

Cracking into Radio

The fiftieth anniversary celebrations of the CBC *in* 1986 *reminded Canadians how very young radio is in this country. Before the* CBC *came into being in* 1936, *amateurs were beginning to fool around with this amazing invention that could bring the sound of the human voice from far distant points into the homes of ordinary people.*

Amateur entertainers saw in radio a platform for their talents which in ordinary circumstances wouldn't have had much chance of reaching beyond the church basement halls of their own communities. They flocked to the early radio stations with their guitars and their songs and they performed for free, just for the opportunity of instant celebrity within their own communities. Most of them continued with their pre-ordained lives, but some, fascinated by the potential of radio technology, stayed with radio all their lives.

Cy Strange, who was still on the air with the CBC *in Toronto in* 1986, *was a dear friend and co-host with me of "Fresh Air."*

I remember the first time so well. There were four of us who had this little group in the Exeter area of Ontario where my father ran the general store. We were all the rankest of amateurs, playing banjos and guitars, but we had ambitions to appear on Doc Cruickshank's Wingham radio station, which wasn't much more than a makeshift affair at the time although it could be heard all over the southwestern part of Ontario. Anyway, one day we piled into an old Model T and drove up to where Doc had his station. Back in those days anybody could get on the air so long as they didn't expect to get paid. Doc welcomed us with open arms and without so much as a rehearsal or an audition we were on the air doing our four or five tunes. We were in heaven! When we were finished Doc came over and said, "That's great! Do some more." But we had to tell him that that was it. He had heard our complete repertoire.

"That's okay," he said, "Do them again." And we did. When I look back on it now, I know we weren't very good but it was enough to give me the bug for broadcasting. I knew then and there that it was what I wanted to do with my life.

Now, that was back in the early thirties, so radio was still very new. Youngsters were still making their own crystal sets. I had built one myself with bits of wire and one of those round oatmeal boxes. Many homes were getting the big cabinet models that were in vogue at the time. My father bought an Atwater-Kent with three tuning dials on the front of it and it did have a speaker. That was a relatively new feature, having been developed from the earphones which up to that time people would put into a bowl so that more than one person could listen at a time. The bowl would magnify the sound.

I remember, though, that our radio used three batteries, as did all radios of the time, — the "A", the "B", and the wet battery which was really a six-volt car battery. In the winter we would put that battery on a sleigh and pull it to a garage where they could charge it. We'd have to leave it for a day or so and then go back with our sled and pull it home again. That would last about two or three weeks depending on how much the radio was used. Of course, that made for very selective listening. There were certain things one just couldn't miss, Amos 'n' Andy being one of them. Then the battery would run down again and it was back to the garage for a twenty-five-cent charge. The trouble with that was that while it was charging you had no radio to listen to, and that was terrible!

Radio was so much fun because of the experimental nature of the programs. All of the stations were trying something new all the time and for us at home the big thing was the mystery of it all. How could that music and that voice and all of that stuff come out of the air? It was so mystifying, and wonderful and it expanded your mind like nothing else up to that time could do. The desire to be part of all this became my all-consuming passion. Today's children take all of these things — radio, TV, and space travel — for granted, but radio in my young days was the ultimate in all that was new. The very idea of stringing a wire aerial outside from a tree to the corner of your house or something like that and bringing in music and voices from all over North America, and indeed on short wave from all over the world, was nothing short of astounding.

I remember being absolutely astounded a year or so after we got our radio when my father came home one day with what he said was an indoor aerial. It was very long like a coil spring and it could stretch across the ceiling from one corner of the room to the other. What amazed me was that this aerial was *inside* the house, meaning that all of that music, all of those voices were inside our room all the time and all it took was this coil of wire to bring it down to our radio set. Oh — the wonder of it all! And yet, when I got over there with my banjo to Doc Cruickshank's station, it all looked so ordinary! It was simply a backroom in his shop with an old wind-up phonograph in one corner which he would crank away at to play records. Like all of those machines it would run down sometimes when he'd forget to crank and the sound of *that* on the air would be pretty hilarious.

By the way, that old phonograph wasn't wired into the broadcasting transmitter. When he wanted the record to go out on the air, he just turned on the microphones. All radio stations were very primitive then. There was a rug on the floor to absorb some of the sound and he had drapes all around the wall. Aside from that it was an ordinary room. Radio was only a hobby for Doc then, and he was having a lot of fun, but it was an expensive hobby and he began to look around for ways to make some money out of it or else he'd have to give it up. That's when he decided to try to get some of the merchants around town to pay a little money to get their names and establishments mentioned on the air. So for fifty or seventy-five cents he began doing commercials, although they weren't even called that at the time. He'd write these messages telling about a sale or something and he'd read them on the air himself for just a few pennies, really. But it saved his station and later he became one of the most respected broadcasters in radio and TV in the country.

I started to become seriously interested in becoming part of the business around 1935 when I'd hitchhike down from Exeter to London once or twice a week to do a fifteen-minute program singing and playing guitar on CFPL which was only 100 watts at the time. It would come on for a couple of hours in the morning, a couple of hours at noon, and a couple more in the evening. Out of that came work with dance bands. A lot of the early radio broadcasters started that way. All the stations were doing remote broadcasts from dance locations so that when I'd sing or play my guitar with a band I was often being heard on radio, and my name, I suppose, was getting to be known.

Where I really began as an announcer was in Timmins in Northern Ontario for Roy Thompson and Jack Kent Cook. I literally had to do everything there, including sweeping the floor. I wrote commercials and I learned how to type. I worked in the record library, looked after the news machines, read newscasts, played at being a disc jockey and answered the phone. There wasn't a job there that I didn't do — not just me, but everybody at that station and every station in the country. Another part of the job was program planning. The station manager and the announcers would dream up ideas for programs — say, fifteen minutes in length, with some special thrust such as waltz music, Hawaiian music, cowboy music, or whatever, and then the commercial salesmen would go out and attempt to sell these ideas to the local merchants. When that was done the announcer would take over and write the program and announce the shows. The programs were never longer than fifteen or thirty minutes. That was the style at the time. If the listener didn't like one style of music, they knew they wouldn't have to suffer very long as in fifteen to thirty minutes it would change to something else — maybe band music or classical or old time or something else.

It was exciting to work that way because you had all the latitude in the world and you could do practically anything you wanted. You were free to try anything. If it worked, fine. If it didn't, you moved on to another experiment. It was all experimentation then. Everybody from the secretary to the station manager would be coming up with ideas all of the time and it was the announcer who got the chance to present all of these ideas on air. Everything from working with the minister who came in to do something spiritual at sign-on or sign-off to being a sports announcer. We did classical music shows and hoedown music. We read poetry with organ background and did special events around town — things like the mayor unveiling a new monument. We did sidewalk interviews and interviews with all of the local talent who came in to perform on air. They got paid nothing and I got paid very little, but we all loved it as we were learning the business.

Love of show business was what motivated an awful lot of us then. It was a chance to perform and where else could most Canadians get a chance to do it? It was an opportunity for experience for all that hidden talent. Asking to be *paid* for that experience never occurred to most would-be entertainers. Outside of the major cities there was no way for singers or musicians to make a living in show business. It was necessary to get known first and the way to do that was through the local radio station which couldn't afford to pay them anyway.

You could call that period of time "non-formula radio," because most of the ideas were being tried out for the first time and all of the stations were doing things that they hoped would appeal to the ethnic makeup of their particular communities.

In Timmins where I started, there were various ethnic groups so that the station was aiming its programming at different nationalities from all over the world. In Quebec stations were programming to the French majority in the same way that stations on the East coast were aiming theirs at the Scottish and Irish majorities. That's the way it went all across the country and the better people from all of those different milieus eventually graduated from the private stations to the national networks of the CBC where they had more of an opportunity to concentrate on the areas of programming that they could do best.

I spent most of my years in private radio, because like a lot of others I could continue doing a variety of jobs without having to give up the on-air work I liked best. Over those years I watched the business grow from the one-man operations such as Doc Cruickshank's to very large staffs like that of CFRB in Toronto. I watched as the new staff positions came into being. Instead of the announcer getting himself on and off the air on time, there came a person who could be known as a producer responsible for such things. Then people were hired to pick the music. Writers were hired to supply scripts for the announcers. Announcers were hired for special duties only, i.e. sports programs and live classical-music shows. The business was growing rapidly and positions such as program planner, program consultant came into being. On the commercial side, advertising agencies began dreaming up and packaging programs and selling them to stations complete with national advertisers. All the stations had to do was provide the air-time and collect the money. Big-name advertisers had big money to spend and we began to see radio programs that reflected this new-found wealth.

In addition to the American big-dollar shows from across the border, now there was money to develop our own. Wayne and Shuster first became big stars on radio, shortly after the Second World War. "Hockey Night in Canada" with Foster Hewitt was another big money show. These were developed by the advertising agencies who paid the CBC for air-time on the national networks. The soap companies gave us the afternoon serials that came to be known as "soap operas" and the patent-medicine companies gave us everything from the Bible to the "Barnyard Follies." But there's no doubt about it, without all of this sponsor money pouring in radio could never have developed like it has. The CBC depended on that money every bit as much as the "privates."

Out of these private stations and out of these advertising agencies came some of the best talent that the CBC ever had — producers like Andrew Allan, idea men like Harry Boyle, actors like John Drainie. They were trained first in the private sector and allowed to blossom in the CBC; so that the CBC had a stable of talent unequalled in the English-speaking world.

I had worked in both sectors. If "work" is really the word that some say it is, then I've never "worked" a day in my life. I've enjoyed every day of my more than fifty-one years. It was a joy working with so many of those people. Kate Aitken, for one, was a remarkable woman with a wonderful sense of humour. I was her announcer for a long time and we did three fifteen-minute live shows every weekday. Some of the creators of those early shows too, will always stay in mind—people such as Bill Byles, the advertising-agency man we called "The Star Maker" because his ideas were always so successful. Bill always was a great gentleman. Another I think of is Alan Savage, who was a naturally superb broadcaster with a fine sense of what was acceptable. Ramsay Lees is another, a performer-announcer-actor, as well as a radio and TV director. He also was a very creative man, as was Maurice Rosenfeld, another advertising-agency man who was responsible for countless shows that went into Canadian homes through radio. Still another was Horace Stovin from Western Canada, one of the founders of network radio. Spencer Caldwell, also a radio pioneer, was the man who later founded CTV.

All of these and countless others stand out in my mind as people that not only I but the whole radio and television industry and indeed the whole country owe a debt of gratitude.

Monseigneur Malcolm MacLellan

The St. F.X. Co-operative Movement

When the Depression hit Canada and the rest of the world in 1929, people hardly noticed in the Maritime provinces. They were already in a kind of Depression, one created by the exploitive companies who had come in to make a killing. Farmers' crops were taken from them for next to nothing. Fishermen received pennies for their catches and miners and steelworkers laboured in virtual slavery as they had for decades. Almost everyone was poor and it seemed as if it would always be that way until two Roman Catholic priests from the area started to change the situation. They began teaching people how they could extricate themselves, by themselves, through education, co-operatives, credit unions, and the like. Dr. Moses Coady and his mentor and cousin Father Jimmy Tompkins started what came to be known as the St. F.X. Movement.

I was a very young priest then, and more an observer of the Movement than a participant when it began. The fishing industry was in a sorry mess and the fishermen had to take whatever the buyers offered them. The mining industry was going through a terrible series of strikes. Strife, poverty, and despair were the norm in towns like Glace Bay, Sydney Mines, and New Waterford. Wages at the steel plant in Sydney were even worse than those in the mines and farming was in a state of decline with people just walking away and leaving the area, because there was just no profit from all that work and the markets were bad. All the young people, practically all of those who didn't complete high school, went off to either Boston or Detroit to make a living. The people at home were living on the small amounts of money that these young ones could send back. In fact they were dependent on them.

As a result of this, a group of concerned citizens, particularly priests, would gather in conferences attempting to find a solution to these problems. They decided that something had to be done in the way of an educational venture and the chief spark in all of this was Father Jimmy Tompkins, who had been to a conference in London, England, shortly after the end of the First World War, where he was inspired by the prospect of adult education. He kept needling these clergymen and those at St. Francis Xavier University to do something about it. The University was small and extremely poor, but finally, as the result of an organization called the Scottish Catholic Society, they got enough money to put some kind of a structure together which was the beginning of the St. F.X. Movement, or the Antigonish Movement as it is more commonly known today.

That was around 1928. The year before, when the rest of Canada was celebrating the fiftieth anniversary of Confederation we were flying our flags at half-mast here in the Maritimes as our part in the "celebration." Nobody around here felt there was much to be joyous about.

Father Jimmy had succeeded in getting a commission set up to study the fishing industry and I believe it was he who got Dr. Coady to make a presentation to the commission. As a result of this the commission asked Dr. Coady to organize the fishermen. That was the first venture into adult education.

It's significant to note that both Tompkins and Coady had sprung from their own ranks. Their fathers were as poor as anyone else down here, and of course being a parish priest in those days meant you were very much a part of the people and you were aware of everything that was going on. You suffered with them and felt a moral obligation to elevate the educational level. A deplorable part of all this was the very young age at which children left school. Very few ever made it to high school. Grade eight was considered a good education in an area where most were pretty well illiterate.

Dr. Coady was unquestionably the right man to lead this whole movement. Father Tompkins wanted Coady to lead it and so did the bishop and all the others involved as they recognized his abilities. Previously he had been involved with the organization of teachers in Nova Scotia and he had been a well-known public speaker. He was an outstanding teacher and he was also a big man in stature and made an impressive appearance. He was a country boy who had the knack of bringing lofty ideas down to the level of the ordinary man and making them understandable.

Now, St. Francis Xavier itself was a university of the people that was started by them, but Coady didn't let *it* escape from his criticism of the whole educational system either, which he described as "a trap door process" by which the children of those who were better off financially were able to escape the so-called tyranny of conditions by getting into the higher professions and making a better living. It was his aim to turn that all around so that education would be the birthright of everyone and available to them freely, in the form of adult education. He wanted to make education popular with those who had never had a chance to get any — with the entire community instead of the select, or elite, group.

Until that time, even those who did manage to educate themselves were leaving and taking their knowledge elsewhere for better opportunities. Even uneducated bright people were not staying behind. We were losing all of our best young people to greener pastures. Take, for example, a newly created young doctor. To stay here he had to depend on the resources of the people for his income. When these people had no resources, this young doctor would have no income. It was similar in all other professions.

Now trying to change all of this, a pattern developed over a lot of years, was a massive task. Dr. Coady hit on what he called "The Study Club Method" through a meeting he had in Margaree, Cape Breton, with a small group of farmers. They met and discussed the immediate problems of the community. Following several meetings Dr. Coady concluded that this was the best way to have people come to grips with their own immediate problems and try on their own to find solutions.

From those meetings grew the particular methodology of the study club. Group discussion became the basic procedure in educating people in their own communities where the problems were largely economic. Teach them first how to get the bread and butter and come to grips with solving those economic problems which are really basic to life in general.

Coady's philosophy of course, was that that was only the beginning. They had to know first all the principles of cooperation. They had to start their own small banks, better known as credit unions and take control of their own lives, away from the companies that were exploiting them. The message of the movement was basically, "The Lord helps those who help themselves," not only as individuals but as groups. There was great emphasis on personal responsibility, social responsibility, and the promotion of those caring not only for themselves but the community as a whole.

That was an important part of it as it minimized the personal emphasis of the past, and emphasized responsibility for the larger community. Coady was very strong on that and also on the assumption that once the citizens began to build their own economic structures, they would develop greater responsibility.

When Dr. Coady first began travelling around to these depressed communities he knew the road ahead would be hard. While they knew they were hard up and hard done by, miners in Glace Bay, for example, didn't really know just how badly off they were. They thought of banks as buildings downtown patronized by businessmen, for example. They never thought of them as something that they could have anything to do with. When Coady told them that they could have their own banks they thought he was crazy. How could we have a bank when we've got no money to put in it? He held meetings and showed them how credit unions could help them — how they could have savings accounts where they could deposit even ten cents at a time. The miners were skeptical, of course, but they joined the credit unions and were amazed to find that after a while, they had amassed enough savings, a dime at a time, to actually provide security for their own loans. This was amazing to people who had never been in a bank before.

When other miners got word of what the credit unions were doing for some, they flocked to join and save their nickels and dimes and they certainly made it work, and as a result of that happening here it spread all across the country.

From that grew the co-operative stores which bought groceries and furniture and other things in bulk and sold them as reasonably as possible to their members — and then paid them a share of the profits as well.

The same thing happened with the farmers and fishermen. They learned to band together to buy and sell and to save. It was making a tremendous difference in their lives. It was very difficult for them to save even one cent, given the economic picture of the times, but Coady kept reminding them that at the end of the rainbow was a totally better life for all — with economic, social, and political benefits. They would advance culturally and in the meantime, for the first time, they would attain a good measure of power in controlling their own destinies. For these people, it was the very first ray of hope they ever had.

The big corporations existed for one reason only, and that was to make money. Social responsibility to the workers was practically nonexistent. These companies provided housing only because the workers needed a place to stay. They were built as cheaply as possible with no thought of comfort and with no thought that these houses should last any length of time — so they were really not much better than shacks. The housing groups gave these workers the first decent housing they'd ever known and they gave them something much more important — self-respect. Governments at that time didn't have much money either, and they were rather lax in any decent social legislation, so a lot of things went on that wouldn't be tolerated today. Laws governing health, safety, and sanitary conditions were very, very rudimentary. The governments took a low key approach to these things and these big companies could do pretty much as they wanted.

Most of the miners, along with steelworkers, were living in company-owned substandard housing. Through study clubs Coady and Tompkins showed them how they could build decent houses of their own in co-operative groups using their own labour and long-term financing. The first group to do it was in a small town called Reserve, near Glace Gay, and it was so successful that many groups followed in Glace Bay and Sydney. The first, by the way, was called Tompkinsville after Father Jimmy, and if you visit there today you'll still be impressed by the quality of the homes they built.

Not many miners had homes with proper basements and furnaces before that. It was a phenomenal aspect of the Movement and it did enormous good for the people. It required that they set up these little corporations with a dozen or so members. There were rules and regulations and there was study required to learn the terms of financing and things such as that. It also required the election of one man to head the corporation and it required others who had particular knowledge of skills in carpentry or electricity to take charge of these departments. Every aspect of the Co-operative Movement was being put to use in these housing groups. Each one had to help the others or else it couldn't work.

Youngsters who survived the very high infant morality in those communities were simply looked on by the companies as future workers, who could be put to work at a very early age, as child education and child labour laws were also very lax. If, by some happenstance, a miner's child ever got to high school or university in those days, it was viewed in the community as almost a miracle. Very few of them ever did.

The St. F.X. Movement was so important in changing all of these attitudes that its significance cannot be overemphasized. It gave hope to the workers and it made them realize that they could do something in a co-operative way themselves, and that there was power in numbers. Coady showed them how they could solve most of their own problems if they worked together as a group. These people trusted and believed in Coady. He was a great communicator who held his audience in the palm of his hand, and when they left a room after he'd spoken, they knew that they had heard something worthwhile.

Coady and Tompkins were a great pair who often differed violently on the proper approach that should be taken. Dr. Jimmy was a great believer in libraries as a main source of adult education, but Dr. Coady, with his economic approach felt that the time wasn't quite ripe for libraries, as a lot of the people could hardly even read. Dr. Jimmy believed in approaching people one at a time and instilling the philosophy on an individual basis, while Coady felt that the group method of study clubs and meetings was the better way. Coady was much more an organizer, while Tompkins was more of a writer. However, they were a fantastic team and what they did was extremely important. It produced many community leaders who never would have attained that particular role in society, and it made the mass of the people more literate. It changed the whole fabric of society at that time.

Many don't see the same needs for the Antigonish Movement in this age of relative affluence, although it does live on in the Third World today through the Coady International Institute, which carries these same teachings to many, many developing countries. The youth from these countries come up here to St. Francis Xavier University every year to study for a period of six or seven months and they go back to their own countries to put what they've learned into practice. So, although Coady and Tompkins are both long gone, their work does go on.

Kathleen Mathers Nouch

Book-in-Hand Theatre

Now in her eightieth year, Kathleen Nouch of Saskatoon is deeply involved in the theatre of that province. She writes, produces, and acts, and she involves other seniors in her "Book-in-Hand theatre," which requires that the actors carry their scripts on stage whether they need them or not. Her theory is that a person's age has very little to do with what he or she can accomplish, and that the mind, if properly used, can overcome the limitations placed on the body by advancing years.

I was always enthusiastic about show business, and it wasn't because I was born into it. My parents were immigrants from England in the early part of the century, and they landed here without two cents to rub together. Father wasn't interested in homesteading as he was a city boy, and I suppose it seemed too much like hard work for him. He settled us down in a shack, with a flat, slanted roof, on the main street of Grenfell, Saskatchewan, and that's where I grew up. He was more of an odd-jobs man than anything, and his greatest love in life was ballroom dancing. We didn't have much money, but his prized possession was a tuxedo, which he put on as often as he could to go to any big dances. It seems he was a good dancer, because he became more or less the darling of the well-to-do ladies around town, who invited him everywhere. He was kind of a happy-go-lucky Irishman who cared more about having fun than he did for his family, I suppose. He never let us starve though, so he wasn't all bad. He loved to drink and he loved to gamble, which didn't go down very well with my mother, who was something of a religious fanatic.

I really had to battle for my education all of my life, because after one went so far in school in those days, there was an extra fee to be paid. I remember one time my parents didn't want to pay it. They said that I had all the education I needed, but in the end, after I made a fuss, they came through, and eventually I obtained my teacher's certificate. They say I was a good teacher, and maybe I was. Instead of simply reading a story to the children, I would act out all of the parts, and things like that. That's the part of it I loved the best.

After I married, I kept on taking courses to upgrade myself, and that wasn't easy with children at home and my husband working all the time. I would trade baby-sitting for tutoring other students in some of those night classes. I was sixty-five years old by the time I was able to muster all the credits for my degree. Of course, the Depression held me back a lot too, as it did everybody who lived through those years. Even today I suffer from "the thirties syndrome." I'll search for bargains till I'm blue in the face, even though I no longer have to. I'll search out auction and rummage sales and crow with delight when I find a dress for fifty cents or a dollar. Then I put that dress on and cover the thing up with my expensive fur coat. My kids don't understand this at all. They think I'm nuts.

Y'know, when Lord Bessborough started the Dominion Drama Festival in 1933, I was one of the people from out this way who was invited to Ottawa to start organizing that. I was brokenhearted when I couldn't go, as there was no way I could afford to buy the decent shoes and overshoes that I would need for that time of the year in Ottawa. I was devastated!

We all survived those years though and I often think that maybe the lessons I learned at that time were the best thing that could have happened—not just to me, but to all of us. We learned that you get nothing for nothing, and you've got to work for it all.

I really love the theatre and I've always been that way. All of my life. No matter where I lived, I was into some group or other that put on plays. If a place didn't have a group, I'd start one, which is what happened in the small town we lived in before we came to Saskatoon. We had this dandy little group going, but some of them were dropping out, saying they felt they were too old and had had enough and so on. It would get very discouraging, and it was only this intense love of theatre that compelled me to keep going.

When we moved to Saskatoon, I joined the Gateway Players, which is the big amateur theatre group in town and which has been going successfully since the mid-1960s. The first thing I was asked to do was to be assistant director of *Midsummer Night's Dream*. That went well, and I decided to try out for a part in a play called *The Happy Times*. I landed a lovely part in it, and after that the French theatre heard about me also being a French teacher, so they asked me to try out for a part in *Tartuffe*. I got that.

Boy, was I on a high! I met an elderly lady at the Gateway who said to me, "You were lucky. Roles for actors of our age are few and far between." It wasn't long before I discovered she was so right. My streak of roles came to a stop. Gateway asked me to do some directing, which I certainly could do, but I wanted to act.

At this point I heard of a woman who was going around to old folks' homes in Toronto, reading plays to the residents. She would do all of the parts herself. Apparently the residents liked it very much and always asked her back for more.

This seemed very interesting, but at the same time, I wasn't interested enough to do that as I wanted to act and interact with others on stage. However, it did give me an idea. I went to see the women's editor of the Saskatoon *Star-Phoenix*, and told her what I had in mind, which was to start a theatre for old folks who always wanted to act but never had the chance.

Although these people were now old, most of them still had the dream but were afraid to try as they felt they wouldn't be able to memorize the lines. I told the editor that it was to be a book-in-hand theatre where the actors won't have to worry about that.

Well, this women's editor — Zoe Dallas was her name — said "Don't tell anyone else about it and I'll write my entire column on your idea." The next day about a half-hour after the column appeared, I got a call from a man who told me he was on the board for these old folks' homes and he thought this was a great idea and that he would back me about getting it going, financially, and otherwise. I was ecstatic and got right at it.

For the first show I put on, I picked out some one-act plays from the old Dominion Drama Festival, ones that had been winners. Well, it was wonderful. The old people loved being up there on stage, and those in the audience loved to see people of their own age performing. A man from the New Horizons federal grants program who was in the audience came backstage and was really enthusiastic. He told me that we didn't have to use old people in parts that called for young people: "Use the young where you need them. It won't affect the government assistance you get as long as you use a majority of the older, and also it's the old who run the actual theatre program."

I immediately put in a call for young people who felt they were too busy to memorize lines and would like to join a book-in-hand theatre. I was amazed by the response, and the mix we ended up with was fantastic. Young and elderly hit it off right from the beginning, and since that time we've done some really excellent work. The only problem that arose after a while was that the young ones would have their lines memorized and would show up wanting to go on stage without their books. I said, "No, if you're acting with us old folks, you must take your books with you. It's the books that give all of us the confidence we need, even if we don't have to look at them." So that's the way it is. Everybody has a book in their hands and now, they use them so skillfully that those in the audience don't seem to notice it.

The idea has taken off like wildfire. It seems that everybody wants us. We went to Regina a while ago, and put on two shows for a big convention, and we were no sooner finished when a woman came up and asked if she could book us for next year. There's no end to it. I even had to turn away a request for another national convention next year as we were already booked up for the time. It's a tremendous boost for many of our old people who probably thought that there was nothing else in life for them. Now, they're getting so many requests that they can't possibly do even half of them.

In putting on these plays we don't simply have a lot of people reading lines, because I insist that they must be good actors too. I guarantee that our actors get training in all techniques of theatre. In fact, five of my actors tried out afterwards for roles with other companies and they got the parts.

Nobody gets turned away. Once in a while an elderly person comes along who thinks they know more than the director, or sometimes someone else thinks that the director is there to wait on them. You get all types. Some are meek and mild and very unsure of themselves, but I tell them that everyone is the same in this group, and that there are no "stars."

I'm eighty, you see, just as old as they, so I don't have to beat around the bush. I tell them that I don't have the time for prima donnas, and that if they really want to be part of the group they'll get all the help they need, but if they've come just to pass the time, there's nothing here for them. After I get that little speech out of the way, everybody gets down to it and starts working together. I say to them, "If you don't like me after the first two rehearsals, then quit; because I'll boss you around, and I don't stand for any nonsense. I'm here to teach you the rudiments of the theatre and if you think you know better than I, you can get out. This is not a social group. This is serious work."

I'm a real sergeant major, but I haven't had anyone quit. They keep coming back. Because I am old myself, I think I know how the old like to be treated. We don't want to be patronized or coddled, or treated like babies. If anybody tried that with me, I'd just as soon belt them in the mouth, so I don't try it on anyone else. I've got people in this group now who are getting on the stage before an audience that they've never seen before, and doing those roles with all the confidence of actors who've been doing it all of their lives. Before joining the group some of them didn't have confidence enough to come out of their rooms. I think that a group such as this is the best tonic a person can find to fight off the effects of aging. It keeps the mind and the body going.

Some of my plays that I've written have been in drama festivals all over this country, and as an actress I still get called to do roles in the professional theatre and occasionally in television. They're not going to get rid of me without a fight, and that's what I tell all of my cronies in "The Ageless Players" too. Like that baseball manager said, "It ain't over till it's over," or "It ain't over till the fat lady sings."

Tauno Lopenen

Work Like Crazy, Have Fun Like Crazy

If you were to believe the romantic stories and songs that have been written, no job could have been more fun than that of the lumberjack. But the man who's been there, the man who has spent his winters in the woods chopping trees and dragging them out, says it wasn't fun at all. It was a life spent half-frozen much of the time, and lonely all of the time. Tauno Lopenen came to Northern Ontario from Scandinavia in the early years of this century and laboured for almost forty years as a lumberjack.

The good old days? Hardly. A bucksaw and an axe made for hard work, hard, brutal work. And the power-saw that men use today is child's play compared to that.

Life in those old camps was really rough. Most of the camps I worked in had about one hundred and fifty men, and the barracks where we all lived was a long log building that had one big stove about four feet long in the middle of it. The night watchman would load that thing up with green poplar in the middle of the evening and you'd see that green wood boiling up in there with the juice running out the ends of it. It boiled rather than burned, and the only guys who were warm were the ones who sat right next to the stove. Those who were farther back would have their hair freeze to the wall. That's how cold it was: we couldn't sleep because of the cold, and the guys who sat next to the stove couldn't sleep because it was too hot.

It didn't smell too good in there either, because when we came back from the woods we'd be soaking wet from melting snow and our own sweat. Everyone would hang his clothes to dry — underwear and socks included — on these wires that were strung up all over the place. Boy, oh boy, when the steam from those things started to rise, the bunkhouse wasn't the greatest place to be. Also, if the socks you hung up were new, you had to hang around and keep an eye on them or they wouldn't be there in the morning. There'd be a pair that had no toes or heels in their place. Socks were a valuable commodity in those camps. As far as the underwear were concerned, nobody would steal *them* because chances were they were lousy anyway.

One of the big problems in the lumber camps was that a lot of the men working there were really the dregs of society. They came from the skid rows of the cities, and others were those who couldn't get jobs anywhere else. They were roustabouts and hobos and anything else you can imagine, who simply wanted a place to hole up for the winter. Of course, there were a lot of good men who were there because they loved working in the woods, and there were others who sent all of their money home to families. The unfortunate part of this is that in the public mind there was only one kind of lumberjack — the kind who worked all winter so he could drink and bum around the remainder of the year. That type of man didn't come to the camps until the Depression began. Before that, you'd find mostly Finns and Swedes, Ukrainians, and a few other nationalities from Europe who were immigrants here. And, of course, a lot of French-Canadians too.

Aside from the roustabouts who came during the hard times of the thirties, most of the woods workers were good, honest, hard-working men who were doing the only jobs that were available that they *could* do. Some were family men, but I would say that the large majority were single.

Gosh, y'know, it was hard to understand some of those fellows. They would work really hard all winter long — cutting trees, hauling logs with teams of horses, working for months on end; patching their own clothes and darning socks, day in and day out. That would be their whole life for all those months, and then in the spring, they'd head into town for a spree. In two weeks their entire winter's salary would be gone and they'd find themselves broke. The girls in town always knew when they'd be coming, and would be waiting for them. That was their life, I guess. Work like crazy, and have fun like crazy.

The food in those camps though was always good and there was plenty of it. Lots of meat and potatoes, pies and cakes and desserts of all kinds; pork and beans too, of course, and soups and the very best of bread. They didn't scrimp in the food department. They knew that they wouldn't keep their workers if they shortchanged on the food. That's why the cook's job was so very important. They were always the best; if they weren't they were shipped out. As the bosses and the men all rate the same food, there was no way that a poor cook could escape detection.

Next to the camp foreman, the cook was always considered the most important man in camp. He was number one — The Boss — nobody was above him. When he was in his cookhouse, not even the owners of the company were above, and he knew it too. He had rules of behaviour which had to be followed or he'd throw you out. He did not tolerate talking at the table. Not one word. He'd stroll up and down between the tables sometimes swinging a meat cleaver, and if he'd hear anyone even raise his voice to ask someone to pass the salt, he'd say, "Shut up or get out!" Nobody ever argues with the cook, and we all learned quickly to eat in silence.

Part of the reason for this rule of his was that conversation tended to make meals longer, and it was the cook's job to get the men in and out of there fast. If you wanted to eat, you could stay, but if you wanted to talk, you had to get out.

We worked every day except Sunday, and we worked from early morning, right up to the time it got dark. When I first started in the camps, I had a nice new wife, and a nice new home, but the only day off I had was Sunday, which meant that I had to stay there all week long. For a young married fellow, it was a long, long week indeed. Some men, of course, went in in the fall, and never came out at all until spring. I could leave on Saturday night, as long as I was back by Sunday night. It wasn't much time at home, but it was better than nothing and anyway, it never occurred to any of us that there was anything wrong with this. That was just the way life was.

Y'know, if you listen to all of these old songs about the lumberjacks and the camps, you get the impression that these were a pretty rowdy lot of men, but really, except for a very few that wasn't true at all. You can understand, though, how even those few would want to live it up a bit when they did hit town. They couldn't wait for the excitement of a few drinks and even a few good fights. They were raring to go.

They mostly were young guys just blowing their corks. The camps didn't allow drinking at all, and even if they had, it was always too far away for them to get liquor. There was a team of horses that brought the mail in once in a while, but that was all. Even if a man could sneak a bottle in, he would be fired if he was caught. It could be dangerous in those woods, and it was important that he have his wits about him at all times.

It wasn't all just cutting down trees and hauling logs, you know. There were all types of jobs in a lumber camp. For instance, there was one chap who was known as a "sand-hill man". His job was to keep sand on the hills to slow the sleighs down. That may sound simple, but it really was a very skilled job. He had to know how to use just the right amount of sand to match the various conditions. If the hill was too slippery, the sleigh would come too fast and bang into the horses and either push them off the road into the bushes, or run over them and they would be killed. If he put too much, the whole thing would stop. The sand-hill man knew exactly how much sand to put on to slow the sleighs.

Another man was called a "chickadee". His job was to pick the horse pebbles off the road. If there was too much of it on the road, the sleigh would stick on them just like it would on too much sand. When those sleighs were loaded with logs, they weighed many tons, and it was important that they kept moving — not too slow, and not too fast. A runaway sleigh could be a disaster. If one came to a halt, it was sometimes hard to get it going again. There were all kinds of strange little jobs like that in the woods and they were every bit as important as actually cutting trees. Each man was part of a team.

It's all so different today. The equipment is different. The work is not drudgery any longer, and most men don't even stay overnight, let alone stay all winter. Now they're driven in by buses, and sometimes even by helicopters and small planes. The camps as they were in the old days are gone, and for that matter, so are the old-time lumberjacks. They don't even call them that any more. They now are referred to as "woods workers" who go out in the mornings to their jobs and come back home at night. The old days are gone, and there are not many people shedding tears for those days. It was a very hard way to make a living.

Hugh MacLennan

Getting It Down on Paper

At the age of eighty-one, Hugh MacLennan is one of the acknowledged masters of Canadian writing. His novels about Canadian places, situations, and events are landmarks along the rocky road to this country's maturity in the arts. His 1941 novel Barometer Rising *told of the 1917 Halifax Explosion, the worst explosion in history up to that time.* Two Solitudes *dramatized the sad situation of French-English relations in Canada. His writings are filled with people and places he has known. Another of his novels,* Each Man's Son *is the often tragic tale of people caught up in an environment over which they have no control — the coal miners of Cape Breton and the town of Glace Bay, where Hugh MacLennan was born to a doctor's family in 1907.*

My father was a doctor in general practice, a very difficult one, working for the coal company. He didn't make much money for what proved to be very severe work. There were many accidents in the mines and a great deal of sickness too, due to the privation of the miners and the low wages they received. Glace Bay was a very young town then. When I was born in 1907, it was only six years old, a company town with company houses, company stores, and all that sort of thing.

The poorly built houses were in rows, two families under one roof, with a wall between them. It was exactly what had been described by D.H. Lawrence of the mines in Nottinghamshire in England. Indeed, the pattern for the town could easily have come from there: there was heavy English investment in the mines of Glace Bay.

My actual, early memory of life there is rather dim, because Father took his family away from Glace Bay when I was six years old, around 1913, but my mother took us back for a while during the 1914–18 war while Father was serving overseas with the Medical Corps. We were back in Halifax at the time of the Halifax Explosion of 1917, but after that, we went back to Glace Bay for another while, when I went to school there. So all in all I remember the place very well.

It was like a frontier town in those years with people coming in from all over the world. I'd stroll over to the main part of town on a Saturday night, where there'd be a lot of those miners with coal dust still on their faces. It seemed there'd always be a fight between two or three of them on Commercial Street at Senator's Corner, with great crowds cheering them on. I remember one old fellow saying, "Why should I go into Sydney and pay to see Black Roddy fight, when I can see Big Alex McKubrie here, fightin' for nothin'?" Oh, she was a wild old town back then.

My father loved Cape Breton with a passion. He was a very, very loyal Scot, and he felt right at home in that Celtic culture, but eventually, the hard work of being a "company doctor" got to him. He was tired all the time and hardly ever got a full night's sleep. If it wasn't an accident in the mine, it would be some fellow pounding at his door with a broken nose, received from a fist fight at two o'clock in the morning. He hated to leave Cape Breton because his roots were there. His father and mother both spoke Gaelic and just barely had English.

It was many years later, in 1951, that I actually finished my novel about Glace Bay, *Each Man's Son*. At the time, my first wife was nearly dying in one hospital in Montreal and I was in another, but somehow or other I managed to write that book. It was the quickest one I ever wrote—also the shortest. I just had to pull all the events out of my head. It was written with some intensity, but I was surprised, really, at its success.

I was also surprised at the success of my book on the Halifax explosion, *Barometer Rising*. I began it before the Second World War, and it came out during the war, and I gave it a life of perhaps nine months, but it's lasted for years. It has come out in paperback and it was extremely well dramatized on CBC. Somebody else is talking of making a movie of it, but I think the technical problems of recreating that event would be very difficult. After all, you can't blow up a town.

In the winter of 1917, the south end schools of Halifax didn't start until 9:30 a.m., to save electricity. So when the explosion occurred at three minutes after nine, on December first, I wasn't yet in the classroom where I would normally be. My first thought was that it was a bomb. I had been tending the furnace at home when I felt this terrific shock which was the earthquake. That was the first thing. Then I raced upstairs to a bay window, where I saw all these objects flying through the air. The whole floor jumped up then, and all the windows came in, and my pants split open, even though I wasn't touched by anything. If I had been four steps forward of where I was, my head would have been knocked off. The complete northwest side of our house buckled. My mother thought it was an air raid, so she herded us all down to the basement.

At this point the doorbell rang, and I went up to answer it. The door was down on the hall floor and there was a soldier out there wanting to know where his captain was. I asked him what had happened and he said, "Oh, a dump went up somewhere. Those damn fools putting an ammunition dump in the middle of town." He didn't know any more than I did what had really happened.

I ventured outside, and the streets were absolutely empty. Not a soul around. Suddenly, one of those trucks that had solid wheels at that time came careering down. This was opposite the Public Gardens in Halifax. It was reeling from side to side and there was a man in the tail-gate with both hands on his face and blood squirting out between his fingers. The truck hit a tree and he was thrown out. I ran over, but he was dead, and the person driving the truck was also dead.

Still there was nobody on the streets. I went down two blocks to see if my sister was allright. She had already gone to school. On the corner of Morris Street and South Park, I heard somebody moaning. It was some poor man in a plasterer's outfit. Evidently he had been plastering above a window when it smashed and cut his jugular. He had fallen out through the window and bled to death. By the time I got a couple of blocks farther down, everybody was coming out of their houses, wondering what was happening to them. My sister had survived, by the way, and we made our way back to our house to find that our father had come home from the hospital to see if we were allright. Then he went right back.

A wonderful thing did happen at Camp Hill Military Hospital, where the wards were. That hospital was about a quarter of a mile long, and when the first shock came, every soldier in every bed knew what it was. They had heard plenty of explosions before. Every one of them rolled out of their beds instinctively, and went under them, at the same time shouting to the doctors and nurses to do the same. Then the windows burst inwards with the glass shards flying in all directions. Not a single person in those wards was injured. It still amazes me when I think of it.

The toll throughout the city was horrifying. The hundreds of people who lost their eyes, people with their faces just cut to pieces, who didn't have any idea what was going on.

Up in the north end of the city, that tidal wave went up the hill about three streets, and anyone who's ever been to Halifax knows how steep the land leading down to the water is. The wave roared in and ripped up everything it reached on land, while out in the harbour it tore ships free of their anchor chains and tossed them around like chips.

I've only known one person who witnessed the actual explosion and lived to talk of it. That was Arthur Lismer, the famous Canadian painter. You see, fortunately the Sydney Express train and the Ocean Limited were both late coming to Halifax that morning. While waiting for the train, Lismer suddenly saw this terrific flash up at the Narrows about six or seven miles away. The concussion reached him about two and a half minutes later and knocked him head over heels.

Citadel Hill protected a great many people in the south end of the city, but in the north, which got the full brunt, it was appalling. I tried to get up there, but the soldiers turned us back. With the war on, the city was full of troops and they immediately took charge.

By this time, people were pouring down from the north end. Every horse-and-wagon brought down loads of bleeding victims and every hospital was full. The schools were getting filled up with the injured, as indeed were all of the public buildings.

It happened on a lovely December morning — about forty-two degrees Fahrenheit [plus 6 Celsius], but then to add to the misery, the temperature began to fall immediately. Snow began falling at about two in the afternoon, and by midnight it was a raging blizzard and the temperature was two above zero Fahrenheit. Something like three feet came down, which helped put out fires, but God only knows how many were buried in it.

Many heroic stories came out of the disaster. I think of those British sailors off *The High Flyer*, who were told it was an ammunition ship, but still they tried to get aboard after the collision to attempt to put out the fires. It exploded just as they reached the side.

The entire thing was an accident pure and simple. Someone balled up a signal. The Swedish ship, the *Imo*,came out of the harbour and hit the *Mont Blanc* which was in the Narrows. The *Mont Blanc* was very badly loaded and it had a tremendous amount of benzol on the deck held down only by ropes. I believe there was about 550 thousand pounds of the stuff and about 2,700 tons of liddite, which is what was used in gun shells at that time. That blew up like a bomb. The benzol was ignited, thrown up in the sky and then fell down on the houses and set fire to them. The north end was a hideous sight.

The railway tracks were twisted like so much spaghetti, partly due to the shock and partly from the heat. The harbour itself was deepened about eighteen feet where the explosion occurred and the bottom there is solid granite. It was the biggest explosion ever until Hiroshima in 1945.

It's very hard to say how many actually died in the Halifax Explosion. The official figures counted 2,000 dead, but who really knows how many died later of wounds? The official wounded list was somewhere about 20,000, with the eye wounded being the heaviest. They actually collected buckets of eyes that had been blown out of skulls. I remember when we finally got back to school again, three-quarters of my schoolmates had scars on their faces.

It took me about twenty-two years before I actually sat down to write about that tragedy. I had written two novels that failed; the second was rejected by twenty-two different publishers. The last one attached a note to my New York agent which said, "We don't know who your writer is. He doesn't write like an American, and he doesn't write like an Englishman." It was then I realized that Aristotle was right when he said, "No work of fiction — he was speaking of drama — is successful unless there are recognitions." That is so true. For example, I think of an American book, *Strange Fruit*, which opens with a very dramatic paragraph: "It's a hot night in Alabama in a small town, and here is a Negro with a white girl." You don't need any more than that, because the world knows what that implies.

So here I was with this story, but who in the hell in the States knew or cared about Halifax and Canada? I knew it had to be published in the United States, because in the hands of a Toronto publisher at that time, it would have been buried. To gain any kind of recognition then, you had to get published either in England or the States. That was almost an impossible task then, because they didn't care about Canada, let alone Halifax. Therefore, it was necessary to create an American stage before putting the drama on it, for which, of course, I was duly criticized by the academics for quite a while.

The Americans were not read widely in England until *The Last of the Mohicans* [by James Fenimore Cooper], because Europeans had the idea of "the red Indian," "the noble savage." They thought Dickens was a far better writer than Melville, which he wasn't. Melville was finally discovered and brought to the fore by D.H. Lawrence. I'll amend that. Melville was really discovered by Archie MacMechan, a professor of English at Dalhousie University in Halifax, who came from Ontario. Rummaging around the Dalhousie Library, he came across *Moby-Dick* by Melville. He read it, and then wrote an article for the *Atlantic Monthly* called "The Greatest Sea Story Ever Told," and that's what started the Melville boom in the United States. Lawrence discovered him a few years later, and wrote wonderfully well about him. That accounts for his popularity in England.

Charles G.D. Roberts was a well-recognized and popular Canadian writer long before I came on the scene. I loved his animal stories when I was a boy. They were very authentic, and beautifully written — romanticized perhaps. I met Roberts just before his death and he was very gracious to me. Apropos of *Barometer Rising*, he said, "Canada is coming of age allright if you could do that now. You couldn't have done it in my time. The land itself is too overwhelming, and too new to be known and felt."

Now, *Two Solitudes*, my novel about the problems found by the French and English trying to exist side by side in Quebec is another story tragically funny in its own way. The Hollywood boys wanted to make it into a movie, shifting the locale out of Canada to somewhere in the U.S.A. I told them that surely the Quebec separatist crisis which was in the news all over the world made Canada something more than an unknown quantity. "No," said this fellow from Hollywood, "I'll tell you what you can do. There's a Mennonite settlement somewhere in the American middle west. You can set it there." This really happened! Not thirty or forty years ago, but sometime in 1980.

Margaret Lawrence's book, *A Jest of God*, was sold to the movies and they transferred it out of Canada to the Midwest. They continue to do that. There are all sorts of funny stories. I remember the film reader for Paramount Pictures recommended *Barometer Rising* very strongly as a book that should become a picture. As a result, I was called to their New York offices. A rather "boiled" looking man took me to lunch. "It's a great book," he said: "I haven't read it, but it's great! You know, though, that Halifax thing kinda kills it. Nice brought up people in New York only know that as a polite swear word. They don't say, 'Go to hell'. They say 'Go to Halifax'. We'll do a switcheroo on the location. What difference does it make as long as it's a good story? Boy meets girl, Paris, France. Great! Boy meets girl, Halifax or Winnipeg. Who cares?" Anyway, *Barometer Rising* never made it to Hollywood.

It was done on CBC Radio many years ago and they did a splendid job of it. Actually, it would require tremendous resources to do a story like that on film.

I didn't start out to be a "Canadian" writer — just a writer. It was the existing conditions of the times that brought that about. I never even thought about it one way or the other. I had a classical education, you might say, although it wasn't up to English standards. I loathed the way they did things at Princeton, which was purely Germanic, yet they could hardly read Latin and Greek. They had to read what Germans said about it. So I did badly there.

I got a job for twenty-five dollars a week in Montreal where I became fascinated with Canada as I had never been in Central Canada before. I was a Maritimer. I discovered that this part of my country had it all — French, English, and everything else. So, out of that came *Two Solitudes*. It was published in 1945, before the end of the war. It did very well in the United States and very well here.

Ninety percent of the people who use the expression "two solitudes" today never read the book, I'm sure, but the phrase stuck and did go into the language. It was a lucky title. I couldn't find a title at first for what I had written, until I came across a review in the *New York Times* of a very bad book. The review ended with the statement, "This writer has absolutely no conception of the profundity of Rilke's line "Love consists in this: 'The two solitudes protect and touch and greet each other'." I thought, "There's my title!" My American publisher didn't want it. He thought it was too gloomy. I said, "Please keep it." He did because he couldn't find a better one.

Two Solitudes had a great impact on the reading public because it came just at the time of our second conscription crisis. In 1944, the casualties in the war were getting pretty bad. The old Bloc Populaire was holding rallies all over Quebec, and in one of them I saw this young man introducing old Henri Bourassa down in Magog. Here was a passionate young man, blazing eyes, locks of black hair falling over his forehead, speaking with a terrible intensity. I said to my friend, "I've just put that man in a book, and mailed him to New York. Who is he?" "Don't you know?" said my friend, "that's André Laurendeau."

Three years later, André, who had a family of six children, wrote a book for children and sent me an autographed copy. I got to know him somewhat later, and admired him tremendously for the very great service he did for this country in making young people aware of what was going on in Quebec. What *Two Solitudes* did was spread that word outside the province. Things have improved in recent years between the French and English, but there's still a long way to go.

For me, writing has always provided a great deal of satisfaction. It's not something one goes into to make money because most writers have to have another job. It's always been that way, not just in Canada, but in other countries as well. It's always been a marginal occupation, and you do it for reasons other than material rewards.

Lucky Lott

Cheap Thrills

Thrill shows were the big form of release for a lot of people during the Depression. For a few coins you could go to an outdoor show that featured daredevils in cars or boats or even airplanes. There were motorcycle shows, six-day bicycle races and death-defying dives from high towers into what looked like a bucket of water. Magicians loaded down with chains and locked in boxes were dropped into lakes, high-wire artists walked across the Niagara gorge while down below others tumbled over the Falls in barrels. Watching someone else tempting death or sometimes embracing it became a universal pastime. Huge crowds turned up for these events, something to take the humdrum from their own lives.

I saw my first show in Chicago when I was about twelve or thirteen and watched some "old guys" who were probably about thirty at the time, roaring around in their cars. I thought, "Well, if they can do that, I should be able to do it better." I had already learned to drive an old Model T and thought I was pretty much of a whiz anyway.

Back home after seeing that show I started polishing up some kind of an act in a farmer's field with a few friends and a bunch of old cars. Our first show was in 1935. We paid the farmer twenty dollars for the use of his pasture and we plastered signs all over the countryside, advertising our big thrill show. We actually pulled in over nine hundred dollars in nickels and dimes. That was a fortune in those days when nine dollars could keep a family going for a week. We just couldn't believe it! We dumped all of that money in a pile and we counted it over and over again. I didn't even *know* anybody who ever *saw* that much money. We knew we were onto a good thing and we decided to go on with more shows, bigger and better ones.

The more dangerous we could make our acts appear, the more people seemed to like them. We used to build huge ramps where we'd have to race our cars up at speeds around a hundred miles an hour. At the top, the car would go sailing through the air until it came to another ramp that would take it down the other side. Now, stunts like that have to be planned and timed perfectly or someone is going to die. We always kept a watchful eye on what some of the other daredevils like Lucky Teeter were doing and we'd take our tips from them. Teeter was the creator of ramp-to-ramp and its greatest practitioner, but he fell short one time and was killed. He was so confident he didn't even wear a safety belt. Needless to say we didn't take *all* of our tips from him. We did learn though from that tragedy, that some kind of a cushion was needed at the other end in case a car did miss — something soft like bales of straw. Our motto became "Luck is only a name — know-how is the name of the game." But you know, no matter how much you prepare or how many precautions you take, you never take anything for granted. It's such a scary thing that you're always filled with apprehension. The night before a show, sleep was impossible and the butterflies in your stomach would have wings like a bat.

The worst thing would be hearing news that other stunt drivers had been killed or maimed. You can imagine what that would do to you as you were preparing for a show. I saw one friend, Carl Suchuk, killed right before my eyes in a stunt that he had successfully performed in my show only six months before. He was the kind of guy who wanted to try everything. He even went over the Falls in a barrel successfully.

Ken Carter was another like that. He'd try anything. On the circuit he was known as "The Mad Canadian." I helped him prepare for many of his stunts but I finally had to walk away when these acts were getting too dangerous. I said, "Ken, you're doing weird things." Sure enough, he was killed in his Rocket Car stunt a while later. When someone dies in that way — literally by his own hand — sure, I'm disturbed and I feel sorry that it happened; but I get mad too because it was something that *shouldn't* have happened. I've had accidents myself, but it was never because I was doing something stupid or careless.

I played at as many as eighty fairs a summer where we wrecked an average of five cars a fair. Over my entire career, I made something like 800 jumps and wrecked in my shows something like 7,000 cars. These weren't accidents — just part of the show.

There were some very good and famous racers on the circuit when I started out in the thirties. Barney Oldfield was one — someone whose name lives on — and I actually worked with Barney for a while. He was the first man to drive a car two miles a minute. He drove Henry Ford's car, old 999, all over the place.

Frank and Patty Conklin of Toronto were the ones who brought me to Canada after I did my stint as a bomber pilot during the war. I was actually from Illinois, but they brought me here to perform in shows. I married a Canadian girl and this is where I've lived ever since. I knew Canada anyway, because of the circuit we travelled in our performances and I always liked it here.

I think most of us stunt drivers are just kids who don't want to grow up. It's exhibitionism, really, but you know when you're getting the roar of the crowd you don't really hear it because you're concentrating too hard on what you're doing. We'd have huge crowds back in the thirties out there in Western Canada, and they'd be yelling their heads off apparently, but the only sound that would get through to me was the sound of my engine. My ears were tuned right into that, just listening all the time to make sure it was ticking along like it should be. We played the "Burning Privy" circuit out there — Estevan, Weyburn, Assiniboia, Lethbridge, and Prince Albert. I remember that the young man who opened one of our fairs there was a lawyer called John Diefenbaker, a beginner politician.

People in Western Canada at that time would drive hundreds of miles just to come to one of these thrill shows. I'd be amazed at that because there was only one stretch of paved road at the time and that was between Moose Jaw and Regina. All the rest were gravel, real washboards. So you can imagine the shaking up we'd get just driving the roads between towns doing two shows a day, seven days a week.

Most of the guys doing what I was doing gradually dropped out of stunt racing — the ones who weren't killed, and as far as I know I'm the only one still doing it, fifty years later. It's not quite the same now. People are more blasé, I guess, and they get their thrills from too many other sources, but back in the Depression we were it. We were the big stars.

Rev. Dr. Donald McMillan

Kirks and Churches, Organs and Bagpipes

When the early pioneers came to this country in the eighteenth and nineteenth centuries one of the first things they wanted after putting a roof over their families' heads was a church, a place of worship, a link with the life they had left behind. This applied to all of the different groups, regardless of their origins or denomination.

As an important part of Canada's beginnings, those early churches are an important source of information today about the way we were, and who we are. They recorded the births and deaths, the triumphs and the tragedies of their members. Their record-keepers were the first unofficial historians of our country.

The Reverend Dr. Donald McMillan, a retired Presbyterian minister and former Moderator of the General Assembly from the Glengarry area in eastern Ontario, which was mainly settled by Scots, became interested in that history while serving in one of his early churches and carried that interest with him when he served overseas during the Second World War.

During my years as a chaplain with the RCAF, I visited many of the districts from which the early settlers came. Later on when I came back and was appointed to a chair in the college in Montreal I had access to the libraries where they had sourcebooks and other papers dating back to those early years.

Ontario's Glengarry area is a district of very special interest to many Scottish Canadians because it was one of the first areas to be settled at the end of the American Revolution by officers and men who fought on the side of the British. They were given land grants along the St. Lawrence River at Stormont and Dundas and even farther west. When I talk of Glengarry, I use the word not to designate a county but in the church sense: I include not only Glengarry county but also Stormont county and portions of Dundas, Prescott, and even a small portion of what was called Lower Canada. So it was quite a large land mass and very appealing to those early Scottish settlers who tried to bring Scotland with them to the new world. They were primarily Gaelic-speaking, although some of them and most of their leaders also spoke English.

Most churches' ministers were Gaelic-speaking too, except for a few in Stormont county, where German was the language of the people who had settled in Canada after having lived first in the New England states. Originally, of course, they came from Germany down the Rhine River, through Holland and over to England, where Queen Anne encouraged them to go to New England to settle. This particular group was so loyal to the British Crown thereafter that on the outbreak of hostilities in the American Revolution they elected to be on the British side, so they received their grants along with the Gaelic-speaking soldiers.

The people of Glengarry have always been very much akin to the Scots who settled in Pictou and Cape Breton Island in Nova Scotia. They retained their way of life, their language, and their customs. It's a real thrill to observe this every year at the annual Highland games. You'll see forty or fifty pipe bands, Scottish singers, dancers, and other musicians and twenty or twenty-five thousand others who are for the most part simply recharging their Scottish heritage.

I believe the church played a big part in enabling them to retain their Scottishness. An early requirement was that the ministers had to be bilingual. In the church where I served in 1930, the vacancy advertisement included the words "Gaelic essential," and it was. When I greeted the older parishioners at the church door I'd have been at a loss if I couldn't speak to them in the old tongue.

The pursuits that they followed in Canada were the same ones they followed in Scotland, except that the area that they had to farm was very different from their native land. The first generation had to contend with the forest and a wilderness area which most had never seen the likes of before. But they transformed it completely to fine farmland in the first half-century. They began by cutting just enough trees to build their homes and clearing a small portion of land to grow some crops. Those who had been fighting in the British army in northern New York had some knowledge of forests and it was in the army that they had learned how to use the logs when they built fortresses. When they came to Glengarry they built their homes the same way and taught others the skills needed. The first churches were all made of logs and these were located in the southern part of Glengarry, along the river.

When their houses were completed, they wanted a minister and a church. Ministers didn't come over with them in the beginning, but it didn't take long before they arrived. The Reverend John Bethune who had served as a chaplain with the British forces originally came out to North Carolina from the Isle of Skye. His stay was short, however, as he enlisted and was soon taken prisoner when the Revolution began. His group was too ill-equipped to fight properly. Not only Bethune but other famous people such as the husband of Flora Macdonald, the Scottish heroine who befriended Bonnie Prince Charlie had the same problem. But Bethune remained loyal to Crown and left the States after the war and came first to Montreal and established a congregation. He didn't remain there too long as the Glengarry area was more what he wanted. He liked its Scottishness and, of course, the large land grants were attractive as he had a large family — six boys and three girls. He settled himself here in 1787 and from then on he ministered to his people. He died in 1815. He accomplished a good deal. He established preaching points at Williamstown, Lancaster, Summerstown, Cornwall, and Martintown. That was indeed a very big area for one man to cover but he did it and became a great source of comfort to these people, many of whom had suffered such persecution by the English after the Battle of Culloden in 1746. Many were stripped of everything and chased off their lands during the Highland Clearances. So the security and freedom of their new homeland were something they cherished.

In Glengarry, we also had those who chose to leave America after the Revolution, and another group of veterans who came over after serving the Crown in the Napoleonic Wars. This group undoubtedly came because they saw better opportunities in the new land, which they had heard of from friends or relatives who had come earlier. At any rate there was a continual migration from the Highlands of Scotland to Glengarry from 1800 on, and most came of their own free will.

Over there, after Culloden, they were forbidden almost everything they held so dear: their language, their bagpipes, and even any sign of their national dress, the tartan. In Glengarry we remember this every year in a religious ceremony we call "The Kirking of the Tartan". On that day everyone is encouraged to wear the kilt and we play plenty of good Scottish music in church.

Speaking of music, there was a period of many many years when the only music in the Presbyterian church was that provided by the voice alone, the singing of psalms and the paraphrases. A paraphrase is a free translation of certain portions of the scripture. The early people in the church believed that it was better to *sing* the word of God and they were led in this singing by a "presenter." He presented the lines to be sung and the church members followed him. This practice goes back hundreds of years to the Westminster Assembly, to the days when most people in the pews were not able to read. So they would have the presenter line out the words, verse by verse, singing them at the same time, and the others would join with him. That became quite a tradition in the churches, and it made for some very long services, as it doubled the time it took to sing something: first the presenter, and then the people in the pews. The presenter occupied a high place of honour in the church and he counted himself a very important person. It's interesting to note that at the time the only musical instrument in church was a tuning fork.

It was a long time before any other type of music made its way into the church. It was a very controversial process in which the Reverend Donald Gordon, the father of the famous Ralph Connor, played an important role on the side of the opposition. The majority of the individual churches opposed the introduction of the organ. They thought they would lose a great deal of the heritage that they associated with their worship in the past. Also, the singing was extremely well done, and the congregation loved it just the way it was.

In the Reverend Ralph Connor's church in "the Indian lands," as they were known then, he writes of how as many as a hundred people were trained to sing the parts. One can imagine how glorious this must have sounded — one hundred trained singers with another four or five hundred parishioners joining in. It must have been magnificent.

When the organ was first introduced there would be times when the presenter and the organist didn't quite know what the other was doing. On one occasion at St. Elmo Church in the Indian lands on one of the first sabbaths, it was understood ahead of time that the organist would play the instrument and the presenter would also assist in the leading of the singing. However, the minister forgot to announce the tune they were to sing, and the result was that the organist played one tune while the presenter sang to the tune of something entirely different. They went through all of the verses, totally oblivious of each other, right to the end. I can only imagine how that sounded and wonder if one was trying to show the other up!

Another reason for the resistance to music in the church was that some of the oldsters looked on musical instruments as "instruments of the devil." Even some ministers who played fiddles or bagpipes themselves were opposed. It wasn't music they were against; it was music in *church*, and the use of any manmade instrument in the service of worship. Some ministers who were against instruments being used were actually very accomplished musicians and composers, and some of our most beloved Scottish tunes were composed by ministers, "The Road to The Isles" being one example. At one time someone remarked to the

Reverend Gordon that it was unfair of him to oppose the use of the organ in that he had the benefit of such a wonderful choir in his church, while other small churches didn't have that advantage. His answer is not recorded, but he didn't change his mind, in any event. Gradually, however, the opposition died out and musical instruments found their way in. Today there are services where instruments of all types are used inside the church.

Today, it's not unusual at all for bagpipes to be part of the service in Glengarry, nor is it unusual to see the minister dressed in Highland costume, welcoming his people to church, or the "kirk."

Within Scotland, the church was always called The Kirk of Scotland. The story is told of one small village where there were three churches. The Kirk of Scotland, the Free Kirk, and the United Presbyterian Kirk — all different branches of Presbyterianism. They say that the ringing of all three of the Kirk bells had a sound which allowed one to recognize which bell belonged to which. The old Kirk had a sound which said: "We are the Kirk, We are the Kirk." The Free Kirk, which had broken away over the appointment of ministers, had a bell which replied, "No, you're not; No, you're not." The United Presbyterian, which was made up of various sects that had broken away from the Kirk of Scotland over the question of government funding and was now entirely dependent on voluntary donations, or givings, had a bell which people said sounded the words, "Collection, Collection."

Bob Hahn

The Harmony Kids

Joyce Hahn was one of the earliest stars on Canadian television. She was pretty, cute, and talented, and she had the appearance of good fortune about her, the air of someone born to the "good life" and who never suffered a hard day in her life. During the Depression, however, Joyce was born into a family that was constantly on the move. Her father took his small flock, wife and four children, all over the country searching for a place to roost, a place where things might be better for them. For a time in the early thirties they lived in northern Saskatchewan on a lonely homestead. Like so many families of the time, they continued to move westward in search of the promised land, the Canadian counterparts of the dispossessed people portrayed in John Steinbeck's classic Grapes of Wrath. *The Hahns' constant moves never seemed to better their lives. Bob Hahn, one of Joyce's brothers, remembers the period as a time when his father was not trying to get into something new, but trying rather to "get* OUT *of some situation."*

When the drought hit the prairies — something Dad couldn't control — he had to do something to get away from it. He made his first move towards the west with us and all of our belongings in an old truck. This brought us to a worse situation. He was making a series of bad decisions in reaction to the terrible circumstances of our lives. Each new place was worse than the one we had left with the homestead in the north of Saskatchewan the worst of them all. It was cold and lonely and the land was totally unsuitable for farming. All we had was each other. There were no schools, no telephones, no railways, no doctors, no dentists — as the saying goes, "No nothing."

My mother took very sick at one stage and it took us two days to get a doctor. He had to operate practically in the dark, except for a flashlight. This really shook us and my dad was more depressed than ever for getting us into the situation he figured he had gotten us into.

In the meantime, Dad's parents down East would be sending us packages every fall, a barrel of dried apples and staples like that. They helped to keep us alive. The things in the barrels were packed with old newspapers and, starved as we were for news of any kind, we'd straighten them out, of course, and read every word. There was a story in there titled "Tin Can Tourists." It had a picture of a trailer and a family who were travelling all over the States; wherever they stopped, they were "home." The story really got to Dad, and before we knew what was happening he began to build a trailer. His real profession was cabinet maker, so that helped a lot even though it did take him eighteen months to finish and find wheels for it and figure out a way to get it out.

He did, and it was our escape from the barren northern homestead. We'd been there for six years. We had nothing when we arrived and nothing when we left except a couple of guitars, an accordian, and banjos plus some singing talent. In fact we had developed into a passable musical singing group during the long and lonely winter evenings. We were the best in the North, but the truth is we were actually pretty awful. We were musically illiterate and we played by the seat of our pants. All of the musical ability we later acquired was picked up on the road in the days and months ahead of us, as that was how we planned to earn our living, with music.

We'd stop in a small town and the only two places where people gathered and where we could possibly perform were the Chinese restaurant that one will find in any little prairie town and the poolroom. We'd stop at these places, put on a show, and pass the hat around. Most times we'd get at least enough to buy something to eat and enough gas to get to the next town. Day after day we'd do this, living hand-to-mouth — but I don't remember that it was awful at all. It was living on the edge, but it was exciting, with new experiences, new people, and new places everyday.

Also, you must remember we were providing some measure of excitement to these dusty little towns. In the thirties this great big rig of a trailer that Father had built would stop people in their tracks. They'd never seen anything like it before. The trailer and the truck were painted green, red, and yellow and you can be certain that when we arrived in a town everybody knew we were there.

At first we called ourselves "The Hahn Family," but when we were asked to appear on the radio in Saskatoon as "Hahn and His Kids," one of the telegrams the station received was from a lady who thought that our name wasn't very nice, and suggested that we change the title to "The Harmony Kids." We thought this was a good title and we took it and stuck with it.

We were in no hurry to get to any particular destination so we just kept moving in an easterly direction, like a band of gypsies, stopping at any little town or village where we thought we could make a dollar or two. When October arrived we had made it to Regina and we were having all kinds of trouble with the authorities — "How come these kids aren't in school?" — things like that. We were engaged to appear on a local Regina radio station for a once-a-week show at five dollars a show for the whole famly. That was a lot of money for us at the time. In addition they gave us ten dollars for an hour on Saturday and they allowed us to sell post cards with our picture on them. Suddenly we were making a hundred dollars a week just selling the cards. More money than we'd seen in total in the ten years prior! A hundred dollars was a fortune when whole families were living on ten or fifteen dollars a week!

We came down to earth from this euphoria long enough to realize that we had stumbled into a field where we could have futures, provided we could learn more about it. We all began music lessons — the girls adding singing and dancing lessons and we were all beginning to know what we were doing for the first time.

Our radio show got a commercial sponsor in 1936, one of the first commercially sponsored shows in Canada, by a soap company, called of all things OGD (Out Goes Dirt), and letters came in from different towns asking how much the Harmony Kids would charge to appear at various functions. That meant we had to put a real show together which would have different things such as magic illusions and so on. Letters came too from towns in Montana and North Dakota, places where the Regina radio signal reached. We'd take off for these places and put our show on there, mainly because the educational authorities caught up to us and stopped us from doing it in Regina — and they wouldn't permit us on the highway with our trailer because they were afraid we'd get snowed in somewhere. We'd been in Regina for sixteen months and we were dying to move on to other pastures anyway.

By now, we had a new truck with a good radio and we had a new sound system for our concerts. One day while rolling down the highway, listening to an American show called "We, the People" from New York, a family who were performing on it claimed that they were the most trailer-travelled family in North America. Well, my dad was so angry that he immediately wrote the producer a snarky letter telling them about us, the Hahns. He said we had done more, gone further and could make that family look like beginners.

Eventually — months later when our mail caught up with us — there was a letter from "We, the People" apologizing for their mistake in presenting that other family as "the most travelled" etc., and they invited us to come to New York and appear on the show. To make a long story short, very soon the whole family was there standing right in the centre of Broadway. We left the truck and trailer in a parking lot in Buffalo in the middle of a snowstorm in January and made it down to New York by train, as we were scheduled to appear on the show the following Tuesday. If it wasn't for that we would have driven the whole rig right down the middle of Broadway.

Our "We, the People" appearance was a great success and it gave us an entré to a whole lot of other opportunities. Booking agents and managers were waiting at the stage door when we finished and we got work immediately all over New York. "Major Bowes Amateur Hour" had us on and we won, and we were offered tours all over the United States. We were riding so high we had to pinch ourselves to believe it. From the homestead to Broadway in the blink of an eye.

However, that's when everything began to go wrong. Educational authorities and do-gooder organizations started to get into the act making noises about children being exploited and so on. We had to more or less go into hiding, playing in out-of-the-way places such as Coney Island and other sites further away from the downtown area. In the end we moved across the river to New Jersey where these busybodies had no jurisdiction. We got lots of work in towns like Hoboken, especially when the war started and people suddenly had money to spend.

By this time my brother and I were nineteen and twenty and we had to make a choice between joining the American forces or coming home to join the Canadian army — which is what we did. The Harmony Kids had had their day. Joyce and Kay tried working without us for a while, but that didn't work. At war's end Lloyd returned with one arm gone. Kay died young with leukemia and that left only me and Joyce. It took her a while, but Joyce later became the darling of the new television service in Canada and I had good success in other areas of the music business.

I often wonder what would have happened to us had the Depression never occurred. People were forced into trying all sorts of things just to survive. It was the Depression that created the musical Hahn Family and the Harmony Kids.

Joe Neil MacNeil

Do You Have the Gaelic?

Joe Neil MacNeil of Big Pond, Cape Breton, was born in 1908, when there were still Gaelic-speaking communities on the island and when English was seldom heard there. Sadly, the Gaelic language is now dying out with the older generation despite the efforts of local folk societies to maintain it. With the island's improved communications with the mainland, the language of its residents' ancestors is heard less and less, and their rich heritage of oral history is gradually being lost. Joe Neil MacNeil is one of the island's finest old-style storytellers and has the Gaelic himself.

I was adopted at the age of six months by a couple living in Middle Cape. They were quite elderly and couldn't speak a word of English, and so it was that I grew up knowing only Gaelic. When I started school I had no English of course, except for a few words here and there. I was taught how to say my name in English and I was able to remember that, but that was about it. The funny part of it was that I could read a bit of English, but couldn't speak it.

At school we didn't use Gaelic except when we were outside playing. Inside the school Gaelic was forbidden despite the fact that most of the children spoke it as a first language. This was around 1914 or '15, and English had already made enough inroads that most families around there could speak both, although they preferred Gaelic. The parents and the younger children were picking up what English they had from the older children who were bringing it home from school.

Little by little, I learned the English language but it took a long time. In spite of this I never lost my love for the beautiful Gaelic and for the customs which my own people had brought over from the Hebrides. I think I may have been a bit different than most children my age which was probably because I was the only child in a home with elderly Gaelic-speaking parents. Most of my time was spent in the company of my elders. When others would come for a house-visit I was very interested in the conversations they would have and even if there were children along, I used to stay with the old folks and listen to them and the stories they told.

These stories were a big part of the social life back then, especially in the long dark nights of winter. No people in particular would be invited to a house-visit. They would just drop by and they were always welcome. It didn't matter how many came — one or a dozen — all would have the same warm reception. In those days the house-visit fulfilled a very important function. It was the only way of getting news of what was happening: whether the blacksmith was active at this job, or if the merchant had received the load of goods he was expecting off the boat. People would also ask whether the miller had begun to grind the grain, and if he had begun to card the wool. They would talk of other people they had met during the day's activities and what news they had picked up from them.

All of this was shared with the others as well as news of when fish started moving up the river. There was not much idle talk in these sessions. Most were interested in hearing news that was important to their lives. Gossip seldom entered these evenings of information and entertainment.

Some excelled at singing songs and others at reciting poems. Still others were outstanding musicians and dancers. I was most interested in the storytellers, the ones who could keep you spellbound by reciting the tales that had been passed down from generation to generation over hundreds of years.

Some were so skilled at this that you would be held enraptured — sometimes for hours — listening to the old stories. I would listen with both ears, noting all the inflections in their speech and later would practise telling the same stories when I was alone.

These gatherings were called ceilidhs, which is pronounced Kay-Lee in English, and they could be all music or all talk or a mixture of both. The code of hospitality also dictated that food, something small, should be given. Sometimes it might be a small dram if there was plenty of it, or it might be only buttermilk or tea, with a little bit of food. These house-visits were wonderful for keeping people together and happy, physically and spiritually. It's a great loss that so much of this has declined and grown so rare.

Something I didn't have but wanted very much at that time was the ability to read Gaelic. Many of the old folks who spoke the language couldn't read it, but there was a man who lived further on from us who would come visit us frequently and he could read it. I used to save every little bit of paper with any Gaelic on it until he came. He would read them for me, and I began to pick up the written language a bit at a time. Then I found a copy of *MacTalla*, an old paper which had gone out of print before my time, which contained stories and other items in Gaelic. This was a great help but it was the ads from various merchants that helped the most. They showed the items and the Gaelic was right there for things like flour, meal, tea, a suit, and things of that kind.

I found copies of some of the classical works but found the words far beyond my capability to understand. Then I borrowed a copy of *Clarsach No Coille*, and started to read the words to the songs, which I had already heard before. That was a great help to me.

Then, too, there was a Gaelic newspaper which was printed in Sydney and I'd buy that from time to time. Another one was called *The Casket* and that was printed in Antigonish, and it had a section in Gaelic with songs and stories and Letters to the Editor. Even the main Cape Breton newspaper, *The Post*, had a bit of Gaelic in it every week. So with all of these things I was able to learn to read it as well as speak it. I graduated to books and finally I got a dictionary to find any words I was looking for.

We had plenty of storytellers in those days, but as with anything else some were much better than others. They could hold your attention for hours just in the telling of one tale. It was the long tales that pleased people the most. When a good story began, I would find myself hoping that it would never end. You also had some idea of what would happen but you never thought about that, because the storyteller was so skilled he could keep your attention and nobody ever got restless or bored.

Although one could go to any house to hear stories it seemed that some houses were better than others. In my neighbourhood, Michael MacLean's house was the best for lore and songs, and Archie Kennedy's was the best to go to for stories.

Any house where a wake was being held was especially good for hearing stories, because there would be a number of people who stayed there throughout the night keeping vigil with the body. Telling stories was the accepted way of passing time. One man in particular was especially good as a wake-house storyteller. He had wonderful, long stories and could carry them on all through the early morning hours.

Most stories are the same ones that have been told over hundreds of years, the same ones that were recited around fires back in the Highlands and islands of Scotland — long before we ever set foot in this country. It's amazing how little they have changed, even though they were passed on orally and not in print. The reason we know this is that there are books that I've seen which were printed hundreds of years ago that contain many of these stories almost exactly the same as I've heard them from people who never learned to read.

Sadly, the art is dying out and there are not many young people who are that interested anymore. There are a few old storytellers like myself around but not too many and what happens after we've gone is hard to say.

It's the same with the Gaelic. I'm afraid there are not many left now who can speak it — or if they can they don't use it much. There's some attempt through Gaelic culture societies to teach it through classes to young people, but the trouble is you can't really get it from books. You've got to use the language in conversation with others. I hope I'm wrong, but the future doesn't look good for "the language of the Garden of Eden."

Florence Bell

The School Cars of Ontario

In the mid 1920s, the northern part of Canada was still very much a developing country with few communities, few roads, and even fewer schoolhouses. In Northern Ontario there were many children of prospectors and trappers and railwaymen who were getting no education at all because of this. That's when the government of Ontario came up with a plan in co-operation with the three railroads. If the railroads would supply some cars, the government would fit them out as rolling schoolrooms, complete with teachers. These school cars would be able to go wherever the rails could take them, which was just about anywhere there were people, and the children could attend a unique kind of one-room school. The plan worked; and it was in these moving classrooms where many northern children received an education. Recently, I travelled to White River in northern Ontario for a reunion of some of these students with their teacher, eighty-one-year-old Florence Bell, who says she remembers all of her students, as well as some of the great characters who lived in isolation beside the railroad track.

The war was still on when my husband and I, along with our two children, took that job. We were the only husband-and-wife team of teachers — that is to say, where both of us actually taught. He would be teaching some students up at one end of the classroom, and I'd be teaching others down at the other end. The classroom was one half of the rail car, and in the other half we had our living-quarters which had all the comforts of a regular home. Two bedrooms, a living room, kitchen, and bathroom. It was very nice really, and there were very few problems except for one winter when we had trouble with heat. Now, in a country where the temperature outside gets down to thirty and thirty-five degrees below Fahrenheit, that could be very serious; but someone came and fixed that up before we froze to death.

When we first took that posting, I was full of misgivings. After all, what was it going to be like living day in and day out on a railroad car, half of which was a schoolroom, parked on a railroad siding? I wondered how we would get any sense of permanence when we would never be in one location any longer than a week. How would we ever get to know any neighbours, and how would our children ever get to have any permanent friends? These were only a few of the doubts I had, but do you know, those fears were all groundless.

Right from the very first day we loved it. When we went to bed we could hear the sound of a nearby waterfall, the roar of the rapids in the river, and the tiny noises coming from the forest that never stop. We slept soundly that first night and after a good breakfast in the morning we sat there and waited for our new students to show up.

The first who came were a boy and a girl from a Finnish family, a couple of tiny tots. Next, from across the tracks, came a little Norwegian-French girl, a beautiful little blonde. Her cousins from Sudbury were staying with them at the time, and they also came. The Pratt children showed next. Their father was English and their mother was Cree, and they told us two things: their father drank beer, and if you tell lies you don't go to heaven.

Our two children stood there looking at these children shyly and the new children just as shyly looked at them. After lunch the children came back to school with two kittens and a pup which they gave to my two. Then they were friends.

I wasn't supposed to teach that first day. I was only the teacher's wife; but we discovered that some of the children didn't really know how to work! So I went out in the classroom and began teaching along with my husband. It worked out so well that I kept on doing that in the days that followed. At the end of our first day we gave the children homework, and we went to our living-quarters and wondered if what we were doing would have any kind of an impact on these children and their families. What would they think of us? Intruders in their midst. Well, we didn't have long to wait. The Finnish family sent over an invitation to us to have a sauna in the little log cabin they had built for that purpose. It was a unique experience for me, as I had never even heard the word "sauna" before. Afterwards, we went up to their house for coffee. We didn't speak Finnish, and they didn't speak English, but we managed to have a great time anyway.

When we left after a week, we left five weeks of homework for the children to complete before we returned again. When the engine came to pull our car away to the next community my only thoughts were,

"Will they do it? Will they be able to do the homework by themselves?" You see, many of the parents had no education at all, and therefore wouldn't be able to help them.

What I really loved about those four years in our moving one-room school was the wonderful people. They were really exceptional, and so anxious to learn that we never had discipline problems of any sort. We never had parents complain either. Homework was always done, and you must remember when I mention homework, I mean a *lot* of it. We would only be in each place for a week before we moved on to the next for a week, and then on to another and another. They always had it finished when we came back.

When we first started, we only had nineteen children between all the stops on the whole line where our school car went. At some stops we'd have only one or two, but at others there would be seven or eight. Those numbers grew as time went on, and by the time we left, we had a total of sixty on that line. There were seven different cars on seven different lines, so a lot of northern children got their education that way.

At our next stop, we had Bella MacAulay's three children. She told me that Gerald and Margaret would be good students, but that Rodney was a little backward and stupid. At the end of the year she said to me, "You know, I think that Rodney is getting smart." Bella didn't want to have anything to do with us at all when we went there, but it wasn't long before she was showing up with all the other parents for our Friday-night poker games, and we eventually became good friends.

Most of the children that came to classes had never before been to school, and it was such a delight to see the way they took to it. You could see those little minds just expanding day by day. They were like little sponges soaking it all up. We taught in English, of course, but we were dealing with children who spoke twenty-eight different languages between them, as the North was full of new immigrants in those days. Even though they didn't speak English, however, they had no trouble understanding. In his report on our students at the end of the year the school inspector said, "They are better than my best rural school and as good as my best urban school." One of my students who had to leave during her grade ten year because her father was moving to the city led her new class in Latin in that city. They all were such very good students.

Like the others, our car was beautifully equipped and furnished. The CPR paid for the furnishing, and the department of education in Ontario supplied all the books and other equipment, so in reality we were much better off than most of the traditional one-room schools.

My own children were better off, too, because of it. They had good friends at every stop, and they were enriched by the experience of knowing children of so many nationalities. They skied, skated, and canoed, and were never bored or asking, "What will we do today?" as so many city children do. Our living-quarters were really modern for the times. We had proper beds, an up-to-date kitchen and the bathroom even had a tub, which you don't often see on a train. The only pioneering aspect of life for me was going down to the lake in winter, breaking the ice, and carrying the water back to heat it on the coal-burning kitchen stove so I could do the weekly wash. After a while that became a bit much for me, and I began sending it to the Chinese laundry in Sudbury.

People who lived in that part of Ontario were strong, individualistic characters. They had to be as the land and the climate would be very harsh. In a way, only the strong could survive.

There was one woman at a small place called Stralich, one of our school stops, who impressed me a great deal. Her name was Turgea. She was Finnish. I had been warned by the men on the railroad to be careful around her. "She has a shotgun and she doesn't like strangers." Well, I wanted her children to come to school, so my husband Cameron and I swallowed our fears and approached her small home nevertheless. She had a big garden with all kinds of vegetables, and she had an old horse called Fanny, who slept in the sun most of the time. Well, when we rather timidly approached Mrs. Turgea, she was working in the turnip patch close to where Fanny was sleeping. I told her how we'd like to have her children come to school. She didn't say a word. She just looked at me and turned back to the turnip patch and began working with her hoe again. I noticed that she did indeed have a shotgun, because there it was, propped up against a stump close by. We didn't really believe she was going to use it on us, but we could see we weren't going to get any more in the way of conversation out of her either, so we said goodbye and threw in an invitation for her to come and see our school car. She didn't say anything in reply, so we made our way out of her yard, and back to the school car, thinking, "You win some, and you lose some".

A few days later, I was in the kitchen of the school car. There was a box of chocolates on the counter, and sitting on one of the chairs was Mrs. Turgea — without her shotgun. She smiled and rather shyly asked us down to her home for a real visit, which we accepted gladly. She turned out to be the nicest person; someone who was just plain shy rather than unfriendly. She proudly showed us her garden and her house, and she had the biggest pansies, the fattest cats, and the oldest horse I had ever seen. The gun, she told us, was for shooting rabbits for her stew pot.

The house itself was a tiny little log cabin, with the inside walls covered with coloured comics from newspapers. My children who came with us were thrilled to find comic papers up there in the wilderness, but when they tried to crane their necks to read them, they found they were all upside down. She became a great friend, and we found there was nothing she wanted more than to get her children into our school for the education she never got herself.

Our school car, which was only one of several that travelled through the north, always seemed to be the one that the visiting dignitaries were brought to see. We had Lord and Lady Wellington from England, and so on and so on, and we never knew when someone would next arrive. Well, one day, Jessie Clement, whose husband worked with the Ontario Northland Railway, had been over with me all day, working in the kitchen, making jam from berries we had picked. She got tired, and she lay down on the chesterfield in the living-quarters. All of a sudden, the door from the outside opened and this big tall man started to come into the room. Jessie got the fright of her life, and she screamed, "Who in the hell are you?"

"I'm the lieutenant governor of Ontario," he said, "and I'm very sorry if I startled you."

One never knew who was going to walk into our lives, but it was fun, and it broke the routine.

When we were at a location, the parents all came down to the school on Friday nights for a social evening. We had a movie projector, and they really enjoyed that. I remember one man saying, "It's the first time I saw a moving picture in twenty years." You see, most of them had left the cities and towns of the south for a different kind of life—hunting, trapping, fishing and lumbering, and so on—and so even an ordinary movie in a made-over railroad car was a real treat.

They showered us with apple pies and cakes, and all kinds of other good things. Those Friday-night gatherings were real special to them and equally special to us. For some of the women, it would be their only night out until the school car came around again in six weeks' time. When we came around again into the community after such a long time away, everybody was there to greet us and welcome us back like long-lost friends. They'd all be there, parents and children, crowding around the railroad siding, waiting for the car to come to a stop. You couldn't help feeling so welcome—eyes would be shining, everyone smiling and waving, and every stop was like that.

The thirst for knowledge was just unbelievable, and the wonderful thing was that the children would go home and pass on what they had learned to their parents.

At Christmas time it was very exciting, especially for my husband and I and our children. We had one Christmas a week for six weeks in a row. One at each of the stops. A ladies' auxilliary group down in Toronto had made a project for themselves to make a Christmas box for every child who attended school on the northern school cars, so on each stop we'd have a fresh tree, presents for everyone, lots of goodies, and songs, the whole works! One year I remember that, as a bit of a joke, someone down in Toronto had put a huge pair of long johns in one of the boxes. They were big enough to hold two people at least. Well, there was never more fun than with those long johns! The little guy who got them in his box thought they were just great! He put them on over his clothes, and paraded up and down, and danced and carried on the whole day long. It really was such fun! Something special like that happened at every spot, and my own kids had more fun than any, because after all, they had six Christmases in six weeks.

Another thing, too, was the wildlife. It was not unusual at all to look out the classroom window and see a big moose or a bear looking back at you. The kids loved that, and these were about the only times I had trouble getting them to pay attention to their studies. There were a lot of black bears up there, and the kids would make a game of it — who will see the first bear today? Nobody, least of all the children, seemed to have any fear of them. They never came too near, and of course we never, never went too near to them. It seemed that whenever you went outside to pick berries there was always a bear off somewhere in the background, watching us, just as we were watching them.

Altogether there were seven of these school cars in Ontario, each one serving a different part of the north. It was the only such system in the world, and it was perfectly suited for the terrain and the times. Later on, Brazil patterned a system after ours, as did Mexico. Newfoundland also put in a system. The state of Arizona in the U.S. also sent people up here to look at ours before they went back to start a school-car system of their own. But ours was the very first, and, I like to think, the best!

I feel so very proud of those children, and I don't forget one of them. They went on in later years to just about any job or profession you can name, and when one thinks about it they would not have had any chance at all without the school cars. There were literally thousands who got an education that way in the almost forty years that they were used.

Gradually, as the North began filling up with more people, and more permanent communities were established with their own schools, the need for the school cars died out. It was in the mid-sixties before the last one closed, though.

It was a terrific thing to have been involved in, and I must say that my four years in them were probably the best years of my life.

Russell Brown

Disaster at the Docks

Russell Brown, of Thunder Bay, Ontario, was a duty officer on board the Noronic *on September 17, 1948, nearing the end of his career as a Great Lakes sailor. He loved the life, but at the age of sixty-seven, he was facing retirement. He savoured each sailing day left to him: but he looks on that night as the worst one in his long life.*

At age one hundred-and-one, he was easily moved to tears as he remembered one of the worst disasters in our history, the night the cruiseship the Noronic *burned at the Toronto docks, taking 118 lives.*

I was on her for six seasons of cruising the Lakes. Wonderful, happy holiday seasons, with everyone having the time of their lives, but that day was the end of all that. There were only two inspectors, and I was one. My partner had a wife who lived in Toronto, so while we were docked there, he had permission from the captain to stay with her instead of on board overnight.

On a ship like the *Noronic*, a duty inspector is required to make sure that his partner is awake and ready to begin his duty, before he can retire to his own bed. When he would be ready to come off duty, he would call me, and I would call him when I was coming off duty to wake him up, you see.

Anyway, with him off ship, the pumpsman was appointed to wake me. I was supposed to be on duty at twelve midnight to take my round for the remainder of the night. Nobody called me. Nobody woke me, and the first thing I knew I snapped awake to hear the sounds of people running up the stairs, which were right by my room. There was a lot of screaming and yelling, and it was while this was happening that I first smelled smoke.

I jumped out of bed and pulled on a few clothes and went running out the door to see where in hell the smoke was coming from. I tore up the stairs to get on deck, but I couldn't get out of this little lobby at the top of the stairs because the door was jammed. I pulled and banged at it, but it wouldn't budge, and this smoke was getting thicker all the time. Then I spotted an axe in a glass case on the wall. I smashed the glass, grabbed the axe, and started swinging at that door. I knocked the panels out and knocked the lock off, and when I got on deck everything was on fire. The flames were going up about twelve feet in the air by this time, and although we were at the dock in the centre of the city, there was no sign or sound of a fire truck. That ship was turning into an inferno, and there wasn't one stream of water directed on her. This was now about twenty minutes before one in the morning. It was chaos! People were jumping over the side, and others were sliding down ropes, or running down the gangplank. These were the lucky ones. Many others were trapped in their rooms. Some just never woke up and were smothered by the smoke in their beds.

What had happened was that the cabin maids used to collect all the rubbish from the various rooms and bring it to one cubbyhole on each deck. They would dump it in there and the bellboys would later come and dump it overboard. That sort of thing was quite usual in those days. The fire started in that trash collection on the third deck, and it was noticed first by the bellboys who had come to collect the trash. But the thing was that, this being the end of the season, they also had some liquor stored in the same room and were having a bit of a party for themselves. They were drinking and smoking, and carrying on. Before they knew it, the trash was on fire, and by this time it was too late. In fact, it was an American passenger who first smelled smoke. He went to the office of the head bellboy, and the two of them went to track it down, but by the time they found it the whole room was on fire. The bellboys were trying to get it out, but without water, and it was gaining on them. The American pulled down the fire hose, but when he went to turn it on, there was no water. It had never been used, you see. When they pulled open the door of the trash room, the fire spurted out, and went racing clean up through to the other decks to the top in no time. Before you could bat an eye, the entire ship was in flames.

Most of those people never even got out of their staterooms. In fact, most were found dead in their beds just as if they were still sleeping. Of the 450 passengers on board, 118 died.

Some of my own friends died too. One was our passenger agent from Detroit. He and his wife were on board, but he went out and tried to get some of the trapped passengers out of their state rooms. He went a bit too far with his efforts, and the first thing we knew, he was gone himself. That happened with several of the crew members.

By this time, the entire ship was just a mass of flames, and we were all running around trying to do something, but really there was very little that we could do. All I could think of was those people who were trapped in their rooms.

I made my way to the centre of the ship's deck where I knew there was a hose, and when I got there, the hose was lying on the deck with water running from its nozzle. I picked it up and pointed it into the staterooms area. I thought at that point that the majority of people were out of the rooms on that deck, because I saw the lights there and I saw one room empty. The door was open. I saw a woman at a porthole and although I could not hear her, I knew she was calling for help. The porthole had a heavy metal netting over it, attached with screws. I had no screwdriver, but I grabbed that axe again, and tried to knock the screen off. I banged at it in desperation and then I smashed through the window and I was able to pull that poor woman through. She said, "My friend is still in there, and she's unconscious." I looked in, and sure enough there was a woman on the bed. I raced back and got two young deckhands who were able to wriggle in through the porthole, and pull her over to where I could get hold of her and lay her on the deck. Then I dragged her down a set of inside stairs to a deck below and over to the gangplank, where we took her to the dock area.

By now, the dock was full of fire trucks, sirens were screaming, crowds were pressing in, and passengers were flinging themselves from the decks — some into the water of the harbour, and others right down on the docks. That entire night was as close to hell as I ever want to get, and even now, about forty years later, I can't think of it without the tears starting to flow. All those unfortunate people — well over a hundred of them — who died that terrible night. A dreadful, dreadful thing. The *Noronic* tragedy brought that whole era of the cruise ships on the Great Lakes to an end. It was coming to a close anyway, because after the war people were able to buy cars again, and the new highways made it easier for families to travel together and of course, air travel was beginning to become more popular too.

It was a wonderful, easy-going and romantic era, and although the *Noronic* wasn't responsible for ending it, it did in fact end with that tragedy.

Jean Louis LaChance

Carving a Town Out of the Bush

The North Shore of the St. Lawrence River in the province of Quebec can be just about the most desolate area in Canada; there is nothing but rocks and trees, and winters the like of which you'd have to experience before you could describe them. However, in 1936 the unemployed were begging to go there. The Quebec North Shore company was building a paper mill and a town to be called Baie Comeau, and thousands of people, many of whom had almost given up, would be given the opportunity to live. Jean Louis LaChance, was there at the beginning in 1936. He's now eighty-two, but he likes to remember those early days when he was a young man of thirty with a wife and a couple of children.

Yes, I was in there from the beginning when there was nothing but solid bush and solid rock. It was the twenty-third of June 1936, and it was only three months before that the company first started cutting trees and blasting rock in preparation for the town and the paper mill that were to come.

It was absolutely wild country with nothing manmade at all—just rocks and trees and water, with a bit of a wharf sticking out into the St. Lawrence River. There weren't many people besides the construction workers, but there was plenty of wildlife including lots of fish. There were more moose and deer wandering around close to the camp than there were workers. It was about as wild a country as you would find anywhere in Canada.

Before I arrived, I was working at Anticosti Island with the Consolidated Paper Company and things began to slow down quite a bit due to the Depression. I heard of the activity at Baie Comeau, and the newspapers were describing it as the town of the future for young people, so I decided to quit Anticosti and move on. I was thirty years old with a young family, and I was very concerned about a future for all of us.

The minute I landed there I began to wonder. I was all alone and the company boat had just dropped me off at this small wharf. I looked around and there was no sign of any civilization whatsoever. All I could see were trees and rocks and from there you couldn't even see the construction site of the paper mill. I thought to myself, "My God, what have I done? I must be insane!"

Nevertheless, I followed a path through the woods carrying my suitcase, and I could hear the noise of blasting and machinery in the distance. I couldn't believe my eyes when I finally arrived at the site. It was a beehive of activity. Jackhammers drilling at rock; saws cutting trees; heavy machinery of every type and at least two thousand men working at the various jobs. It was very exciting seeing so much activity and I knew immediately I was in the right place for me. I was a part of something that was literally being built from the ground up. I put my roots in from that first day, and now, more than fifty years later, I can truthfully say that I was never sorry.

The accommodation was pretty primitive, of course, as it was really just a camp with a few buildings for a kitchen and an office and bunkhouses for the men. There wasn't one woman in the entire place. A couple of times a few would come on visiting tours and it was amazing to see how all work stopped as everyone tried to get a look!

It stayed that way until the fall of that year, 1936, when the Company brought in some of the wives of the men — those who were lucky enough to have been assigned one of the new houses being built. I was one of those lucky ones, and when my wife and children arrived in November I was the happiest man in the world. I hadn't seen them since April — about seven months or more.

There were about two thousand of us workers and the reason there were so many was that the Company wanted to get the new paper mill in production by 1938, so there was a real deadline for what was a huge job. It wasn't only the mill but all the services and even the town where the employees would live that had to be built.

Each and every street had to be blasted out of the solid rock as did every foundation for each building. It's amazing what was accomplished in that first year alone. Some streets already had rows of houses with running water and electricity. Even the trenches for these had to be blasted out of rock. The drilling and blasting went on for twenty-four hours every day. For a while it was hard to get any sleep, but eventually we got used to that. Nothing was done haphazardly either. Each and every project was on a master plan — every road, every street, every water line — everything from the mill site to the town site. Because of this special care all of us knew that this entire operation was something special, and we were fortunate to be part of it. We knew that this was going to be our new life and so we were willing to work extra hard to make it all work out.

You must remember also that the whole world was in a depression while this was going on, and Baie Comeau was the opportunity we all wanted in order to break out of that cycle of terrible poverty. Those of us who had work there felt like the chosen people; it seemed as if everyone else was out of work. Companies could pick and choose all of the labour they wanted. At one point there were so many looking for jobs that the company had to erect a fence and a gate at the wharf to keep them out. We who had jobs treasured them because we knew if we were fired, the company would find ten men that same day to fill our places. Despite this, the companies couldn't have been better in their treatment of the men. They paid us well, gave us entertainment, and even made sure that our spiritual needs were looked after.

When the big paper storage warehouse was finished, it became kind of an entertainment centre for the men's families. On Sunday mornings it was used for the religious services, and then in the afternoon we'd go back for boxing and wrestling matches, card games, and things like that.

This was very necessary because we were really isolated at that time, summer and winter. The only way to get there was by boat. There were no roads, no railroads, and for sure no planes. Everything came by boat from Rimouski or Matane, across the St. Lawrence River. When a man felt really bushed he could get out for a few days on a ferry boat which came three times a week. Later on, in 1938 and 1939, it came in daily when the river wasn't frozen. In winter the sense of isolation was greatly increased.

As you can imagine, that was a busy wharf. Everything had to be brought in by boat — all machinery for the mill, all material for building the town, all provisions, and all the people. Everything you couldn't get in the Baie Comeau stores had to be ordered from the catalogue and then you had to wait for it to come by boat. If it didn't come on one boat, you'd wait and maybe it would be on the next. You had to learn to have lots of patience. In 1938, the Hudson's Bay Company put in a general store, where we could get groceries and dry goods which made quite a difference.

At first there were only two or three families with small children like mine. When they got to be five or six years the second year we were there, they got a teacher in and built a school. At the same time they built a Catholic church and an Anglican church, and life for most began to be very normal.

In the beginning it was a company town and therefore everything was strictly controlled by the North Shore Paper Company — and this is the way it had to be. They didn't want a shack town, but rather a place they could be proud of, and the ones who lived there could be proud of too. They decided it would be "closed" — that is that they would control whatever or whoever went there. If the company decided that the town needed one barber shop, then that's what we'd get, one barber shop. Why bring three and have two go bankrupt? It was the same thing with stores. If one drugstore was enough, that's what we'd get. We got one tavern, one theatre, one dance hall; until it was found that more than one of these facilities was needed. Everything was built according to the needs of the population.

There was a good deal of criticism in the Quebec newspapers all over the province about this, but not in Baie Comeau itself, because we who lived there felt that the Company was doing a good job of keeping things under control and keeping it from turning into some kind of a wild boomtown.

It was the right thing to do, as anyone can now see by the way this town has lasted over the past fifty years. It is still a wonderful place to live and work and bring up a family. At one time I thought I'd probably live in Quebec City when I retired. Well, I did retire a few years ago and did try living in Quebec City. I'm sure glad I didn't sell my house when I left Baie Comeau, because after a few months in the city, I couldn't wait to get back where I belong. I'll never get ideas like that again, and I'll stay here until the day I die. This place is part of me and I am part of it.

Isabella Scott Knowles

My Husband Was Good with his Hands

The early years of the twentieth century in Canada were the homestead years; but not everybody who came at that time was looking for a life on the land. Others simply wanted to take their old-country skills with them to a new country and see if a clean slate would start them on the road to a better life.

Isabella Scott Knowles was seventeen when she arrived along with her father and mother and the rest of the family in Vancouver in 1910.

My parents were really just looking for some place where their three children would have a better chance at life than was available in Scotland, in Edinburgh. Father was a carpenter over there, and managed well enough so that the family could get by, but we didn't seem to be improving our lot at all. We got along, but just barely, and the future only promised more of the same. So there was a great deal of talk about Canada and I remember my parents discussing all the pros and cons of trying it out in the New World. Finally it was decided that we should go.

I remember coming over on the ship where we booked the cheapest passage that was available in the hold, and I thought we had made a big mistake. We all were so seasick for the eleven days it took to cross the Atlantic to Quebec City. From there we boarded a train and we thought that that ride would never end. I think it took an entire week before we finally arrived in Vancouver.

At first, we felt only relief that we had at last stopped moving. It was June when we got to Vancouver, and the weather was pretty good, so gradually our spirits began to rise. Father found a house for rent and we moved in right away while we looked around for something that he could buy. It took a couple of months, but he did find a place in the

1800 block on Georgia Street. When we moved into that, we felt that we were indeed Canadians.

Vancouver was only a small town really at that time. It was very young, of course, about twenty-four-years old, and there wasn't much to it beyond the immediate downtown area. After living in Edinburgh, which was a very old and beautiful city, we felt kind of let-down. However, we were glad it was Vancouver that we had decided on, rather than some place on the prairies. When we were going across there on the train, it all looked so dry and flat and lifeless. That made us look forward even more to Vancouver.

When we got there, the only thing that really disappointed us was its size. It didn't seem much bigger than some of the villages in Scotland, but it didn't take us very long to fall in love with it and to realize that some day it was going to be a wonderful place. In all of the years I've been here I have never been disappointed, and I have never even wanted to go back and see Edinburgh again.

After only a few days here we all got jobs. My sister and I found work in a paper-box factory, which was about a block from the house we were renting at the time, and it was there, on the very first day, that I met the man who was to become my husband. He was six years older than I, and we were married five years later, when I was twenty-two. We had been saving our money all this time that we were going together, so we had enough of a nest egg to buy this old house for five hundred dollars. It had been partially burned in a fire but we could see it had possibilities. My husband was good with his hands, and could do just about anything in the way of building.

It wasn't long before he had a new roof over the part that had been burned and the inside repaired so we could live in it. The rest we just left as it was and finished it little by little. He was such a hardworking man. He never stopped, day or night, when something was still to be done. It's a nice house too, and perhaps it's too big for me now, but I just can't bear to leave it because for thirty-seven years we lived here, brought up our children, and it was here that he died suddenly. We were very happy in this house, and I figure that as long as I can manage to live here, I'll continue to be happy. I still love to do all my own work including gardening, even though everyone tells me that I shouldn't be working so hard at eighty-eight years of age, or that I should be in a nursing-home or some place like that. I just tell them that if they really want to see the end of me, then that would really do it. I'd be dead in a week, I'm sure, if I was sent off to one of those places.

Aside from the few years that I spent with my parents after coming from Scotland, this house is where I've always lived in this country. It *is* Canada to me and I love every inch of it. My children were all born right in this house. That's the way it was done in those days. We didn't even have a midwife. My mother came in and looked after me for the first couple of days, and that was all. I continued on as if nothing happened.

I always seemed to have lots of energy, even though I never weighed any more than eighty-five pounds, which is still my weight to this day. God gave me good health and good strength, and I thank Him for that. I try to pay back by doing what I can for others through volunteer work. Meals-on-wheels is my main one. I go out with a driver and deliver meals to some other old people who are not in very good health, but are still trying to live in their homes or apartments. I'm probably older than most of the ones I take meals to, but I seem to be able to get around better than they do.

They enjoy the little chats that we have as much as they enjoy getting the meals. Most of them spend too much time alone, and I really think that that makes them older than what they are. In my case, I don't feel any older than I did when I was forty or fifty. Perhaps I should feel old because I've certainly been around a long time.

I was at the very first Pacific National Exhibition in 1910, and I was there when Sir Wilfrid Laurier opened it. I can see him still, in an open coach pulled by horses, and he had this great tall hat on his head as he came in through the gates. That was the first exhibition I attended, and I've been at every one since that very first one. I do volunteer work there too while it's on, looking after children in the Lost-and-Found. I also give a couple of days a week to volunteer work at nursing homes. I like to do these things as I think it sort of pays back the country for all the happiness it gave to me.

My parents made the right decision back in 1910. None of us ever regretted it.

Captain John Thomas

Men Who Make Their Living from the Sea

For centuries, the wild Atlantic ocean that surrounds the province of Newfoundland has been both a friend and an enemy to the people who depend on her for survival. Newfoundlanders fear the sea and they respect her. They bless her for the largesse of her crops, and curse her for her foul moods which can come suddenly to take away life and property.

John Thomas, an outport fisherman's son left the dories behind when he grew up to become captain of one of the large ferry boats that ply between the Nova Scotia mainland and Newfoundland's Port-aux-Basques.

It never occurred to me that there was anything else but the sea when I was young. That's how all of the men in the outports made a living, so why should I think I was any different? Fish is what outports are all about. If it weren't for the fish, nobody would be there. People settled in those rocky little coastal harbours and inlets, because it put them near what they considered to be good fishing grounds. Nobody lived in the outports unless they were involved in some way with the fishing industry, and that includes the merchants who bought the product, and sold them the other things they needed in return.

The clergy were there to serve the fishermen, as were the doctors and a few others like that, so the codfish — and that's what most Newfoundlanders mean when they say "fish" — the codfish has always been king.

I was out in the boats as a full-fledged fisherman with my father when I was fourteen years old. That was just along the coast here, about twenty miles from where we are now at Port-aux-Basques. I graduated from that dory to every type of boat there was in the trade — schooners, long-liners, and so on. My world was the little outport and the waters off the coast from there.

As far as I was concerned, everybody in the world earned their way in life by fishing. It's only now that I know that it was very tough. The fishermen didn't get much for the fish — two or two and a half cents a pound, so you had to get an awful lot of fish to get even one dollar. My family had been doing this for many generations, since the first one came over from Wales in the early 1800s.

His name was George Thomas, and I suppose he came because the waters off Newfoundland were, even at that time, famous for the amount of fish in them. Perhaps he had been over this way before that, as part of the crew on a schooner. In any case, he knew what was here before he came. He didn't come for the land, that's for sure. It's a hard, hard land, just a big rock really, and it must have been something for him to set about building that first house here. I often think of that.

At that time, the fishing grounds were all good, so a man like George Thomas would just pick out a little harbour close to his favourite fishing spot and claim it for himself. That's what those early people did, and if you go along the coast, you'll see that every little cove and harbour has maybe just one or two families in them. The fact that they were far away, or "out" from the centres of population is what gave them the name "outports."

There were no roads in or out of any of them, no cars and no bicycles, so the boat was the only way to travel and the sea was the highway. After a while, of course, that one man who came to the port originally would marry and have children, and they would eventually marry too, so the average outport would expand to maybe five or six families. The men would find their brides just up or down the coast in one of the other outports.

Our connection to the outside world was by telegraph in those days, and by the coastal boat that ran from St. John's up to Port-aux-Basques. It would stop at these outports, bringing in mail and supplies, and take out whatever had to be taken out including any people who had some reason for going to the city. It would only come once about every two weeks, but boy-oh-boy did we ever look forward to seeing her.

She'd bring the latest newspaper, and that would be put in the post-office window so that everybody could see it. And she'd also bring in parcels that were ordered from the stores in St. John's. Everyone would be down at the dock when the coastal boat came in.

The only thing I remember that caused more excitement was when the first radio arrived in our outport. That was about 1940, and I couldn't get over it! I thought it was wonderful! I just couldn't believe it! To hear those voices coming in from the outside, from all over the world. It really made us feel for the first time that we were part of the world. We would glue ourselves around that radio and we didn't really care what was coming out of it.

On the short wave, we'd listen to Chinese and German or whatever. It didn't matter at all and the wonder of it was that these people on the radio were speaking at that very moment, thousands of miles away, in places we had only read about in school books.

All of my friends were fishermen and so were their fathers and brothers and everyone else. I don't remember thinking of what there might be in the outside world very much until after we got that radio, and it wasn't until after the war in about 1945 or '46 that I began to think seriously of life in other places.

By this time I was part of the crew on fishing boats that went out for six or seven months at a time. We'd go over to Cape Breton, to Glace Bay or Sydney, and I'd get a taste of life in a larger community. When I got married, I felt that it was time to get away from the outports and try something else.

I landed a job with CN Marine, the company that ran the big ferries. I took the first job I was offered which happened to be the lowest, but I put all my spare time into study, so that within two years I was an officer on one of the boats, and now I'm what is called a ship's master. It was a lot of hard work and hard study to qualify for that, but I guess I wanted it bad enough to do that.

My job keeps me in daily contact with the sea and the ships and actually I can't ever imagine being happy away from that. I don't think I could survive without hearing the sea roaring and the seagulls crying or the smell of the salt water and mixing with men who make their living from the sea. I feel very comfortable when I have all of these things, and I can say there's no happier man than me right now.

Johnny Wayne and Frank Shuster

The Making of Canadian Humour

For all its importance during the 1930s and 1940s, perhaps Canadian radio made its greatest contribution to its listeners' lives in its power to make people laugh. During the dark years of the Depression in particular, such entertainers as Amos 'n' Andy, Fred Allen, Jack Benny, and many others saved the sanity of North Americans.

Canadians eavesdropped on these American radio shows and at the same time set out to develop a humour that was distinctly and uniquely Canadian, something halfway between British music-hall and American radio sketches. A team from the West, Woodhouse and Hawkins, graced Canada's air-waves before and during the Second World War, but it wasn't until after 1945 that Canadians recognized two full-fledged comedy stars in Johnny Wayne and Frank Shuster.

The two young Torontonians had performed as servicemen in "The Canadian Army Show" and had been as great a success during the Second World War as the Dumbells had been in the First World War. Today Shuster and Wayne, or Wayne and Shuster as they are now called, are still big Canadian stars after almost half a century in the business.

In an interview they almost speak as one voice, one beginning a sentence and the other finishing it. And they take their humour very seriously.

When we came back to Canada after the war, we were approached by the CBC to do a show which would explain rehabilitation credits to veterans. "Johnny Home" was the name of that program and it ran for fifty-two weeks.

Our first evening show was on CBC and it was called "Blended Rhythm." It was a big show with Eric Wilde's forty-piece orchestra and we were to do short comedy sketches between the musical numbers. There was to be no live audience, but we were told the orchestra members could supply the laughter. Now that didn't seem too good to us as we were familiar with the Jack Benny and Fred Allen shows which did have audiences who laughed heartily where a laugh was needed. That sounded just marvellous. After doing two shows with only the orchestra supplying the laughs, we knew that wasn't good enough. We went to McLaren's, the ad agency which packaged the show, and told them that unless we could have an audience we were going to leave. This was a pretty chancy thing for two kids just starting out to do, but they gave in and put us in a studio with an audience. It made all the difference in the world and those shows went over as well as any of the American ones.

Here we were, two Canadians, being funny! Instead of hearing Benny or Allen making jokes about smog on the San Fernando freeway or of Brooklyn or Hoboken, here we were making jokes about Vancouver, Toronto, or Prince Edward Island.

The audience had a sense of identification with us. We'd joke about hockey. They'd never heard hockey jokes from the United States. This, then was theirs and it was Canadian! We would sit down for hours and think about what would be funny and Canadian. "Hockey Night In Canada" with Foster Hewitt was certainly Canadian so we hit on the idea of getting Foster to come on our show to describe a game between the Leafs and our mythical team, "The Mimico Mice." We dressed it up with crowd noises and cheering and everything else, which was relatively easy to do on radio. Anyone just tuning in would swear that a real game was in progress, what with Foster using real names of Leaf players and that sort of thing. The radio audience loved it so much that we made it into an annual event — The Toronto Maple Leafs versus The Mimico Mice.

Many of our skits could have been easily translated to American radio, but the hockey game was so uniquely Canadian it was a great favourite with our audience.

Our very first show on radio was a little thing back in 1941, before we went into the army, on CFRB, a big Toronto station. It was a program of hints for housewives and called "The Wife Preservers." We did three fifteen-minute shows a week and in retrospect I think we were terrible, but the fact that we were being at least amusing in the morning — in commercials no less — helped the show to catch on. Back in those days there was no humour in commercials at all.

A lot of entertainers like to refer to that period as the "Grand Old Days," but in fact they were not that at all. Once a person begins talking of the good old days, you have to assume that they think the time they're living in is terrible. I think what most entertainers mean is really just the days when they were working. In this business a good day is a day when you've got a job.

Everyone in this business or any other for that matter has to thank so many who helped them up on different steps of the ladder. The ones in the business at that time were good people, and we remember them with great affection. In our case, it was Maurice Rosenfeld who got us that first job, and Bill Byles the advertising agency man who thought we were right for the first big network show. Without people like that we'd be nowhere.

They were different old days for sure, the horse-and-buggy days of communications technology, although we never thought so at the time. The technology now is unbelievable and it's changing day by day. What they call state-of-the-art today could be obsolete before this year is over.

Even though we shifted over to TV a long time ago, both of us still love radio and we listen all the time. We don't like to see it downgraded by people who run it. Most of us spend more time with our radios than we do with our TV. We have it all over our homes and we have it in our cars. We still get most of our information and a lot of our entertainment from radio.

We've always felt that there should be no separation between radio and TV and that there should be a sort of cross-pollination between the two. Stars of radio should be also doing shows on TV and vice versa. There should be specials on radio which I'm sure everyone would tune in to hear. I think CBC does a wonderful job with its radio service, but even there, I think it could be made better. The good old days can be improved on, although the good old days or whatever you may wish to call them, in radio particularly, are something we can all be proud of in this country more than any other country in the world.

Radio was the vehicle that opened up this country and it's still such a magical thing. Because you build them in your own mind, the sets and the costumes on radio are much more exciting. We knew *that* when we first moved over to TV. We did a show on radio where we were supposed to be on the moon and it was so realistic with the music and the sound and all the rest of it. We realized then that on television people would see right away that the sets were painted, no matter how well. It couldn't be recreated the way that one can do it in their heads just by listening. We felt badly about that.

Radio still has great opportunities but so much of the good directorial talent is being attracted to the more visually exciting area of TV and films. I'd like to see more young people begin working on the great scope that radio has. In many ways I think that radio hasn't picked up the challenge of technology and it is still working in the forties — technically. I think we should be able to do a lot better than that.

Harry Gairey

Black and White

In its treatment of the black man, Canada's record is not bad; but it's not that good either. It's true that our country was a haven for runaway slaves from the United States—the final stop on "the underground railway." However, once they arrived here the blacks didn't find a society free from discrimination as they had hoped they would. They were able to live here in comparative freedom as long as they didn't expect to get anything but the lowliest of jobs and they didn't mind living in places deemed undesirable by whites.

As in the United States, blacks were looked upon as workers predestined by God to serve the needs of whites until well into the present century.

Harry Gairey was born in Jamaica in 1895 and came to Toronto in 1910. He found that dramatic changes in social attitudes in Canada have taken place in the course of his lifetime, and he helped bring about those changes.

Before we came here my family kept moving around looking for something better in countries other than the one where I was born. I spent my fifth birthday in Cuba and my sixteenth in Toronto with all of the other ones in between in many other places. It was simply a case of looking for the promised land, I suppose.

Today I love this country and I especially love this city where I've spent most of my life, but it was a love that came in spite of many negatives. Before I came here I didn't know what colour discrimination was, I had never seen it or experienced it, but it didn't take me long to find out.

I came here with skills as a cigar maker—something I'd learned in Cuba so I figured this was going to be a way of making a living in Canada. Anyway there was a cigar factory down here with a sign in the window saying: "Cigar wrapper needed." I went in and applied, but they told me that they didn't need anybody at the moment. A few days later I passed by the place and the sign was still there and there was a telephone number to call. So I placed a call, and the person who answered told me to come over right away, which I did. They took one look at me and said, "Sorry, the job's filled." It didn't take me long to figure out it was my black face they didn't want. I learned from friends that cigar-making was considered a white man's job. Black men could dig ditches and sweep streets but skilled jobs were in the territory that blacks must not enter. Blacks were meant to serve.

One day a friend who knew that I still had no work came over and said he could get me on with the Toronto-Hamilton and Buffalo railroad as a cook and waiter. This was considered a job that blacks should be allowed to do as it meant service to whites. I was hired and I stayed there and did my job faithfully until 1930 when the Depression caught up and I was laid off.

I wasn't too worried because in those fifteen years with the railroad I had been very careful with my money and my wife and I had savings of around four thousand dollars. I thought I'd be able to pick up some work here and there and only have to dip into the savings in emergencies. However, it wasn't to be that way. There were very few jobs for anybody and almost none if you were black. In the hiring halls we were always pushed to the end of the line. I couldn't get anything even though I was willing to take any job at all. I found myself unable to get in the lineups at the soup kitchens because of my pride and I couldn't accept the tiny food handouts that were being made to the destitute. The four thousand dollars kept getting smaller and smaller over the next four years until the day arrived when there wasn't a penny left. My little son came into the house that day and asked me for one cent to buy a candy and I didn't even have one to give him. That's when I knew we had hit the very bottom. It brings tears to my eyes even to this day when I think of it.

That's when I was finally forced to go on relief where they would give you coupons instead of money which you would take to a grocery store and exchange for food. As far as I was concerned, that was the end of the line. I can't tell you how depressed I felt.

After a period of about two months of this I received a call from the Canadian Pacific railroad. I had applied there for a sleeping-car porter's job a long time before and nothing was happening so I more or less forgot about it. I grabbed it even though I didn't know a thing about sleeping-car work, but I figured I could do it as I had seen it done when I worked on the railroad before.

It wasn't an easy job at all and was made even worse by the hours upon hours of constant travel all the way out to Vancouver and back. It was dusty and hot and in those days there were no air-conditioned trains, and the conditions of work could almost be described as slave-driven. If you lost a towel for example, or anything in the way of equipment — even a pillow slip, it was noted on your work sheet. This would be followed by a reprimand and after a couple of incidents you could be fired. As you can imagine, I put up with everything just to keep that job, and I eventually became a charge-porter, and alternated also in cooking and waiting on tables in the dining-car. I made myself one of their most valued employees, willing to do anything they asked.

Despite this though, I came to work one morning and the platform agent said, "Harry, I'm sorry, but I have to lay you off." I was devastated, of course. I could just picture another long period of unemployment ahead again just when things were going so well. Well, I went home and paced around the house all day wondering what I should do. At six o'clock the phone rang and it was the platform agent telling me to forget about what he had said in the morning and to get in there to work. I never got laid off again.

You must remember that in those years a porter was as low on the scale of railroad jobs that one could go. All the porters were black and there was no such thing as job security. One could be fired for something like forgetting to be extremely polite with a difficult passenger, someone who was drunk and violent. You were always expected to call him "sir," no matter what, and believe me in those days there were many passengers travelling who treated blacks like dirt.

Later on I was promoted to porter-supervisor, which was about as high as a black man could go. Now, I determined in this new job of porter-supervisor to use whatever influence I had to better the lot of my fellow blacks who had just traded one form of slavery for another, when you think of it. Porters could never aspire to being a conductor: that was a job for a white man. The black man could not rise above duties such as what we called "spreading sheet," making beds. That's all we could get.

I knew my job was lowly but I never thought that way of myself, so I determined to be the best sleeping-car porter there was — even though it was hard at times with some of those customers.

One time when I had a special party on board I did lose patience. They were drinking and making a terrible racket which didn't upset me as — after all that was their business. But then they started calling me "George." "Come here, George," and so on. I wouldn't respond at all. "Why don't you come when you're called, George?" one of them said.

I said "My title is porter. It's on my cap and it's on my uniform and my name is not 'George,' so if you want me to serve you, please address me properly." I thought there'd be trouble over that but there wasn't, and from there on, they didn't call me George.

But you know, there were other insults that couldn't be dealt with so easily. There were many places where blacks weren't permitted to enter—restaurants and dance halls, etc. even some skating rinks as I discovered when my young son went to one to try out his new skates. I heard of this unwritten rule at the rink, but I couldn't believe that young children would be treated that way. My son had gone there with a white friend. They let his friend in and told my son to go home. He came in in tears and when he told me what happened I was in tears too.

I couldn't sleep that night, so first thing in the morning I went down to see Joe Salzberg, the Jewish member of Parliament. Joe knew what I was talking about as Jews suffered a lot of discrimination at that time also. He said, "We are going down to city council chambers together tomorrow morning." We did, and Mayor Saunders was there to receive us. I said, "Mr. Mayor, I'm not here asking for anything. I just want my right as a citizen in a demoracy." The mayor listened sympathetically and then the whole thing hit the newspapers, and we found that the majority of Toronto's white population were outraged, too, by what had happened to my son. From that time onward blacks and whites could skate together on the same sheet of ice. The important thing was, though that we were beginning to realize that in a country like Canada we didn't have to suffer these insults, and that by rising up and protesting we could change them.

Shortly after that incident, I joined a delegation to Ottawa to protest the government's restrictive immigration policy which kept family members from joining husbands and fathers who were working in Canada.

When I returned from Ottawa and that weekend trip my railroad bosses said I had no business taking time off work for something such as that and they threatened to penalize me. I took out my work sheets and showed them that I didn't take time off work. Everything was done on my own time.

I felt that it was time for the porters to form a union and change their poor conditions. Most of them, conditioned by years of subservience, were scared to death they would lose their jobs. It took a lot of persuading and a good deal of time, but eventually we got it and that made a big difference for black men on the railroad. Our wages were greatly improved, but the biggest thing was that we gained some dignity. We didn't have to take being treated as children any more which is how we were treated, even though we were responsible men and heads of families.

I'm not taking credit for all of this. There were many, many people involved in changing the way blacks were treated. It's much different now, and there's still a way to go, but today we can truly feel equal.

Frank Smith

Stairway to the Stars

"You'll never get me up in one of those." That's what people said back in the mid-1930s when multiple-passenger planes first appeared in the skies over Canada. Those big planes of the time were really quite small by today's standards, but compared to the small ones used by the bush pilots, they were huge indeed.

We've come a long way in the skies in the past fifty years, with monsters of machines routinely lifting off runways, carrying passenger loads in the hundreds — more than the entire population of many small Canadian communities. While there were very few souls back in the thirties who had ever experienced the thrill of flying, today only a very few can be found who haven't.

Our forefathers could never in their wildest dreams have imagined travelling from the east coast to the west coast and back again in one day. At the turn of the century, one could travel only twenty-five miles a day in a horse-and-wagon.

The twentieth century banished forever the barriers of distance and time and the five most important technological developments in accomplishing this were the telephone, the radio, the automobile, the train, and the airplane. Between them they've turned the whole world into Marshall McLuhan's global village, changing the measurement of distance from miles or kilometres to mere hours and minutes.

I've crossed the Atlantic at least two dozen times, never by ship. I still can't get used to the idea that it takes less than eight hours to do it. I've never done it without thinking of my poor ancestors who came here from the Hebrides of Scotland in leaky boats, on journeys that took four or five weeks.

Frank Smith is a man who represents both ends of the air age. He began flying two-seater moths in 1931 at an RCAF flying school, and twenty-five-thousand air hours later, he was at the controls of TCA (present-day Air Canada) 747's and DC 1011s with hundreds of passengers in his "rumble seat."

In all my years of flying, there's been nothing to match the thrill of that first small plane. It had no brakes, no tail skid, no instruments to speak of: the air speed indicator was a spring steel vein bent against a graduated scale on the inboard strut. The instructor told me that it wasn't very reliable, and we were taught to judge air speed by sound. If it was too noisy, we were going too fast, and if it was too quiet we were going too slow. It wasn't what you might call very scientific, you know, but I don't want to give the impression that there hadn't been much progress from the days of the Wright brothers because there had been. This progress wasn't reflected in the small flying school I attended, because in 1931, the RCAF wasn't exactly in the vanguard of development in the art of aviation. They progressed a long way, but really those years of the early thirties were only the beginning years of big planes. Airline flying was just starting in the United States, and in Canada, there wasn't anything like that at all.

Our front line fighter in the RCAF in 1931 was a late First World War model, developed around 1917, a biplane strung together with wire and struts as you might imagine. But don't get me wrong, lots of progress was taking place.

Charles Lindbergh flying solo across the Atlantic was a tremendous milestone. He became a hero to the whole world, and he helped to focus attention on the development of better aircraft. The biggest boost, of course, came because of the Second World War. The airplane leaped from being regarded as a small-capacity machine into something that could really do big work.

The DC-3 was the first really successful commercial transport, and it was also one of the largest airborne weapons of the war until the late stages, when they got eight or nine thousand of them in the forces and began to use them for aerial supply. It was a tremendous weapon when properly used. Mind you, this was true only when there was good fighter cover.

Shortly before the war, two years before actually, the Lockheed 10A became a familiar sight in the skies with the formation of Trans Canada Airlines. It was this plane that was used in the inaugural flight of TCA in 1937, and for those days it was something of a wonder. It was a ten-passenger aircraft, with two 450-horsepower engines. That particular plane is preserved today at the airport museum [National Aviation Museum] in Ottawa. It was a very good plane that was kept in service for many years. In fact, during Air Canada's thirtieth anniversary they took her up again and she performed well. The company had her restored, and George Lothian, one of the original pilots from 1937 and some other fellows flew her all the way from Montreal out to Vancouver, retracing the first flight.

The Lockheed 10A was one of the pioneers of commercial transport. I flew it myself on an airline-type route, while I was in the air force. It had a service ceiling of around ten thousand feet or so. There were no flight instruments on the first officer's side of the cockpit. It had what we thought were good radios, although you would not call them good today. All the higher frequency VHF we use now didn't even exist at that time. There was a standby navigation receiver which was battery-powered and sat under the first officer's seat. If you needed it, you had to lean down and fiddle with the volume under him. So there was still a lot of seat-of-the-pants flying. We did use instruments, but it was tougher in many ways because you didn't have the performance or the power, and you didn't have the reliability of engines, and there was no such thing as weather-radar.

Our radio navigation system was the old radio-range, which you listened to get a "dit-da" on one side, and a "da-dit" on the other, and if you were where you supposed to be, you just got a solid hum. Of course, we couldn't use anything like that today. If you go into a busy terminal like Montreal or Toronto, with all the radio chatter and the traffic-control instruction, you can't be sitting there listening to a radio-range at the same time. What we have now is an instrument landing-system that is much better, much more accurate.

A big improvement that came about shortly after the end of the Second World War was the change in the aircraft compasses. Prior to that we were using magnetic compasses and you can't steer an aircraft on a compass. You can do a full 360-degree turn in a plane, but your magnetic compass will stay on one point the entire way. They changed those into gyroscopic things that are mounted and are very accurate. They are not affected by acceleration of the aircraft. Before these came along, it was very difficult to maintain a straight course, especially when I first began flying.

I flew just about every plane there was — from that first small Moth in 1931 right up to the largest of the modern monsters, the 747s and the 1011s. I remember sitting at a banquet one night, next to a fellow who had been in Burma with me. I had been his flight commander in 1945, but through those intervening years he had progressed to head of flight test engineering for the Boeing Aircraft Corporation. He asked me if I would be flying the 747 which Air Canada had just bought. I told him I was too old and too junior to get a chance. He said, "Well,

I'll tell you, Frank, I think you ought to fly it. At least once. We'll work it out some way." He arranged that I should go down to Seattle and fly it on one of the test flights. I had four and a half hours as a co-pilot with one of the Boeing aircraft pilots. That's how I'm able to say I flew them all, with the exception of the North Star. I regret not having flown one of those. They were noisy old planes, but they were sure reliable.

I've had more than fifty years behind the controls of aircraft, and in many ways those years were the most important ones, where the airplane moved from being almost a novelty, to what it is today — a part of all our lives and a stairway to the stars.

Ella Trow

The Way We Were

Canadian cities today compare favourably with cities anywhere in the world. The downtown cores are filled with architectural triumphs of glass and steel that reach far in the sky, served by express roads that wind around, over, and under each other like those in the futuristic cartoon books of the Depression years. Canadian cities are all glitz and glamour on the one hand, but overcrowded and too expensive for the average person on the other.

But has the urban explosion which followed the Second World War really improved the way we live? Those who remember Toronto before and after the war remember simpler times. Perhaps, as Ella Trow of Toronto believes, we have given up too much for the gains we have made.

I was born in 1911 — too young to remember much of the First World War, but I can remember with clarity what it was like in the years that followed. Toronto, where I was born and raised, was well under half a million people until the Second World War ended. It was small enough that there was always a feeling of familiarity no matter where you happened to be within the city confines. It was like a group of small communities linked together rather than a big city. It's natural for me to think of the twenties and thirties as the best.

It was certainly a simpler way of living and we had much more freedom to get around. On public transportation there was never any of the crush you find today on buses and subways. Just about everyone went to the Canadian National Exhibition, "the Ex." You wouldn't think of *not* going. It marked the end of summer and the beginning of autumn. Families would pack a picnic basket for a day there, and away they'd go on the streetcar. They'd find a place on the grass somewhere

Photo Album

1. Life in the Newfoundland outports was always hand-to-mouth with no luxuries of any kind. David Pitt remembers that it was almost impossible, too, to have even a small garden: "The land was extremely rocky and the soil was very shallow. Most of it had to be carted in from the outside. Even the cemeteries had to be built on solid rock with wooden retaining walls to hold the soil that was brought in from ten to twelve miles inland."
Public Archives of Canada C-30760

2. The Klondike Gold Rush brought adventurers from all over the world to Canada's North, including Toronto-born Joe Boyle. As "King of the Klondike", Boyle owned a kingdom of fancy stores and fancy women, as seen in this street scene in Dawson, Yukon, in 1898. Ed Bennett of Woodstock, Ontario, describes Boyle as "a true Canadian hero".
Public Archives of Canada PA-13406

3. Gordon Jackson of Port Credit, Ontario, recalls joining the Royal Navy Canadian Volunteer Reserve and the attitudes of the British petty officers: "Most of them had never been near the sea, let alone a ship. They were giving orders to these *real* sailors from Canada without having any knowledge to back up their orders."
Courtesy Ruth de Boerr

4. Cy Strange died in 1987 after fifty-two years in Canadian broadcasting. For the last seventeen years of his life, Cy worked as co-host of CBC Radio's "Fresh Air" program. "It was a joy working with so many of those people. Kate Aitken, for one, was a remarkable woman with a wonderful sense of humour." Here, "Mrs. A." is seated at her desk with some of the CFRB staff around her in the 1940s. Cy stands on the far right.

5. Big timber was floated down Canada's rivers for later export. This big raft on the St. Lawrence in 1870 is heading for the port of Quebec, where it will be broken up and loaded onto transAtlantic ships. Of the life of a lumberjack, Tauno Lopenen says "A bucksaw and an axe made for hard work, hard brutal work."

Courtesy D.D. Calvin, Ontario Forest Industries Association

6. The Halifax Explosion of December 6, 1917 killed 2,000 people and injured another 20,000. To cope with the diaster, Canadian soldiers were called in. Canadian author Hugh MacLennan was ten years old and remembers vividly that "every horse-and-wagon brought down loads of bleeding victims and every hospital was full."
Public Archives of Canada PA-22744

7. Joyce Hahn was one of the first real stars of Canadian television when it went on the air in 1952. Her brother, Bob, remembers the Depression years when their father took "The Harmony Kids" on the road as performers in an attempt to put food on the table: "People were forced into trying all sorts of things just to survive."
Courtesy Robert Hahn

8. Florence Bell and her husband were teachers on one of the old school cars that moved from community to community from the 1920s to the early 1960s. The students, like these children in Chapleau, Ontario, were sometimes distracted from their lessons by bears wandering past the rolling one-room schools. *Public Archives of Canada* PA-142372

9. Russell Brown recalls the burning of the cruise ship, *Noronic* on September 17, 1948 in Toronto harbour. "That entire night was as close to hell as I ever want to get." This photo of the twisted steel decks gives some idea of the intense heat of the blaze.
Public Archives of Canada RD-900

10. Baie Comeau as it looked when Jean Louis La Chance arrived there in 1937. Two thousand men were carving a new town and a new paper mill out of the bush.
Credit: Al Plosz

11. The Newfoundland outport of Port de Grave. Captain John Thomas explains the existence of the small settlements: "Fish is what outports are all about. If it weren't for the fish, nobody would be there."
Public Archives of Canada PA-139014

12. Harry Gairey, born in Jamaica in 1895, has lived in Toronto since 1910. He worked for the Canadian Pacific Railroad during the Depression years: "You must remember that in those years a porter was as low on the scale of railroad jobs that one could go. All the porters were black and there was no such thing as job security."
Courtesy Harry Gairey

13. As Frank Smith notes, Canada entered the international commercial air age with the establishment of Trans Canada Air Lines, the predecessor of Air Canada, in 1939. Among the first passengers was C.D. Howe (third from left), the most powerful minister in Prime Minister Mackenzie King's Cabinet.
Courtesy Air Canada

TOP RIGHT
14. Arthur Raymond Bates served as the lone RCMP officer stationed on Baffin Island for four years and came to love the North and its people. These Inuit were photographed at Dundas Harbour, North Devon Island, N.W.T. in August 1925.

BOTTOM RIGHT
15. In the course of his pilot's training, W.W. ("Mac") MacGill says that "a great many of the boys cracked up their planes on their first solos."
Public Archives of Canada PA-138555

16. Sir Frederick Banting (above left) and Dr. Charles Best, discovered insulin. Sir Frederick's niece recalls that "when he was a very small boy in Alliston, Ontario, one of his best friends was a little girl who lived just across the road from him. Well, she got sick and eventually died from diabetes, and Grandma said that Uncle Fred was almost uncontrollable in his grief." Both Banting and Best later worked at the Connaught Laboratories in Toronto, where Dr. Robert Wilson (right) of Vancouver continued their research in the development of vaccines.
Courtesy Myles McCormick and Robert Van Exan, Connaught Laboratories.

BOTTOM RIGHT
18. Canadian diplomat George Ignatieff assists Prime Minister Lester B. Pearson in laying a wreath at the war memorial in Stalingrad (later named Volgograd in 1955). The man in the light-coloured suit with recording equipment over his shoulder is CBC reporter Rene Lévesque, later premier of Quebec.
Courtesy U.S.S.R. Information Services

17. HMS *Rainbow*, the first ship in Canada's navy, guards the *Komagatamaru* with 400 Sikhs aboard during the 1914 immigration controversy concerning their entry to Canada.
Public Archives of Canada C-26546

19. Of building fishing schooners in Lunenburg, Nova Scotia, David Stephens, himself a boatbuilder, says "I'm afraid that very soon shipbuilding will become a lost art."
Public Archives of Canada C-8599

20. Sandy Downie of Kapuskasing, Ontario, describes the hardship of creating a home in the bush: "Dad was as tough as they come. Those virgin trees were huge, and the task of cutting just one of them down could take an entire day. It took many logs to build a house."
Public Archives of Canada PA-12761

21. Paul Martin, "the politician's politician", at Canada House in London, England with the Queen Mum and Mrs. Martin.
Courtesy Paul Martin

22. "King" Clancy was one of the all-time great hockey players in the NHL. He retained his front-office connections and his love for the Toronto Maple Leafs until his death at the age of eighty-three in 1986.
Public Archives of Canada PA-49024 *with permission of the Hockey Hall of Fame, Toronto*

23. Following the tragic shipwreck of the USS *Pollux* and *Truxton*, the worst disaster in U.S. naval history, the residents of Lawn and St. Lawrence, Newfoundland rescued 187 survivors although 203 sailors died. Ena Edwards was the only person to photograph any of the incident with her five-dollar Brownie camera: "Funerals were a daily occurrence here for a while after that."
Courtesy Ena Farrell Edwards

24. Hugh Mackay Ross's arrival at the Hudson's Bay outpost in Northern Ontario was memorable: "I was picked up by two Indians and taken up to Grassy Narrows. Those noble red men must have had a great laugh later over this greenhorn in the double-breasted suit and brown pointy-toe shoes who was loaded down with books and violin."
Photo: anonymous

25. Jeff Wyborn, the new bush pilot, stands proudly beside his Hudson Bay Beech 18-CF-BMI at the Dominion Skyways base in Roberval, Quebec, in 1941. A few months after this photo was taken, the plane was swamped in a storm and sank in Richmond Gulf, Quebec. After a life of flying, he says, "I can't think of ever wanting to do anything else but fly."
Courtesy Jeff Wyborn

26a and 26b. Two views of Victoria Harbour — in 1886 (left) and in 1910 (right), as Gordon James Duncan knew it before he was stationed in Peace River country as its first lawman with the RNWMP.
Public Archives of Canada PA-62200 *and* PA-59895

just as they'd do for a day at the beach, and everyone would go wandering around, looking at whatever they were interested in.

Families went together to the museum, the art gallery, to one of the three live theatres or to Massey Hall, where the best artists of the world appeared. The Royal Alex, the Princess, and the Grand Theatres would have live productions by touring companies, and there were also two very good vaudeville houses. Vaudeville is sometimes thought of as a place of jugglers and magicians. Sure, you could see those acts, but you'd also see great artists.

I saw all of the Barrymores, for example, performing in plays in vaudeville houses. One didn't have to book tickets six weeks in advance as they do now. You could make up your mind on a Thursday and go on a Friday, the next day. Simple as that. I saw Pavlova perform; Paderewski; all of the great ballets; and just about anyone who was anyone in the performing arts at the time. They all came here.

We would dress in our finest for Massey Hall and the Royal Alex. The Princess and the Grand were a bit less so the attire we wore was also not as fine. But the point is that everybody dressed *up*, but not necessarily always in evening clothes. People wouldn't dream of attending the theatre in the clothes they wore every day. It was a big thing to go out for an evening of theatre, where you'd expect to see at least several of your friends.

It was a big treat for children too. They would be taken along with their parents. It was quite usual to see entire families at these performances. It was considered part of our education. We would go out to dinner first at one of the good hotels, follow that up with the theatre performance, and then home and to bed with a head full of memories. As children, we never misbehaved on these occasions, because this was always *the* big treat we looked forward to for weeks. We didn't have to be warned to "be good"; we wanted to be.

Toronto was a city full of horses in the twenties and thirties, lots of delivery horses and still a few carriages, although the automobile was taking over. Even then, it was a wonderful sight to see people in carriages. It looked rather grand. Children loved to chase after the ice wagons, which were pulled by horses, and they'd scramble for the little bits of ice that would fly off when the ice-man chipped a block off for delivery to homes which still used ice boxes. It wasn't considered nice for girls to chase after the ice wagon, so it was mostly a pastime for the boys.

Little girls were supposed to be polite and quiet at all times. At school, we played games, but we weren't allowed to play on the street the way boys did with their hockey and baseball. We skipped rope, and we were allowed to ride bicycles, but girls were always more supervised than were the boys. It was the same for women, really. Wives stayed home and looked after the house, and the girls were expected to learn how to do the same. Manners, behaviour, voice, and all of those things were taught in school. There were classes in home economics, in with cooking and everything else to do with running a household. In those days it was called domestic science where we'd also be taught subjects like food chemistry, etc. Many girls, who had no intention of going to college would specialize in domestic science as its aim was to make a girl a better housewife.

Private schools patterned after those in England were, and still are, a big part of the Toronto educational scene. Ones who could afford it would have their children go to these schools, because there was a very structured pattern that taught the children to be self-disciplined. One got out of bed at a certain time, studied and played at certain times, and ate and went to bed at certain times. My own children still ask how I could possibly stand all that regimentation, but when everybody else is doing the same thing, you don't seem to mind it at all. We all took cold baths every day, and we all had to open our windows at night no matter how cold it was. It sounds dreadful now, perhaps, but I remember only what a good time we had. Sometimes, when I'd complain to my parents about something at school, they'd say, "What did you do to deserve that?" Or "How many other girls in your class? Did they all get the same?" There was never very much conflict between teachers and parents over discipline. In fact, if we did get punished, we'd hope our parents wouldn't find out. We might get additional punishment rather than sympathy.

There was a great deal of entertaining at home in those days. The theatres and the vaudeville were special occasion things. People would have others over a lot — for listening to the radio, and simple things like that. Food would be served and maybe some liquor for the grownups — hardly ever to the young ones. In my family, which was strictly teetotal, it was never served at all. The food would be wonderful though, and I can remember we had marvellous times. We played Ouija board, checkers, chess, and word games. There was always something for all age groups to do. The point is that we did things that hardly ever cost money. Even our big nights out didn't cost much. A couple could go to the Royal Alex for about five dollars, and then afterwards, for about the same price, you could go to a supper dance at the King Edward.

We girls would dream about being asked to these supper dances. We'd see all our friends there because it was *the* event in town that was geared to young people in my teen years. We'd know all the waiters by name because they never changed, and it was just like a big party that took place every Friday night. At other times you could go to the dance pavilions in the resort areas near the city. The Brant Inn always had good orchestras. The Palais Royale was on one of the beaches right inside the city and it would be crowded with young people who loved the music of the big bands. The period between 1927 when I graduated and the Second World War were the golden years for those events.

When the Second World War came along the supper dances became big goodbye parties for the boys going into the services. It was a romantic, almost dream-like sort of time. We'd be dancing and singing, and saying goodbyes to the music of bands like the Romanellis, Trump Davidson, Mart Kenney, Horace Lapp, and many others.

Our tastes were very simple really. We went out with our friends and just had fun. Very few young people in my age group drank, and in fact it was considered kind of shocking if someone showed up at a party with too much to drink. I think abstinence or moderation was partly because of a consideration for your family. I knew Daddy would absolutely drop dead if I ever came home with someone who had too much to drink. He would not only be upset, but you can be sure I wouldn't be allowed to go out with that boy ever again. We were expected to conform or be punished, and we accepted that. We felt that parents were entitled to that kind of control until we left home for marriage, or to follow a career. In fact, even after I was married, I wouldn't dream of doing something my parents didn't approve of. It was simply just not what was expected.

In families that were a little better off, the maxim was "Much is given — much is expected," meaning, since we have been favoured, we owed it to the community to give back in the way of public service or charity, or whatever. It was "woe betied" any of us who ever got the feeling that we were something better just because we were better off financially.

My father came originally from a small Ontario town to Toronto and found success here. Maybe because of that he thought Toronto was the greatest place in the world. No matter where we travelled, he would always say on the return trip home, "Back to good old Toronto." He felt it was a miracle that this city allowed a young lad who was only nineteen when he came with nothing much to start his own business and succeed at it.

Now the Toronto of those years was best for those who were at the top end of what was a very stratified society, along English lines. You had the governor general of the country, and the prime minister on top, followed by the lieutenant governor, the oldest families, successful newcomers, and so on. Unlike England, it wasn't a strict class society, as there was always the opportunity there for anyone to move up. Most people in the top bracket had come to Canada as immigrants in the early years, and they only started to get grander in the second and third generations. The "old families," therefore, were really not that old, and the class they belonged to wasn't an impenetrable fortress as was the case in England. Torontonians were always aspiring to move up.

The church played a very important part in the lives of the people in those days, regardless of where they were in society. Our family always went to church on Sunday mornings, and if we children weren't going with family, we would certainly go to Sunday school in the afternoon. After church in the mornings we often went to a hotel dining-room for lunch, and after Sunday school, a group of us would go to somebody's house for afternoon tea. Of course, you weren't allowed to dance or anything like that, but you could play games. Sunday was a "good" day, when everyone got dressed up.

When we began dating, the things we were expected to do were always in somebody's house with other friends — playing games, listening to the radio, singing, or whatever. It always surprises me when I hear people talk about the horrible boring Sundays of Toronto, but I think they are referring to the absence of outdoor events like baseball or public entertainment like movies. On the contrary, I never wanted Sunday to be over.

Family life was of great importance back in those days, and there was hardly a home that didn't include several generations. My grandmother lived with us, and in most of my friends' homes there was at least one grandparent or an aunt or an uncle. It was really considered some sort of disgrace to have anybody in your family looked after by anyone else, in an institution or whatever.

Houses were bigger then, of course, so that made it a lot easier, and most families, even in the bottom end of society, had some domestic help. When you consider that girls from the country were willing to work for five dollars a month, it is easy to understand why most families could have a maid. These girls were anxious to get away from the drudgery of life on a farm, and housework in the city was one way of doing that. They became part of the family rather than servants and after a short time they usually moved on to other jobs, or to a marriage. So it was beneficial all around.

During the Depression, things changed drastically for all classes of society, but in our family, strangely enough, we were better off than before. Father was in the advertising business, the one business that seemed to improve with the downturn in the economy. Manufacturers and others who had anything to sell had to work a lot harder at selling it, so they had to advertise their wares more aggressively. The advertising agencies were booming when everything else declined.

It was a sad time, though. You'd see these really nice people coming to the door trying to sell things like cheap silk stockings, magazines, and books. Most of these people had lost their jobs and you could see that this door-to-door selling was just killing them. We would always invite them in for something to eat or a cup of tea, and sometimes it was obvious that they were starving.

Families that were better off would more or less "adopt" others that had fallen on hard times, bringing them food and clothing. I remember one time especially. My mother was putting together all these little things in a suitcase to take to a lady who recently had a new baby at home. A lot of the babies were delivered in the house in those days. Mother stayed on there with the woman until she could manage by herself. It wasn't a case of Lady Bountiful sending a basket with the chauffeur or anything like that. She went and helped look after the other children and all those other things that had to be done.

The Second World War seemed to change everything in everyone's life. In my own case, my brothers and my husband were in the war. Most of my friends were in the same boat. A lot of my friends and neighbours were killed in it. The city itself began to get tremendously crowded because of servicemen and their families, along with workers in the war industries. I don't believe that the Toronto I've been talking of existed at all after the war started.

When the men came home, things weren't as good as they thought they would be. The war wasn't as decisive as all of us hoped. We thought that surely this would be the last war the world would see.

I don't like what has happened to the city I once knew. My Toronto was a much better place in which to live. It was prettier and not so polluted. I think people were nicer to each other, and I know there was more politeness. The crowding and crushing, and lineups for everything didn't exist. It would be foolish to deny we now have some gorgeous buildings we didn't have before, but as far as I'm concerned, we had everything we needed before all of this took place. The galleries and museums may be bigger and better now, also the theatres, but they're overcrowded and expensive too. There's a new kind of elitism now that's based simply on whether or not you have enough money to do all of these wonderful things. Most do not. Many people who were instrumental in bringing things like ballet and opera to Toronto years ago can no longer afford to pay the very high ticket prices to see them.

So many things have changed that it's very hard for my generation to absorb it all. Take marriage, for instance. In my day, marriage was forever and divorce was so unusual that most people would only talk of some couple getting divorced as if it were a great scandal. Now, it seems as though divorce is as natural as marriage itself.

Hardly anyone lived in apartments before the war. Everybody had a house: some big, some small, but with a front and back door and a yard where they grew something. Now, more people seem to live in apartments than in houses.

Even in the matter of meals, everything is so different. Back then, the table was set for meals, and everybody sat there till everyone else was finished. Children had reasonable table manners, too, but now everyone is on the run all the time, and it's seldom that families sit together at the table.

They tell us that bigger and faster is the way of the new world, but that doesn't necessarily mean that it's better.

Dr. Ben Gullison

Ten Minutes, Ten Dollars, Ten Days

In our long list of Canadian heroes, you'll find many who will be remembered for acts of courage and humanity performed in other parts of the world. Dr. Norman Bethune and Dr. Robert McClure are two of the names that come readily to mind. For many Chinese, these two Canadians achieved legendary reputations for their selfless medical feats, tending to the sick and the poor.

Another man not so well known here but idolized by thousands of the poor in India is Dr. Ben Gullison, who was raised in Yarmouth, Nova Scotia. Dr. Ben spent more than sixty years of his life giving sight to over two hundred thousand people in India who would otherwise have spent their lives in darkness. Dr. Gullison, a medical missionary himself, was also the son of missionaries.

My parents went out from Nova Scotia in 1896, and served one term in India before returning to Port Maitland, Nova Scotia, where I was born in 1906. It must have been the good Maritime air. They didn't return to India until I was about three years old, but from that point until I was sixteen they stayed there and that became my home. During those years I got to know the Indian people very well. They were my friends, my schoolmates, and my neighbours. I spoke their language as well as I spoke English, and I was one of them as much as it was possible to be.

They were terribly poor and disadvantaged and they suffered from many diseases that were easily preventable with western know-how. It was impossible for me to see these people without having a deep caring and a deep desire to help them in some way, as young as I was. I thought then that I might some day earn some medical qualifications elsewhere, and return to put what I learned into practice. I didn't know how I was going to do this, but it was a boyhood dream.

To cut a long story short, I was able to continue my studies and qualify as a medical practitioner, and I married a lady who was every bit as dedicated to the task of missions in India as I. We went to India together to do whatever we could, however little that might be, in the face of the tremendous need there. It's an immense country with immense problems.

Blindness captured our interest, simply because there is so much of it. There are two causes for this. One is the parasites and the lack of proper diet and the other is the ordinary reason for going blind, which is old age. Most of us will develop cataracts as we grow older. Some will be serious enough to require surgery, some not, but there will be an incipient cataract in almost everybody's eyes. It's part of growing old. At first the lens of the eye becomes a little cloudy until finally light is blocked out entirely. However, as the cataract material solidifies, one is able to cut down and remove this obstacle so that the light will again come in through the cornea and fall on the retina. With an adequate pair of glasses, at least ninety percent of the sight can be restored.

There is more of this in India because the aging process begins much earlier. People there begin to develop cataracts when they are only forty and fifty years old, whereas here in Canada, it's usually after sixty-five or seventy-five. A person who lives to fifty is considered lucky, and to have lived a long life. Comparatively few live to be sixty and after that age one is looked upon as an ancient person.

My wife and I went out there in 1933 to tackle this problem, as volunteers with the Canadian Baptist Mission. We volunteered to do anything that had to be done. Well, the committee picked an area where there was no church, and no hospital. We were the first couple ever sent to that area, which was so totally impoverished that we wondered if there was anything at all that we could possibly do in the face of such tremendous need. We were overwhelmed until we reached the sensible conclusion that no one could possibly ever do it all, but one could start by doing just a little each day. That's what we did, and then, gradually, as the routine of this became noticed by the people, we were called on more and more to tend to medical problems that we could indeed help with.

In the course of this, we were appalled to see so much blindness that could be prevented. So many children were blind simply because the mothers had acquired rubella, or German measles, in the first trimester of their pregnancies, with the result that some children were born mentally retarded, congenitally blind, or congenitally deaf.

In the case of congenital blindness, we can remove the cataract and restore sight quite easily. We did so much of that, and, you know, what was heartbreaking was the thought of all the children who had gone through life blind, when all that was needed was this relatively simple operation. It takes only ten minutes or so in the hands of a skilled surgeon. We were, and still are, able to do it at a cost of about ten dollars. We used to say "Ten minutes, ten dollars, ten days." The ten days was because we liked to keep patients in hospital that long so we could be perfectly sure they were all right when they returned home.

The full scope of the blindness in that area became clear to me as the word spread among the people. For a while, I thought that everyone must be blind, because I was doing those operations from morning till night and still there was no end in sight. I literally did thousands of them until it reached the point when it got completely beyond me. I couldn't look after maternity work or general surgery, and I couldn't look after the many leprosy cases. We had about eleven people in every thousand who suffered from leprosy in the area. So our general hospital, which had a commitment to help anybody who came in, was getting bogged down with these cases of blindness.

Fortunately, I met a really splendid Indian Christian eye surgeon at this time who was very committed to the responsibilities of his talents and his training. He realized that he was able to help his people. His joy in life was not in amassing money. He actually came to work with me on a missionary's salary, which was around a hundred dollars a month — a bare subsistence.

One day, when he had been with us a few years I asked him in a casual conversation about his eventual aim in life. He replied that all he wanted was to restore sight to a hundred thousand sightless. I thought at the time that he was reaching for the sun and the moon and all of the stars. Well, in the thirty-one years he was with me, he not only achieved that goal, but went well over it before his death.

Our hospital had to keep expanding to meet the increasing demand, and the blind were making their way to us from a radius of well over seven hundred miles, speaking ten different languages, but we found that among our native staff of doctors and nurses we had people who could speak fifteen languages, so we were never stuck. We could always receive them in their own language and make them feel comfortable. Most of them were poor and destitute, and in many cases, crippled as well, but they would make their way to us somehow, over hundreds of miles of difficult terrain in the hope of being able to see.

In those years we've been able to restore the sight of about a quarter of a million, and the work goes on at a steady pace. Sometimes we'll get a group of maybe ten blind people coming in, hands linked together and led by one little sighted child. We get many groups like that, people who have maybe taken a month or more to reach our hospital, begging their way from village to village. How often, after seeing something like this would Christ's words come to me, "a little child shall lead them." I have often seen that little child, when they finally arrived, ask the question, "Is this the hospital for the destitute blind?" When the answer was given: "Yes, it is," he or she would collapse on the ground, completely worn out by the journey.

I can't even begin to tell you the great joy and satisfaction my work has given me over the past more than fifty years, the first ten years of which I worked only as a doctor. Then I returned home to become an ordained minister of the Baptist Church, because there were other things I wanted to do. Only an ordained minister can marry them or bury them or tend to their spiritual needs. We had a policy there, of providing services of the church only if our patients asked for them. There was no compulsion whatever. However, when they did ask, I wanted to be able to provide the spiritual sustenance, as well as the medical.

After my ordination, I returned to India to continue the work. We wouldn't be able to do this, of course, without the tremendous support we get from the people back in Canada. The church-operated organization, Operation Eyesight, supplies the money, along with the government-sponsored Canadian International Development Agency. The work has spread over the years to sixteen other developing countries in forty centres. In addition to the centre, we have also developed what we call "eye camps," where we go to certain prearranged places. Our doctors and surgeons take all the nurses and equipment to some rural setting, and set up camp-hospitals. We examine and treat hundreds of rural people that way, and operate on an average of eighty a day for three or four days, from morning to night.

Although it began in the Baptist Church, the entire thing is now completely trans-denominational, and trans-national with many religions and countries working together. The barriers of religion and nationality went down very early on after we started. All denominations, Catholic and Protestant, are involved, as well as the various nationalities. It goes to show what can be accomplished when petty differences are forgotten and we can provide life, instead of taking it away.

Arthur Raymond Bates

Northern Legends

The Mounted Police force of Canada has long been part of this country's almost legendary history, along with snow-covered wastelands, polar bears, Eskimos and igloos. In fact, many people in other areas of the world still form a mental picture like that whenever the name Canada is mentioned and they are surprised when they hear of great cities such as Toronto, Montreal, and Vancouver. Perhaps they prefer the legend to the reality in an age when the last frontiers are all disappearing. Or is it a legend? Has Canada's last frontier really been conquered or can it ever be? The answer to that has to be "Not really." The frozen North will always be frozen and it will always be daunting, even to the ablest of adventurers. It always will be home to the polar bear and the native people who were once called Eskimo but are now known as Inuit, and it will always be patrolled by men of the Royal Canadian Mounted Police.

When Arthur Raymond Bates joined the RCMP *during the Second World War, he too was taken with the legend of the Force. He wanted to uphold the law in a way that would satisfy his urge for adventure, but he also wanted to make enough money at it to help support his widowed mother. His first posting to the urban sprawl of Toronto proved disappointing in satisfying these goals. Minor city crime was hardly adventure and the cost of living left little money for his mother. He found that volunteering for outpost duty in the north would mean added recompense and possibly the adventure he craved. The* RCMP *had difficulty in getting men to serve at Baffin Island, site of the magnetic pole, as it was so far north, so they made it a policy not to force officers to serve there.*

It was strictly a volunteer thing, and in the first six months I was there, I was sorry I had done it. I couldn't believe how cold it was

— forty and fifty degrees below zero — and there just didn't seem to be anything except snow and ice and mountains as far as the eye could see. The very first thing I had to get accustomed to was that if I needed something I wasn't going to be able to pop down to a store and buy it. For example, in the first week I had to go on a walrus hunt with three Eskimos in the Davis Strait between Greenland and Baffin Island simply to get food for my dog team. We were gone five weeks, during which time we lived mostly on the fish and game that we'd caught. We slept in snow houses and never once got out of our clothing. It was so cold that the ice would constantly crack with loud explosions and I didn't even have the luxury of conversation. I couldn't speak the language of my companions, and could only communicate by way of a makeshift sign language.

The dogs were an important part of life there. I never travelled with less than sixteen dogs and as many as twenty-four, so it took a lot of effort just feeding them. For a city boy this was a good deal different than jumping in a car and pulling into a gas station. I quickly found out that simply to survive I had to forget everything I had known before and learn to live another way of life.

One starts off by just learning to cope and then you're taught by the natives. You've got nothing to teach them, but they've got plenty to teach you. They've been there for centuries and they know everything there is to know of survival, and that's what life is up there — survival. I always travelled with them, never alone, and I learned how to build igloos every night. It takes an hour to build one, and you learn to carry your fur-skin blankets with you. One to go down on the floor, fur-side down, and another over it with the fur side up. With a sleeping bag over that, it's as comfortable as if you were back home in a bed.

Building an igloo is not all that difficult once you get the hang of it. One looks for a bank of snow with just the right consistency and then, with a saw and a knife you cut out the blocks that are needed, and begin laying them in circles, each circle just a little smaller than the preceeding one, until you get it to the top where you place the "key-block.". You don't leave windows, but there is a "punch-hole" near the top that you leave so that the stale air can get out.

I really got to appreciate how wonderful those Eskimo people were during my three years there from 1944 to 1947. We were more or less in charge of looking after their welfare, but the only thing they needed from us was permission to do anything out of the ordinary. We had to approve when some of them went to Frobisher Bay to work for the United States Air Force for a period of six months. We wouldn't allow them to stay any longer, as they lose their sense of hunting very quickly and we found that if they stayed any longer they couldn't survive if they went out anywhere on their own. It's hard to believe, but they forget how to hunt unless they do it every day. When you think how they managed to get along without the white man's so-called civilization for hundreds of years, it makes you sad to see what we have taken away from them. We've given them things they don't need and taken away the skills they need most. We've introduced them to alcohol, which they just can't seem to handle — at least not right now, they can't — and we've taken away their independence and given them welfare. I was there before this spoiling process began.

I found them to be extremely good people with a unique culture of their own. I think they had a lot of fun watching us greenhorns trying to adapt to the North. We were very clumsy in our attempts at living within their system. I found them to be a very interesting and kind people and I was amazed by the number of them who had natural artistic talents. Their carvings, which have become popular only in recent years, are truly beautiful.

The first half year of living there was truly horrendous for me. Adaptation to the way of life compared to living in a city of a million was very difficult. All of the things I had grown up with were suddenly gone, and I found myself in an area of vast nothingness without one familiar object or person around. It took those first months to turn my mind around, and then I fell totally in love with the North. I enjoyed everything I did: travelling with the dogs, going on the walrus hunts, and all of those things.

Once a year a supply ship would come in and bring our mail and the items we couldn't get. Boxes of oranges, bags of potatoes, and onions. Our only fresh fruit and vegetables for a year would be there, and as we'd be so starved for food like that we'd dive right in. I remember that out of all that stuff the first thing I'd grab was an onion which I peeled and ate like an apple. You can't imagine how good that tasted, but I gradually accustomed myself to most of the native food and got to like it, with the exception of walrus, which was a popular staple of the Eskimo. They liked it best when it turned rotten, which they considered a delicacy.

Deer meat was wonderful when eaten frozen and raw. Ptarmigan was eaten right after being killed and skinned and still steaming — everything — including the intestines. That was another thing I couldn't manage; but again, that was one of their delicacies. I had no difficulty, however, with any of the other things on their diet, meat or fish.

They lived very comfortably in snow igloos in winter and skin igloos in summer — deer or caribou skins stretched over a frame. For a stove they used what they called a "cood-lee" which was simply a piece of soapstone hollowed out and filled with seal oil with moss around the edge. This provided them with heat and it was also what they baked over.

At night they would take off their outer clothing only, and they'd sleep on kind of a bench with their heads in and their feet towards the side of the igloo, with everybody, of course, in the same room.

One of my duties there was giving inoculations and the natives went along with it without complaint, although I'm sure they didn't know what it was all about. They humoured us in all our other white-man ways, so I suppose they thought they might as well go along with that strange practice of sticking needles into people. There were three of us who were responsible for inoculating all of them when the medicine came in during the fall of the year, and we gave them second shots three months later. This meant travelling all over the territory making sure that we got everybody. I remember going out to the Savage Islands, the end of the Eskimo camps, and living there with them for three weeks and then retracing my way, doing the same thing in all the other camps. All I had with me besides the medicine and needles were three books, a gun, and my skis.

I never learned to speak their language — not well — although I could converse with them a bit. I'd just pick up words as I went along. "Nikwami," for example, means "Thank you." "I-endamut" means "It can't be helped," and that's truly an important one as it embraces their whole philosophy. Anything that happens, no matter if it's death, is "I-endamut": "It can't be helped."

One time, a little Eskimo boy, six months old, had been sick for a long time. We had been giving him sulpha drugs, but it wasn't working. Finally, I had them bring him in to our establishment and I put a small steam tent over him, but I could see that he was dying. I began mouth-to-mouth and kept it up for hours, until I had to quit from exhaustion. The parents were there, but they didn't seem to want to help. They just watched me all through this like I was crazy.

Anyway, I went over to my quarters for a cup of coffee and when I came back, the parents were putting that little boy in a box which I didn't know they had already prepared and brought with them. They knew all the time that the child would die and in allowing me to go ahead with my attempts at saving him, they were simply humouring me again. That was their I-endamut philosophy — it can't be helped.

I remember an Eskimo engineer on our boat that we used in the summer. We were on a walrus hunt and this old engine in the boat was really decrepit, and it just broke down. It was a bearing. That meant that we'd have to resort to sails to get us back which could take a long time. When we got up in the morning, prepared to make the best of it, the engine was fixed. This fellow had gone ahead and carved a mould out of wood, melted some lead and made a brand new bearing while we slept. Whatever it is, they all seem to have remarkable mechanical abilities. They can take apart machinery that they've never before seen—have the pieces lying all over the place—and then put it back together, working perfectly in a matter of hours.

That fellow, by the way, sent word to me at the Post in 1946 that he was going to die and he would like to see me. I stayed with him for a week doing everything I could for him, but he did die as he said he would. He just seemed to will himself to do it. When they say, "I'm going to die," they are going to die, and there's nothing that anybody can do about it. Old people always did that sort of thing. When they saw they were a burden on the community, they would say that their time had come, and they would simply walk out into the weather and die. That happened all of the time. In their culture that's a perfectly natural thing to do, and the rest of them accept that, as they are not productive and they're using up the valuable food that others need to survive.

After spending three years with those people I left them with a tremendous amount of regret and a great deal of respect. Although I was there primarily as a police officer, I never had to deal with even one case of crime. Not one! I hope that our "civilization" doesn't eventually destroy them.

Anna Russell

The Only Chick in a Nest of Cuckoos

Anna Russell, the internationally famous comedienne, now in her late seventies, had a difficult time playing by the rules and taking life seriously. Even as a child she loved to "take the pomp out of pomposity and crack the eggs of egocentrics": Describing herself as a proud Canadian, she was, in fact, born into Britian's upper classes to a Canadian mother and an English army officer.

My mother became a terrible snob; worse than those whose ways she tried to emulate. Her head was completely turned by those people. What happened, you see, is that my father was given some time off from his regular duties with the jolly old British army, and he was sent over to the Royal Military College in Kingston, Ontario, to teach map-making for three years. While there he fell in love with one of the locals and married her. The local, of course, was my mother. After that, they were sent off to India and China, and places like those, where children weren't allowed to go, so I would be just off-loaded to my grandmother in Toronto for the long summer holidays and the rest of the time I spent at boarding school in England. Later on, I also went to college there. Naturally, I grew up with this ridiculous English accent which strangely enough served me well when I did my debut Town Hall concert in New York.

I was doing my routines in this rather exaggerated high class accent, and they seemed to think it was uproariously funny. After that success I became terrified that I might lose it and start speaking with an American accent, so I would get up every morning and practice my how-now-brown-cows and that sort of thing. After a while it just stayed on its own and I had a grand time over the following ten years or so, running around giving concerts all over the United States and Canada.

When I was invited to do concerts in England, I thought I was going to fail as they wouldn't think my accent was funny in the way that the

Americans did. I tried to change it a bit for the British, but I'd been practising it so hard for ten years that I found I just couldn't. It was stuck permanently. However, the English seemed to laugh as much as the Americans, so it was okay.

I don't know exactly how I got to be the way I am. I started off in life thinking of myself as an ugly duckling — mainly, I suppose because my mother thought I was, and then too, I *was* a bit of a nuisance to the family. My parents were somewhat elderly when I was born. Father was forty-four and Mother was thirty-eight, so I don't imagine they were exactly thrilled by the prospect of having a child.

The English side of the family seemed to consist of all men. My grandfather was in Queen Victoria's glorious army in "*IN*-Juh", and all my father's uncles, the same. *And* on top of this, my father had five brothers in the English army, and one maiden Aunt Jessie, who was the only other female, so when this bunch were confronted with a female baby — me — they had no idea of what to do with it.

Father did his best trying to bring me up on the Royal Engineers Manual, I think, but all the others were completely at a loss. "Give her to somebody else, and let them try" is what I think they said.

Even though people think I never took myself seriously, I was actually the opposite when I was young. I was so very solemn, and my aim was to become a gorgeous singer despite the fact that I had a voice like a crow. People would fall about laughing their heads off when I'd sing as a child, and my feelings would be terribly hurt.

On top of this, I got mixed up with BBC Educational Music, and there's nothing more boring and dull than that, as you must know. I was in this Hey-Nonny-No department — folk music research. Oh, I could see that I was going nowhere fast.

Then my father died, and Mother wanted to come back to Canada and I came with her. Some time after I came, I ran into my Uncle Harry, who worked with an advertising agency in Toronto. He heard me sing some of this BBC folk stuff and he said, "That's absolutely *terrible*! No one wants to hear that awful crap here in Canada! Why don't you try writing some comic songs. Try one about Wrigley's gum, which is one of my accounts."

Well, I did that and he tried it out on the radio station, CFRB in Toronto, and Wrigley's immediately cancelled his account because of it. Harry was a good sport about it though, and didn't give up on me. "Just loosen up a bit" he said, "They're going to laugh anyway, whether you try to be serious or funny."

That's what got me going, really. Good old Uncle Harry was right. When I'd walk out on a stage to do something in a serious vein, the audience were practically rolling in the aisles. They'd have tears rolling down their cheeks and the harder they tried to control themselves so that they wouldn't offend me, the more they laughed. I guess it was something the same as trying to control yourself in church. It was then that I made my decision to avoid trying to be funny, and to continue on being serious.

As a child in that odd British family, I found myself always trying to get someone to pay attention to me. I had eight uncles in all, and one aunt, and some very very old cousins of Father, but I was the only person of my generation. Each of them had a different idea on the way to bring me up, and they'd get together and row over what should be done with me, but of course in the end they'd get tired of that and tired of me and I'd be sent down to Nanny in the kitchen. In our family, I was the object of the expertise of this group of Englishmen, each of whom was highly opinionated. When one lot of them got tired of me, off I'd be sent to a different lot, and each time something different again would happen to make me think I was the only chick in a nest of cuckoos.

My dad's mother was an Australian girl from a "frightfully" wealthy family. She was one of six daughters — all of whom had noses like the Duke of Wellington, with great humps in the middle. There was also two sons, but they got themselves killed steeplechasing. Anyway, my grandmother, who was quite a realist, said to herself, "I'm never going to be able to marry off girls with noses like theirs." So when her husband died, she sold everything off and took them all to the south of France where she managed to get them all married off to some underemployed foreign royalty of sorts, all of them, I should say, with the exception of my father's mother who married Francis David Millet-Brown of the Royal Fusiliers. How about that for a name? The Browns were frightfully "correct" missionary types of Englishmen — so that in later years, when one of the brothers dragged home his Canadian wife — my mother — things didn't meld too well. It was more Mom's fault than theirs, because they were actually very nice to her. Mom got delusions of grandeur and got to thinking that she was Madame Makaterina Serina, right up to the end of her life.

Of course, when Father died, and she came back to live in Canada, this just drove her brothers up the wall. One of them was a farmer, and the other had an ad agency. You can imagine how they reacted to this duchess pose of their sister. It was like the fall of the House of Usher down there in Unionville where the Canadian family lived. They were the Tandys, and I got along famously with them, much better than the English side of the family.

It was in Canada that I first made my way into show business. My very first job was in Toronto, on a CFRB program called "Round the Marble Arch," with singers like Wishart Campbell, the glorious baritone, and Ruby Ramsay Rouse at the piano. Ruby and I were great pals, and I remember one time when I took my laundry to this little Chinese place. The radio was blaring away inside, and I asked the man who owned the laundry, "Lee, what is your favourite radio program?" Without hesitation at all he answered, "Luby Lamsay Louse." When I told Ruby about that, I thought she'd collapse.

I think the funniest things in life do come out of real situations, and where people are being their most serious selves, and not trying to be funny. For instance, I get most of my funniest material straight out of the *Encyclopedia Britannica.* I always maintain it's the greatest source of comic material in the English language. If I've got an idea for a routine, I look it up in the *Encyclopedia* and most of the time, it's all there. For example, there's one popular routine I do on "How to play the bagpipes." The first thing I did was learn a couple of pieces on them and then I just did a précis on what it said there. It's hysterical: people fall off their chairs laughing, but all I'm doing is telling them exactly what's in the encyclopedia. If you look it up, you'll find my act right in there. It's as simple as that.

I think, too, that there's something very hilarious about opera. Just from the nature of the beast, it's got to be hilarious. The main reason is that the hero is always the tenor, and to make a tenor sound, you've got to be a sort of moon-faced person with a barrel chest, which usually goes with being very short, and probably rather fat. *This* is the great lover! Then, of course, the handsome, tall, gorgeous one, who makes the baritone noise is always the old father or someone or other like that, so the whole thing just looks ridiculous right away. Then you have people like Mimi in *La Boheme* who is supposed to be a delicate, sweet young consumptive beauty dying all over the place. The problem is that Mimi is the type of role you can't sing until you're forty-five with good underpinnings and a large bosom. If I go to the opera I always find myself laughing in the wrong places.

Things like that, I find, are so easy to satirize. It's the same with all the things I do. I simply take these things and put a little extra here and a little extra there, and the audience doesn't take long before they recognize how ridiculous so many "serious" things in life really are. I think it's uproarious that my mother spent so much time putting on these silly airs, trying to make people think she was better than they were.

I think it's funny, too, how she never really wanted much to do with me. That might shatter some people, but not me. What's funny is purely a matter of opinion to every individual, but there is also a universal funnybone. I've played in church basements, basketball courts, and on many of the great stages of the world, and I've found that most people, no matter where they come from or from whatever level of society, are essentially the same. *Everybody* likes a good laugh.

W.W. (Mac) MacGill

The Royal Flying Corps in Canada

Canadians who wanted to fly airplanes in the First World War couldn't join the Canadian Air Force because we didn't have one then. Many young men therefore had to join Britain's Air Force, the Royal Flying Corps. A number of these Canadians distinguished themselves as air aces in those early planes over the battlefields of Europe: men like Billy Bishop, Don MacLaren, and a young pharmacist from Vancouver by the name of "Mac" (William Weir) MacGill, who joined up in 1917 when he was twenty-seven years old. His name is recorded in the honour roll of Canada's ace pilots for the Great War of 1914–18.

There were four of us who decided to go in together, two bankers and myself, and I can't remember what the other fellow did for a living. Anyway, we were talking one day about the war, and we said, "Let's all go and learn to fly." Everyone thought this was a great idea and so the four of us went tramping up to the recruiting centre chock full of enthusiasm and had our medical examinations. Not one of us passed. They were pretty strict about physicals at that point in the war. It was 1917. So we were a very disappointed lot going out of there, but we could do nothing about it.

About a month after that we were told that over in Victoria they weren't quite as strict and so three of us got on the ferry and hustled to that recruiting office. Well, this time I was the only one of the three who passed. About two weeks later, I got a note from RFC headquarters in Toronto that I was accepted and that I would be called on at a later date, which turned out to be in May or June of that year when I was told to report in Toronto; but they gave me enough time to see my mother and brother and sister, who were living in different parts of the country.

In Toronto I was issued big boots and big socks with a uniform and a cap with a white band around it, signifying that I was a cadet. We were sent out to Long Branch just outside Toronto for our training. There wasn't much there with the exception of two wooden buildings, one for meals and the other for sleeping. As there was nothing else for us to do right then, we were put to work digging ditches for the latrines. That's how I began my career in the RFC.

That was just after the United States came into the war, and they didn't have the facilities to train students, whereas the RFC was already eight months to a year into its program and they were pretty well organized. They were opening flying fields here and there and were bringing in chaps who had been at the front already to train and look after the new recruits like me. Our group, as it turned out, was sixty-percent American.

In a few weeks we were moved to the University of Toronto's School of Practical Science where we were lectured on everything from the theory of flight to the theory of everything that related in any way to flying—the theory of the flying corps co-operating with the artillery; the theory of bombing; wireless; and even the theory of life itself. That's how we spent our mornings.

In the afternoons we'd sit behind a Lewis and Vickers machine and work it to death until we knew it upside-down. We were grilled on every kind of airplane motor that existed—how they were built; what they were built of; and why they were built that way. It really was a terrific course and they were never able to give such a one again. Those men who taught us came from the battle zone and certainly knew their stuff; they could never assemble a team of teachers like that ever again. We lived and breathed those lessons from morning to night for an entire month. The only other thing we did was marching which we did before we even had breakfast, very early in the morning. During that whole month, though, we didn't see the inside of an airplane. It was all theory, theory, theory, and at the end we were put through a real university exam on what we had learned.

After this, we shipped to a place called Deseronto, where they had Camp Mohawk and Camp Radcliffe and two aerodromes. By now there were only two Canadians in the group, a chap by the name of Anderson and me. The rest were all American, a mixture of army and navy. The Desoronto set-up was brand new then, and when we got there the carpenters were just finishing the two buildings where we were to eat and sleep. Three hangars were ready. One wasn't, and neither was one of the aerodromes. We were kept sitting around for a few days until the workmen were finished and finally a few airplanes were in and each of us was lucky if we managed to get fifteen minutes in one in a matter of two or three days.

The instructor would take us up first to fly us around and see if we got flying sickness, and then we were permitted a few minutes at the controls. There were just too many students for the number of planes that were there. After a month there, I managed to get about three hours altogether of dual flight, and then one morning my instructor said, "Okay. Take it away. You're on your own. Go to it!" I said, "Do you really think I'm good enough now?" "Sure, you are," he said, "You didn't know it, but the last three times we landed you did it by yourself." "Oh," says I, "I guess that's why I'm here, isn't it?"

Anyway I went on my own. I took her up, made a few circles and landed her. I can't tell you how tickled I was with myself. It's like going from here to the stars in one giant step, and you stick out your chest and look down on all the others who haven't yet made their first solo. Talk about walking on air! You know now you really are a flier and there's no one can say you're not. I'll never forget that little plane either. It was Number 202 Curtiss JN4, one of the early ones. Later on at Camp Borden I flew an even earlier Curtiss, Number 127, so I was really very much a pioneer airman.

Before that there wasn't a great deal of flying in the war. There was a small bit in 1915, but they didn't have much in the way of guns, and the planes had very poor power too. That was the year that they really began to experiment with planes in warfare. For a short time the Allies were superior and then the Germans, and it went back and forth like that as each side worked on improvements.

The officers in charge of us new recruits kept stressing that we should get to know those planes as if they were part of our bodies. The importance of the rudder and getting so that your feet and hands would do the right thing automatically. Our training in the air increased every day, and then they sent us to Camp Borden after about three and a half months. A great many of the boys cracked up their planes in their first solos, because they would forget to shut the engine off before landing, so they had to put up this bag banner on the landing strip: "SHUT OFF MOTOR."

At Borden, we got much less time in the air, but we were taught formation flying and a few things like that. I remember flying a Curtiss JN4 in a formation, and in order to fly the plane straight ahead, I had to hold that stick against the side of the fuselage. That's how poorly the plane was rigged. One of the problems was that all of the mechanics were being trained at the same time as we were. Flying was still in its infancy.

About a month later it began to get very cold in Borden, so they shipped the whole operation, planes and all, down to Texas. Incidentally, those planes were all built in Leaside, which is part of Toronto. That reminds me that the very first long-distance flight I made was from Camp Borden to Armour Heights, to Leaside and back again. It was easy. All I had to do was follow Yonge Street which passes all those places.

The trip to Texas was all done on the QT (in secret) so that most of us didn't even know that our final destination was Fort Worth. We arrived okay, but they weren't ready for us — no place to eat, sleep, or fly. We were put up in pup tents, two to a tent, with a little stove in each as the weather can get pretty cool in Fort Worth. One night we had three feet of snow which caused the tents to sag and touch the stoves and go up in flames. Tents were going up all over the place and the boys were jumping out and running to the hangar to sleep. Fortunately no one was hurt.

The entire Texas exercise turned out very badly. Because there were no regular airports there, they had us taking off from fields that were nothing but pure gumbo which packed up on the wheels. It turned out that our bombing practice was simply dropping this gumbo quite unintentionally all over the area. In the end our flying in Texas ended up being all bookwork rather than in airplanes. We were supposed to do bombing, wireless, artillery contact, and all sorts of things, but we did practically none of that.

When we'd been there for about three weeks, we were given our second lieutenant commissions and were sent off to England with a week off beforehand to visit relatives.

We were sent down to Halifax for our trip over and this was about three weeks or a month after the Halifax explosion in December of 1917. I can still remember seeing from the train window all these cement steps standing alone. The houses had been blown away or burnt by the explosion. In town there wasn't a glass window to be seen. Everything was boarded up. I remember buying underwear in a store which still didn't have its electricity back. They were using kerosene lamps. It looked like you would expect it to look in the war-torn cities of Europe. Very, very strange.

Finally a boat arrived to take us across the Atlantic. There were about two or three hundred of us — all RFC student officers but down in the hold were two thousand Chinese labourers who were being taken to France to dig ditches and trenches. They had come through from Vancouver by train, and they were loaded on this ship of ours, the S.S. *Tunisia*, like so much freight.

About half a day out of port, we joined a convoy with a destroyer out front; the *Mauritania* after that, then the *Devonia*, and another one or two behind. On the left side was our ship and another ship behind us; I don't know if it was carrying troops or supplies. Two lines over there were ships carrying lumber and others with munitions. We zig-zagged safely across the Atlantic until we reached the northwest corner of Ireland. Just at dusk we were ordered up on deck. That was the one and only time I ever saw a torpedo. I was at the stern of the ship when I saw this white streak go past in the water about a hundred yards away. It continued past us and hit the *Devonia* which was in the centre of the convoy with thousands of U.S. troops on board. I remember seeing the flash and then the rockets going up, but our instructions were "Every man for himself and show no lights."

We had a good skipper on this old ship, which I think had been a cattle boat at one time. He had made twenty-six or twenty-seven convoy trips across the sea, and boy, did he have a head of steam driving that old tub. In the dead of night, this huge ship came out of nowhere and nearly rammed us. It came so close that those two skippers could curse each other from the bridges. Our skipper successfully veered off and we were the first ship in front of the submarine gate at Liverpool Harbour. By now, a whole flock of torpedo-boat destroyers were already on the way out to pick up any survivors from the *Devonia*, which eventually sank. Most of the troops were saved, except those who were killed by the explosion. We were a relieved lot of rookies as you can imagine by the time we docked and made our way off that ship, and here we were, not yet even part of the battle. That was still to come.

Angus McGovern

Scotland's Loss Was Canada's Gain

Almost two hundred years ago, towards the latter part of the eighteenth century and the early part of the nineteenth, Scottish landlords forced tenants off the land on which they and their families had lived for hundreds of years. By removing the crofters during these Highland Clearances, the landlords could replace them with herds of sheep, which were far more profitable to them in those days of the booming wool trade. Many of those evicted tenants found a new home in Canada, especially in the Maritime provinces where they form the backbone of the economy even today. Angus McGovern of Montague, P.E.I., was born in 1906 and he grew up on the tales of the treachery and cruelty of the landlords towards his ancestors.

All of those people had lived on that land so long they had come to think of it as their own, so of course they couldn't understand it when the landlords, some of them their own clan chiefs, put them off. Those who refused to go saw their houses burned and their pitiful possessions and crops destroyed, giving them no alternative but to leave.

In many cases they were driven off by the sherriff's men and some were trampled under the horses' hooves as they attempted to escape. They had no place to go except eventually to the docks, where unscrupulous ships' captains took what little money they had to pay for a place in the hold of a leaky ship. They were packed in like animals with inadequate supplies of food or water, and sent across the oceans to the wild colonies of Canada and Australia. That's how most of the early Scots, my own ancestors among them, got to this country, and those terrible stories are passed from one generation to the next.

It was dreadful for them when they finally reached their destinations, too. Those who managed to survive the voyage had to start out practically from scratch. Most of the time there wouldn't be a doctor so they relied on some old lady — a "granny" they'd call her — who had some skills in folk medicine. My own great-great grandmother was one of these, and she delivered five hundred babies during her lifetime and she raised a family of her own at the same time. People would come for miles to see her. She was known as the granny of the Belfast district of Prince Edward Island, where the ship *Polly* landed with a group of settlers.

There was a Dr. MacAulay with that group who was also a clergyman, but he died in 1827, and they had no doctor for the next fifteen years and they had to make do with "grannies." Then in 1842 a Dr. Munro came over from the Isle of Skye and he was the doctor for years. It's wonderful when you think how those early settlers were able to get along even in the cruellest of circumstances.

The Micmac Indians were very important to those early people in helping them to survive. They showed them how to use the trees to build log houses and they showed them how to use plants and the barks from the various trees as medicines. I often think of how hard it must have been for the settlers to be dropped in the middle of nowhere with nothing to sustain them, and to see nothing but the dark and thick forest of trees, something they didn't have back at home at all. It must have been frightening.

Many people don't know that the Lord Selkirk who took a big group of settlers to Manitoba in 1812 had brought a group to P.E.I. even earlier than that, in 1803. The Manitoba Selkirk settlers had a hard time of it, but not as hard as the ones who came to P.E.I. because there were no forests to contend with in Manitoba.

Those Scots on P.E.I. were a hardy lot who didn't give up easily. After all, they never had it easy back there in the Hebrides, trying to scratch a living between fishing and farming on that rocky land. If it hadn't been for the cruel way that they were driven from the land they loved, they would have realized that the move to Canada was the best thing that could have happened to them.

But while they were working so hard to establish their roots, all they could think of was the land they had lost. The truth was that here they were founding a much better society, where the land was *theirs*. They were able to keep their Gaelic language and their Gaelic culture, something that had been forbidden back in Scotland after the Battle of Culloden in 1746. They were also able to build a pastoral life.

They didn't have to hide their bagpipes and their tartans anymore; and they could resurrect the old songs and dances and enjoy their ceilidhs. In their log homes at night, they told the old stories, and played the old games. They did plenty of visiting, and built up their churches, something that was very close to their hearts. It took a while, but eventually they found a real happiness.

Something else that they loved to do in the evenings was tell ghost stories. Everyone would have a ghost story and the older people still tell them by the hour. I have to admit I still love an evening of ghost stories.

I had an old grand-aunt who lived nearby by herself and my mother would send us kids out to keep her company. There were ten kids in our family, so there were always a couple of us over with her. She was just full of ghost stories, and we'd be scared out of our skins at some of them. So scared in fact, that we'd hardly get to sleep afterwards, but they were still great fun. I remember one story which is supposed to have happened about 1880.

This tale concerns two brothers named Murchison. One was the captain of a ship named the *Alexander* and the other was the mate. They were my grand-uncles. They were coming from Europe on this sailing vessel and they were stopped in New York with their crew before proceeding to Prince Edward Island. They had a man called McLean with them, and he had a dream that they were going to be shipwrecked. He refused to go on the trip, and sure enough they *were* shipwrecked off Newfoundland. Now that's not what we call a ghost story. Rather it's called a message from an angel.

There was plenty of that kind of thing in those days, and the Scots were great believers. They're always on the lookout for signs and messages of something that is going to happen. There was one man I remember who lived out in the country, who would make all the caskets when someone died. He was a very skilled cabinet maker, and when there was a death people would bring the lumber and he would build a casket. He never charged for his services.

Well, this day he told his wife that he was sure that someone had died overnight. He said he didn't know how he knew this except that he had a very strange feeling come over him. At any rate, he had hardly finished his breakfast when he heard a horse and wagon pulling into his yard. When he went out; sure enough, there was a man with some lumber on the wagon asking him to build a casket for his mother who had died overnight.

There were lots of cases like that one. And still are. It's called second sight or a "forerunner," something that warns you of something that is going to happen before it actually does.

Once upon a time and not long ago a burning ship used to be seen regularly out in the waters between P.E.I. and Nova Scotia. Some try to explain it away by saying it's an illusion caused by the sun, but that's not so because it's been sighted many times in the dead of night. My own brother who is a Presbyterian minister told me that he had seen it one time over near River John. Another man by the name of Donald Campbell was on the other side of the river that night, and he said he had seen it too. Still another man who was on the Wood Island ferry saw it one night, and he was so positive of it, that when he came on land he went over to a ship's captain's house and said, "There's a ship burning out there in the Northumberland Strait." The captain looked, and sure enough he saw it too. They decided to go out and see what they could do to help, but when they got near, it disappeared. I can't explain that, and neither can any of the responsible people who say they've seen it; but every so often somebody reports again, that they've seen it. There are those who say it's an "after-runner" of a disaster that happened near where that burning ship is seen. It seems that a ship's captain and his crew abandoned a ship in a storm, leaving all the passengers to drown. Certainly an awful lot of people have seen it.

I don't know what it is about the Scots, but it does seem that there is an ability with many of them to see into the future. I do know that a lot of the things that have been foretold did indeed come true. Perhaps it all comes from their strong belief in a world beyond. Many people don't have that belief today. But the Scots had a lot of faith then and they sure needed it when they first landed here.

One group had to survive the whole winter by digging down through the ice on the seashore to find clams. They were in rough shape when spring came, but they did manage to survive. Wouldn't they be proud today if they could see what a great island they made out of this?

Jean Banting Webster

Banting's Best

Canada has produced many giants in all fields of endeavour, men and women whose unusual accomplishments have helped to change Canada and the world for the better. Their legendary feats eventually overpower these remarkable individuals in time, and we tend to forget that these great people were first and foremost ordinary human beings who went beyond the ordinary in one area of their lives. In other ways they were much like the rest of us, with everyday joys and problems.

An Ontario doctor, Frederick Banting, is a good example. His discovery of insulin along with another Ontario doctor, Charles Best, has established his name forever in the annals of great discoveries. Millions around the world bless his name daily for the extension of their lives. However, in the beginning, Fred Banting's colleagues considered his experiments doomed to failure like all previous research into diabetes. But Banting persevered and he and Dr. Best discovered insulin, giving millions of diabetes sufferers a chance to live.

The resultant acclaim brought a knighthood for the farm boy from Alliston, Ontario, accolades from the medical profession, and the enshrinement of his name alongside that of other great medical scientists like Louis Pasteur. Fred Banting, who had been born to the wearing of overalls all of his life, had become a legend overnight, to be known to the world as "Sir Frederick."

Sir Fred really was a farm boy, whose parents had to scrape to send him to university, where his marks were only mediocre as they were in high school. In the Great War, he came within a whisker of being killed. After the war, he chalked up a failed marriage and a failed medical practice. He didn't have a lot of enemies; but he also did not have many friends either. Fred didn't go out of his way to be nice, or to avoid conflicts with colleagues and acquaintances. Within the family circle, however, "Uncle Fred" was a much-loved member, as one of his nieces remembers.

Uncle Fred was my father's oldest brother, the oldest child in the family. There were two other boys in between them and there was one sister.

I remember him very well, even though I was very young when he was getting ready to go off to the First World War. I was six at that time, and I was wearing a bandage on my arm which I had hurt in a fall. Uncle Fred refused to open the bandage to look at the arm because of what he called "doctors' ethics." We had our own family doctor, you see, so I suppose he figured that he shouldn't interfere. However, two weeks later when he came to say his final goodbyes before heading off to the war, he did open it up and discovered that it was broken right at the joint. He felt sorry then that he hadn't examined it the first time.

Up to the time he left for the war, he would come home to see his mother, my grandmother, every two weeks, and I remember how glad she always was to see him. When I think of it now, he was still just a boy even though he was a practising medical doctor. He was at the Toronto Hospital for Sick Children at the time and he was only twenty-four.

There was great rejoicing in the family when he came back in one piece when the war was over. I suppose he had a few close calls, though, because he had great big gouges out of his arm where he had been shot. He came home with the Military Cross for bravery, too.

He tried to establish a medical practice in London, Ontario, but it didn't work out. I guess to attempt to start in another city where he was unknown and didn't know anybody wasn't such a good idea. He had all the qualifications though. He was a surgeon and had plenty of experience from his time at the Sick Children's. In spite of all that, his practice never got off the ground, so he had to close up and come back to the University of Toronto where he worked at research. He didn't get much of a welcome there either, because they looked on his diabetes research as a waste of time.

He was the only one in his family to go to university. In those days it was the practice of families who didn't have much money to concentrate on getting at least one child, usually the oldest, a higher education. The other children accepted this and there wasn't any resentment. In fact, they would all pitch in to bring it about. It was the same way in my father's family, where my older brother was the one who got a higher education.

I liked my Uncle Fred a lot. He always seemed happy and playful when he would come to visit us. Even when he came back from the war I didn't see any change in his attitude. We looked on him then as a returning hero, but I remember he never talked much of the years he spent overseas. I can't say what he was like in his outside life or in his marriage, because I don't know about that. I only saw him on his visits to Grandma's farm where he was very much a well-loved son and kindly uncle.

When I was a bit older, I remember one time when my cousin and I went to visit him after his divorce, and we stayed with him for a week, helping him with his young son, Bill, who we were very fond of. Bill used to come to our place for short holidays, and also to my cousin Helen's, who lived on the next line. We had a wonderful time during that week with Uncle Fred in Toronto. He couldn't have been nicer.

Although he had a reputation for being sort of aloof, we never saw any evidence of it. With people he knew very well, he was always warm and friendly. There were times during the trouble in his married life that he seemed a bit distant and distracted, but that's understandable, I think. I only remember the niceness, the times when I was young and he would take me up and dance me up and down on his knee.

During that period of research, leading up to the discovery of insulin, the only thing we in the family knew was that he was having a pretty tough time. All of his colleagues were saying that he was such a fool to be going into something where so much unsuccessful research had already been done. They'd say to him, "Well, Banting, I guess you think you know more than all the rest of us." In the end, of course, he had the last laugh.

Many people were down on him during that period, because he used dogs in the research. They said that this was cruel and so on, but the truth of the matter is that Uncle Fred was a great dog lover, but there was no other way to do what he wanted to do without using dogs.

When he was a very small boy in Alliston, one of his best friends was a little girl who lived just across the road from him. Well, she got sick and eventually died from diabetes, and Grandma said that Uncle Fred was almost uncontrollable in his grief. He would say that when he grew up he was going to find a cure for diabetes. He was so young then that he could barely pronounce the word. It must have made a tremendous impression on his young mind though. It just broke his heart that this little playmate died at such a young age. I suppose we all have childhood dreams of what we're going to do when we grow up, but his dream was realized, even though it took a long time for him to get at it, what with having to become a doctor first, then going through a war, a failed medical practice, and a divorce. He just perservered in spite of everything.

When he and Dr. Best got insulin to the point where they were sure they had it, they got news of a man who was supposedly going to die shortly from diabetes. They got his permission to try the insulin on him, and miraculously, the man immediately began to improve and get better. They knew then that they had what they were looking for.

There were great celebrations all over the world when the news got out, and some American doctors tried to buy the discovery from him but he said, "No, it belongs to Canada"; and he stuck to that decision.

Mart Kenney

Music for Canadians to Dance By

Radio brought many things to Canadian homes that had never been there before — instantaneous news from all over the world — commentary, drama, and for many the most important of all, music. Until the advent of radio most homes had musical instruments and someone who could play them. They also had hand-wound phonographs and records of a tinny and dubious quality. Families did sing together and play together, but all of this did not satisfy the thirst that most of us had.

Listening to Caruso on one of those early recordings required a great deal of imagination on the part of the music lover to appreciate how good he was. The sound of his voice came to the ear complete with the primitive quality of the recording and the many inevitable scratches. Today we can wonder how anyone could sit down to an evening of such sound, but they did and they loved it, and they marvelled at this magical invention.

Radio was a giant step beyond the phonograph. Right into our own homes came an amazing variety of live music from all over the country and the world. The excitement of picking up a live orchestra from New York, Paris, Montreal, Vancouver, or Halifax more than made up for the poor reception and frequent static that accompanied the program.

In a country whose small population was spread thinly over one of the world's largest land masses, radio shattered the isolation that most of us felt. The early networks of the Canadian National Railways and the Canadian Radio Broadcasting Commission brought Vancouver Island and Cape Breton Island as close together as two buildings on the same lot. Through radio, a musician in Sydney could be heard in Winnipeg or Regina, St. John's or Vancouver, Montreal or Toronto. Best of all as far as musicians were concerned, a local orchestra lucky enough to get on a radio network broadcast could gain instant fame almost over-

night. Such was the case with Mart Kenney of Vancouver whose dance band dominated the air-waves for many years.

Until we got on the old CRBC network, we were just another local band. In fact we didn't even pick a name for our orchestra until that happened. Horace Stovin, who ran the network, selected us to play from Waterton Park in 1934 and he told us we would have to pick an identifying theme song and come up with a name. In those days all the bands had more or less geographic names — Guy Lombardo and his Royal Canadians, for example. One of our fellows came up with the idea of "Western Gentlemen." I thought that was fine and I recall seeing a piece of sheet music on my mother's piano called "The West, a nest, and you, dear," which seemed to exemplify not only the area where we were to do our broadcast but also the style of music that we would be playing. We became Mart Kenney and his Western Gentlemen and our theme music, "The West, a nest, and you, dear," eventually became familiar from coast to coast, thanks to radio. Before this time we were simply a bunch of musicians struggling along, barnstorming around Calgary and other Western towns and cities.

I remember going to play a dance outside of Calgary one night. We drove many miles, wearing tuxedos and all the rest of it, and not a single soul came. This was before we got on radio so nobody knew us and nobody cared. Getting started with network radio from Waterton brought us to the attention of the Canadian Pacific Hotels. It was really necessary to "have a wire" as it was known then, meaning a radio station, broadcasting the sound of your band on location. That's what built all of the big bands. The golden age of radio ran concurrently with the development of the Big Bands.

In the United States, for instance, I'll never forget one of the boys in the Casa Loma band telling me, "Listen in tonight because there's a new band and they're going to be broadcasting every night from the Meadowbrook. It's going to be the band to watch." He was so right! That band was Glenn Miller's. Even Glenn could not have done it without radio.

The Music Corporation of America was *the* big powerful organization, musically speaking, at the time. They could take a band and put them into a hotel or some other location where they'd have a network line every night and that would go on for weeks and weeks. After, when they would go out on the road, crowds would flock to see them. Instant fame.

Now in Canada that was difficult to do due to our geographic problems. It's a long way from Vancouver to Halifax, and that's why we were the only band that ever really became a coast-to-coast commodity, because we did have the network spot and we did get out and tour once or twice a year.

When we were in Banff in the summer of 1936 there was a small group of executives there from RCA Victor. Included in the group was E.C. Grimley, the new president of RCA Victor Canada. He'd just come from New York and this man Ernie Hammond brought him down to the room where we were playing to hear us. Mr. Grimley said, "Why haven't we got this band on records?" Within the next two years we did start to do some recording. Now *that* certainly helped in gaining us national recognition, but it wasn't nearly as important as radio. I believe that those who bought our records did so because they knew us from our radio shows.

I knew right from the beginning how demanding this radio thing was. The microphone was like a big magnifying glass and if every note in a chord wasn't perfectly in tune, the chord didn't ring properly going out on the air. Listeners may not have known whether it was in or out of tune, but they sure did know whether they liked it or not. As a result we were cranks about that. We would work for hours making sure that each instrument balanced.

Our music was geared to our audience's tastes. People in southern Alberta liked waltzes, so we became experts at waltz music. Musical taste varied all across the country and we worked very hard to provide a proper balance in the radio shows that went on the network.

I can't stress enough how important radio was to us. For example, when we finished up at Waterton Park in 1934, I only had two other dates left to play. One was in Pembroke, B.C., and the other someplace on the way there. In effect that was the end of us and our band, so I was pretty sick about that. I hadn't fully realized what these network broadcasts were doing for us. When we got to Cranbrooke, B.C., there was a telegram waiting for me: "Would you be interested in booking your orchestra for the Hotel Saskatchewan?" Boy, was I! What I had forgotten was that my orchestra was gaining widespread recognition through radio.

Shortly after this the CRBC was thinking of putting some popular music on Sunday night. Now that was dangerous, as in those days the sabbath was pretty important. The board of governors of the Commission was strait-laced and afraid to offend anyone so we were asked to come up with something "middle-road." We suggested a program we named "Sweet and Low." Well, that apparently satisfied everybody's fears. We went on the air and it went on for years. We had all sorts of letters from our listeners telling us how much they liked what we were doing and offering suggestions which helped us greatly in shaping those early programs.

All during those years I was very conscious of one thing and that was that I didn't want to copy any other orchestra. There were Big Bands all over the radio dial by then and it was easy to keep track of what they were doing. I knew that the successful ones were those who had a sound of their own. That's what we aimed for and that's what we achieved. Guy Lombardo's sound was distinctive, as was Glenn Miller's and other recognized orchestras. As you moved across the dial you'd always know which band was playing after just a few notes.

We did two national tours with our orchestra every year — maybe three or four weeks in the Maritimes and perhaps seven weeks in the western provinces. That took up about half of the year, and then the rest of the time we were around Ontario and Quebec. Wherever we went people knew us and they came to see us. We never forgot that it was on radio that we gained that recognition.

Edith Hewson

A Wonderful Growing-Up Time

Large families tended to be the rule on prairie farms in the early part of this century. "The more the merrier" seemed to be the general philosophy, and "there's always room for one more."

Edith Hewson, who is now "pushing eighty" as she likes to put it, was one of fourteen children born to hardworking parents on a farm near Hazelcliff, Saskatchewan on the Cut Knife Creek, where it runs into the Qu'Appelle Valley. Hers was a happy childhood in a household that boasted twenty-two cats and several dogs in addition to the children. Food from their own land was plentiful, there was a piano and lots of simple fun, but very little money for extras.

Today Edith Hewson still lives in Langbank where she writes a weekly newspaper column. She has also written a book about her life called We Swept the Cornflakes Out the Door.

We moved away from Hazelcliff to Langbank, near Regina, when I was a baby, and Father took up farming there. So it's life at Langbank that I really remember. Our family filled that big old farmhouse and we were really a noisy, rambunctious lot. There was always something going on.

Surprise parties for no particular reason at all were popular events in my teens. Everybody would decide that it was time for a party at someone's house, and the surprise was supposed to be that the person at whose house it was going to be held wouldn't be told. However, word usually leaked out so that when they all arrived at *our* house, the whole place would be clean and shiny, and Mother would have a mountain of sandwiches ready, along with a big tub of coffee. We'd pretend we were surprised, of course, but that too was part of the game. We'd dance and sing around the old piano until midnight, when we'd break for our meal and then we'd go back at it and carry on until maybe two in the morning. We'd square-dance and round-dance, and have a great time of it.

In winter the same crowd would come out and have a skating party on the old marsh back of the barn, and once again my mother would make up a big boiler full of coffee and a pile of sandwiches. We really had a wonderful growing-up time, even though I suppose that if one thought about it in terms of today's young people, we were poor. But we never had any feeling that we were poor. We had just the basics, but the basics seemed to be enough for us.

When I think back on it all, I think mostly of Mother and what it must have been for her, looking after a house with fourteen children and two adults. She would make twenty-eight loaves of bread every two or three days, and I can still picture her with a couple of the neighbouring farmers in their sheepskin coats, following her around from one room to the other, talking a steady stream, while she punched the bread dough and punched a couple of misbehaving kids without missing a beat. She was a great talker, and very interested in politics and everything else going on.

When I talk about sixteen people in the house, I mean that as a minimum. There were always a couple of neighbours, the hired man, and at least a couple of dogs and all of those cats, wandering in and out. It was the type of household where people had no compunction about dropping in, and my poor mother didn't know half the time who was at the table anyway. We had a big long kitchen table with a bench all down one side and chairs along the other side. As the older children left home and the younger ones reached their majority, they graduated from sitting on a bench to a chair of their own. That was quite a landmark in the process of growing up.

I remember one old bachelor neighbour who occasionally visited. He had fierce blue eyes and a big red beard. We were all kind of half afraid of him and we didn't really like him at all, but he always stopped by for a meal. At that time there were a few empty chairs because of the older children who had left the nest, and it was on one of these chairs that the redbearded man was sitting. When I came in, all of the other children were on the bench. I saw that my chair was right next to his, and I went around on the bench side and yelled, "Move over" to the one on the end, and pushed my way onto the bench. Well, Mother's face went scarlet, and she grabbed me by the arm and just threw me into my chair alongside the neighbour. She wasn't going to have any kind of rudeness in her home.

Sleeping was always done three to a bed, and we'd have turns getting the baby in one of the beds. Also, we always had fox terriers who liked to sleep with us, and a few kittens and cats. We'd fight over getting one of the fox terriers as they were little and warm, while the baby wasn't always comfortable to be with, especially in the morning, as you can imagine. On the really cold nights we piled lots of blankets on, but usually it was pretty cozy with three in a bed, one body heating up the other. Anyway, we were always tired and went to sleep before anyone could complain about being squashed in. I remember that the first time I left home I was very lonely sleeping alone.

Mother was very easy-going with our cats and dogs. They had full run of the house day and night, and were considered as much a part of the family as we were. With such an animal and human population in one house you always had to be careful not to bump into someone or step on a cat or dog, but actually you learned to cope and it simply became a way of life.

In addition to all of those house pets, we had horses too, and every one of us rode horseback from the time we could walk and always without saddle. Can't ever remember any one of us falling off either.

I forgot to mention that Grandfather also lived with us, and he was a great one for mischief. My mother was a real Carrie Nation where booze was concerned. She *hated* the stuff, because apparently someone in her family was a terrible drinker. She wouldn't allow a drop of it around the place, and she didn't even want to hear anyone talk about it. Anyway, Grandfather was reading the Bible to me one day, and he came to this part about Christ changing the water into wine. I said to him, "Is wine booze?" "Yes", he said, "It's booze." "Well, how come Christ would change water into booze? He must have approved of it." Grandfather just looked very thoughtful and kind of perplexed and he said, "I think you'd better ask your mother about that." Of course, I did what he told me, and Mother stopped punching bread and walloping kids long enough to scream, "Where does that kid get all these strange ideas?" If she'd looked behind the door, she would've seen Grandfather laughing his head off silently. He was always full of tricks like that.

Our school at Langbank was about three miles from our home, so we were driven there in the Democrat in the fine weather, and in the horse-and-sleigh in winter. As we got older we went to the Collegiate school in Moosomin. The Depression was on by the time I went to teachers' college, so I earned my way through by telling fortunes in a restaurant in the afternoons and evenings, and I went to school in the mornings. Fortune-telling was a favourite pastime then. Everybody wanted to have palms read or their teacups, so I learned how to do that and it put me through school.

People would pay ten cents for a cup of tea and that would include the services of a fortune-teller, which was me. My wages at the restaurant were thirty dollars a month and out of that I paid fifteen dollars a month for my room. My meals during the week were provided by the restaurant, but they expected that I should spend at least part of my money eating at their place on the weekend, in order to get some of their money back. That's the way it was then. You worked for everything you got, and what's more you expected to. Even during our high school years in Moosomin, we worked for our board, doing housework and babysitting, etc. People liked getting farm girls because we were used to hard work.

Getting an education during the Depression wasn't at all easy. It was looked on as a privilege, and those who gave any trouble of any kind were soon booted out, and that would be the end of your education. The teacher wouldn't put up with any nonsense.

Although we never had a lot of money, my father was a very successful farmer until the Depression came along. He had to be with that big family, but in the thirties not even the vegetable garden grew. Besides the financial crash, we had the drought and the crops were so dry that they just blew away along with the soil. Someone said that Saskatchewan simply blew away across the border into Manitoba and Alberta.

There was no way that the farm could support the family any longer, so those of us that could had to leave in search of whatever work there was. I found a job in Regina, and anything extra I had, including my old clothes, was sent home to the family. I had a teacher's license by this time and when I'd go home to the farm for a few days, I would spend the time filling in applications to schools all over the province. My mother would say, "Edith, never mind about teaching. You know how fond you are of your stomach, so stay at the restaurant. You get good meals there." She'd tell me horror stories of girls from our district who took teaching jobs away from home. "May Jukes' mother told me that all she gets up there is fried potatoes, so just you stay where you are."

It's amazing how fast things happened to us. The Market Crash and the drought seemed to come at the same time. Nineteen-thirty was a disaster with hardly any crops at all, and even those that did manage to struggle above the ground were eaten by the grasshoppers. Dust storms were also common, and we found ourselves suffering from poverty, something we had never experienced before. Father's health, physically and mentally, really deteriorated. He was always such an active and ambitious man. He just couldn't stand it when everything he had worked for disappeared. He had to sell or practically give away his herd of purebred cattle that he used to show off at the fairs.

One of our neighbours had raised a prize steer which she sent off to be sold at auction, hoping to get some needed dollars. All she did get was a bill for seventeen cents from the railway. The cost of shipping the animal was more than she got for it at the market in Winnipeg. In those days there were no freezers on farms, so we couldn't even slaughter the animals and keep the meat. It was a very sad time for everyone because if the farmers didn't have money, nobody did. The storekeepers were as poorly off as we were.

The churches helped out as much as possible and the various denominations down in Ontario sent along these "poor barrels," which their parishoners filled up with food and clothing, and anything else they could spare. It was hard, though, for the Saskatchewan farmers to accept this charity, something they never had to do before. Barrels of apples would come in from British Columbia to the town council, who took on the task of getting them distributed to the most needy. There was also some kind of meagre relief system, where a person would get a small bag of essentials such as sugar and flour, but most of the farmers would rather starve than go to pick it up.

Our family lasted there until 1933, and our going was just like those classic tales in *The Grapes Of Wrath*. I don't know if it is sadder than it is funny.

There were thirteen of us in this old truck. Father had gone ahead to British Columbia with my uncle, so there were twelve of us and Mother, along with our big Chesapeake dog and my father's favourite cat. We had to leave all the other cats behind. I guess we were quite a sight as we made our way towards the west coast, cooking meals by the side of the road and sleeping under the stars, but it wasn't that bad. There were many others in the same fix.

When we got to Chilliwack where Father had managed to rent an old house, it was pouring rain, and it continued to rain for days on end. It struck us rather ironic because we found ourselves praying for it to stop here in British Columbia, whereas in Saskatchewan we had prayed steadily for three years for the rain to come, and it never did. The Lord certainly does work in ways that are mysterious, and sometimes odd.

Archie Wills

The La-Di-Das

Some call Victoria on Vancouver Island "the garden of Canada" because of its mild year-round climate. The British were the early settlers and they made it an upper-class haven in the last century — more English than the City of London.

Archie Wills was born there in 1892, and he remembers with great affection what old Victoria was like around the turn of the century.

Oh, it was very British, there's no doubt about that, with lots of noble estates and English gardens and the officers and ships of the Royal Navy, which were always in port but it was also an ideal place for the average person to live, as it is now, of course. I've never wanted to live anywhere else. The waters at that time were full of salmon, and you could catch them with a bent pin. It was the right size too, with about 30,000, and everyone knew everyone else. I was eight years old when the century turned, old enough to remember all of it, and it was like paradise.

We had very few racial problems even though the makeup of the population took in about every type there was. We had Chinese, Japanese, Hindus, Canadian Indians. You name it and we had them. Growing up with all those different peoples was the best thing that could have happened to me. It broadened my outlook immensely.

At that time there was a great drive on to bring in new people who would settle the prairie provinces and mainland, B.C., but here on Vancouver Island we were all settled in. When they finished the CPR, we got a lot of those 30,000 labourers brought in from China, and at the same time we got a lot of railway workers from California. You see, while the CPR was going at it in this country, they were building railways in the States too, and they brought the rails as far as San Francisco in 1869. The gap between Victoria and San Francisco was filled in mostly by ships operating up and down the coast. It was important to maintain that connection for mail and supplies so that when British Columbia came into Confederation in 1871, we insisted that the federal government maintain it.

So for years afterward, until they had regular roads, we always had a steamship service from Victoria to San Francisco. Because of that we have close bonds with the Californians. Many people from this way settled in California, and conversely many former Californians settled here in Victoria. The bonds are strong to this day.

We have always been sort of cut off from the rest of Canada, the barrier being the Rocky Mountains, of course. Prior to that time, immigration to Vancouver Island from England was all the way down around Cape Horn. Missionaries came that way and also those English settlers we call "the la-di-das." They came here and put on the airs of nobility and they ran the country. They, and the Scotsmen. However, they all absorb in time, as all immigrants do, but at that time, the style of life here was pretty well set by the British. They brought their societies with them, and continued to behave as they did back home.

They thought they were the salt of the earth, and the Scotsmen thought they ran it. All of these people took big plots of land — big estates one might say — and they put their stamp on the whole of Vancouver Island in that way. That, of course, was away back around 1843. By the time I was born in 1892, the pattern was set.

All of our officials, such as the first attorney general, the first judges, all came from England. The Hudson's Bay Company was the big power who really ran the place. The Royal Navy headquartered in Esquimalt, and the Royal Engineers under Colonel Moody were an important factor also. All the forts were manned by the British garrisons so you can see how it was that we were considered "more British than the British." They had a very strong presence.

It wasn't until 1905 that the Royal Navy left, and we took over manning not only the forts, but also the communication and shipping and so on. Eventually we set up our own Navy in 1911, when the *Rainbow* came here, and another ship established itself in Halifax. I remember all of that very well as I was nineteen at the time and very proud of my Canadianism. The man who owned that venerable newspaper, the *Victoria Times*, was fiercely Canadian, and he was powerful also in politics, being minister of the interior in the Laurier cabinet. He officially welcomed the *Rainbow* to Victoria on behalf of the federal government. That was just before Laurier's government was defeated on the question of free trade with the United States, a question that is a hot topic to this day.

Canada was a land full of contrasts then. Cricket and rugger set the tone of the sports world in Victoria, while settlers on the prairies were breaking their backs trying to bite their ploughs into virgin land. While the government was trying to give the homestead land away, here in Victoria the biggest real estate boom ever was going on. Everybody and his uncle was into real estate, especially in 1912. It was a crazy time, and the fact is that many people got in over their heads and went broke. It was the time they were building the Project Pacific and the Canadian National. Both of those, like everything else here then, went bust and things were really tough until the war came along in 1914 and gobbled up all the unemployed. That real estate boom, which was really sparked by the general move towards the West—"Go West, young man"—was insane!

Everyone was into it, including the usual crooks who were selling lots under the water in Prince Rupert. Everybody wanted to make a fortune, and quickly. As far as the rest of Canada was concerned, that's when the West was discovered, in 1912. Before that, they didn't acknowledge that we even existed.

You know, there's lot of talk of the drug culture today, and one would think to hear them that drugs were recently discovered. Well, let me tell you, there were plenty of drugs around Victoria at the turn of the century, especially cocaine and opium. There were fourteen places involved in the business right here in the city, some of them right on the main street. One area called Fan Tan Alley and another called Spudge's Cove were places where ships coming from the Orient docked. These ships were all heavily built for steerage passengers who were smuggled into the country. Y'see, there was a five-hundred-dollar head tax on Chinese immigrants who came in legally, so smuggling them in was a lucrative racket. Anyone who had five hundred dollars over in China at that time would be considered wealthy, and there was no way he'd spend it just to come to Canada if they could get in for less. These ships could get them in for considerably less, or else the owners would put up the five hundred bucks just like a loan shark, and these poor people would be in bondage to those smugglers forever.

They'd sign papers that they would work for that smuggler, and pay so much a month on what they owed, but the smuggler would keep piling up interest so the debt could never be repaid. Those smugglers, by the way, were always white men, dealers in human flesh and misery.

These were the same people who were bringing in opium and cocaine, most of it going to the United States, just as we did with liquor during Prohibition in later years. There were those fourteen opium dens operating here, using the stuff they didn't send across the border, and it was amazing to see who some of their customers were. These classy women would go to these places and get a pipe and a container of opium and then would lie down in a dirty old bunk and smoke themselves into a coma. The thing is, too, that it was legitimate at the time. Anybody could go in there as long as they had the money to pay for it. There would be some police raids, but they would be there to catch gamblers playing fan-tan and games like that.

It was always white people who were behind the scenes in those days. Our early treatment of the Chinese is not something this country can be proud of. That was a time when the government really worked hard to keep the minorities in their "places" or keep them out of the country altogether. For instance, the case of the *Komagatamaru*. I was working as a reporter on the *Victoria Times* and I was told to go over to Vancouver where this ship had docked and to see what was going on. Well, this ship had arrived with six hundred Hindus aboard, Sikhs, and they were going to immigrate to Canada but the government didn't want them. For no other reason than that they were Sikhs, I suppose. So they reverted to this law which said that the immigrant must come directly from his country to this with no stops in-between. Now, this was impossible for these people because the only way to get a ship to Canada was from Hong Kong, so this fellow who was a Calcutta businessman organized this voyage to test that law.

When they attempted to disembark in Vancouver, they weren't permitted to get off and their boat was pushed out and anchored in the stream. It stayed there for weeks, while the case was argued in the Supreme Court. In the end the court ruled that, although the Sikhs may have had credentials saying they were carpenters or plumbers or whatever in India, they were not qualified to do these jobs in this country as they didn't meet Canadian standards. When this was going on, these people were cooped up on that ship in the harbour. There was a riot on board at one point and when the Vancouver police chief came alongside, the rioters showered his boat with bricks and he was killed. It was a heck of an uproar. Then the *Rainbow*, our only navy ship on the west coast, was called into it. All they could do was to train their houses on the decks of the *Maru* to try and quiet things down. Finally, after the Supreme Court decision, the ship had no alternative but to go home and anyway, by this time, the First World War had broken out and there were other things to occupy the public's attention.

The *Rainbow*, our glorious warship, was sent off to chase the German ship *The Leipzig*, which was working off our coast, and we who were acquainted with the *Rainbow* prayed that they would never meet, as our poor ship didn't have power enough to break a paper bag.

George Ignatieff

From Russia With Love

Despite some unfortunate incidents in our history, Canada has always been a haven for refugees from political and religious oppression in other lands, a role it continues to this day. In this way our country has gained some of its finest citizens, people who are a credit not only to Canada but also to the land from which they had to flee.

The Russian Revolution of 1917-18 turned that country and its social order upside-down. The aristocracy became the oppressed as the masses rose up and took control. Those who were in any way connected with the deposed czarist regime — families that were aristocratic and highly placed politically like that of George Ignatieff — eventually joined Canada's diplomatic corps. His family left everything behind when they fled for their lives.

I was only three years old when it happened, but the events of those years were so violent and traumatic that I still remember most of them with perfect clarity. Our family, like so many others, was slated for the firing squad and we only escaped because there happened to be a student on the judging tribunal who remembered that my father had carried out many reforms in his role as minister of education in the deposed government. He said he wouldn't agree to this man being shot. My father was astounded by this intervention, because in his own mind he had already accepted the inevitability of his death at the hands of the mob. Even at this point he told the tribunal that he just couldn't accept the reprieve unless they delivered him back to his home where he could protect his family. Surprisingly, they agreed, even though we found out later that it wasn't only Father's name on the list to be shot: his whole family was on that list. That's when he decided that we'd have to escape from Russia altogether.

There was a lot of luck involved. We were lucky first of all when that student on the tribunal recognized Father, and we were lucky at the moment of escape too. The White Russian general commanding the Southern front was in our town recovering from typhus, which was rampant at the time, and he knew our family. He told my mother that she should get us on his armoured train that was heading back to the front through the Red lines. "It's your only chance of getting out," he said, "There'll be White guards on the train and there'll be shooting, but you should get through all right."

Well, we did. We got to the coast where there were some British transport vessels. By this time the White Russian movement was collapsing and the Royal Navy was taking off supplies and refugees like us, as well as some Turkish prisoners from the First World War, who were being taken back to Turkey.

Mother was the heroine of all this, because by now Father's health had been totally broken by his experiences in the revolution and civil war.

What really happened was that Russia had been defeated in its war with Germany, and those who were involved in governing the country had to do so under conditions of defeat and growing unrest. Father had disagreed with his colleagues about how to deal with the situation. As a reformer he wanted them to bring the legislature into greater responsibility and he thought that every minister of the Crown should be required to have a vote of confidence from that legislature. The czar wouldn't accept that the only way to save the situation was to move to responsible government, so it ended with Father resigning just before the Revolution. Then he had to go through endless enquiries until he became totally exhausted and seriously ill.

Mother had to carry the whole load in everything that followed. All the household staff had to be let go, including the nanny who had been just like a mother to me. I think that in itself was the most traumatic moment of my early life, even including those times when we were under heavy gunfire or when we were on a train where most of the passengers were dying typhus victims.

I don't think people realize even today that it is the civilian population that suffers most; and that at a certain point civilization begins to disintegrate and that it's out of such a situation that Communism grows. People have the impression that it was communism and capitalism vying for control that caused the Russian Revolution. That wasn't the case at all. Communism grew out of the misery of the masses later. The communists didn't just seize power. There was a disintegrating society brought about by defeat in the war with Germany. The mistake was in trying to put down communism with guns. They should have concentrated their efforts on solving the misery of the people instead. Out of situations like that, you always get extreme regimes of the left or right that are hostile to a democratic society.

What my father was attempting to do in Russia was build on what little blocks there were at the rural-municipal level. He hoped to develop self-government with the farmers organizing themselves for community effort in building roads and barns and establishing better educational opportunities. He hoped that this would spread into the cities too, and that a proper democracy would result.

He wasn't alone. Many other members of the aristocracy felt the same way. They were of the same school as Leo Tolstoy, who brought the Doukhobors to Canada. It was a school of thought that subscribed very strongly to the idea that members of the aristocracy owed it to the community to serve as well as lead.

All of this upset in Russia almost killed Father. It broke his health, but he realized that the disintegration of the old society was complete and that there would never be any going back again, to the way things were. The issue was just that those who had enough of war wanted peace, and they wanted the land given back to the peasants.

In any event, here we are on the run to escape from our homeland alive with a determined mother and an ill father. We took the same route as many other refugees, through the Black Sea to what was then Constantinople, now Istanbul. We stayed there long enough to get visas to France and we were taken on a French hospital ship which was evacuating Allied wounded from the Salonica front. In Paris Father applied for a visa to England which was granted to him as a former czarist minister. It wasn't too easy to get because England didn't much want czarist ministers around any more than they wanted the czar, but eventually we were granted asylum in England, where we stayed on a farm while Father recovered. We were able to buy this farm with a small sum that had been sitting in an English bank to Father's credit, the result of some investments he made before the war. It wasn't much, but it enabled us to buy that farm.

It was a very lean time for us, and it must have been especially hard for my parents, who had never experienced want before. Mother had been a Russian princess and my father a count, but they knew that was gone, and they never complained. She adjusted immediately to her new role as housewife, walking to market every day for supplies and making a home for her family.

It was ten years later that we sailed off to Canada, where our first home was a forty-five-dollar-a-month apartment in Montreal. There, too, Mother continued her homemaker role, walking every day the five miles to Bonsecours Market and back again, just to make sure that we got the best vegetables and fruit she could find. She was a solid rock of a woman in the true tradition of the pioneer women of Canada, absolutely undaunted by any of these experiences.

There were no silver spoons in any of our mouths. All of us had to work for everything, including our education. I had a job for a while as an axeman on the CPR, cutting brush for a survey party. It was a tough job, but on the plus side it was really the first time in my life that I was accepted for myself. Although they called me "the Douk" because we were in Doukhobor country, I was happy being taught the crafts that made me self-sufficient in the bush.

When the Depression hit, a lot of these jobs just disappeared and I soon found myself in Toronto, working where I could find work, washing dishes in hotels and things like that.

It was at this point that I realized that if I was ever going to have anything better in life, I'd better get some decent education. My only vision up to this time was survival by picking up whatever I could in the way of work, as a delivery boy or whatever.

It was around this time, too, that my brother, who had done his own pioneering in the West, and was now a Hydro engineer, took me to the University of Toronto and introduced me to this wonderful man who was the registrar. In those days the University of Toronto was quite small compared to what it is now — I believe there were only three thousand students — so the registrar had some time for waifs like me. He sat down with all the reports from my previous schools, and after weighing them all in his mind he said, "First of all, you'll go to Jarvis Collegiate and you'll take these twelve subjects for your matric. He told me exactly what I would have to do and how I should progress along the road through high school and university. He pointed out my strengths and my weaknesses and he said, "You have the makings of a good student. Get out of here and get after it."

So I did. I went to Jarvis and then on to the University of Toronto, and I won some scholarships,ending up with the Rhodes Scholarship for Ontario in 1936. I worked my head off for all of those things, including a scholarship for Canadian constitutional Law. I wasn't even a Canadian citizen by that time, but I was fascinated by this country and how it worked. All of those things helped me much later on to enter and win the competition to enter Canada's Department of External Affairs in a junior capacity.

Lester Pearson, who was the official secretary of Canada House at the time, took a great interest in all of the Canadian students, mainly because he was looking for Foreign Service recruits. He had brought me into External Affairs when I came to London as a Rhodes Scholar, and had been following my progress at Oxford and he told me one day that he wanted me to write the exams. This was just prior to the war. I wrote the exams, but then when the war broke out, I joined British Army intelligence before the exam results came. When they did come, they showed that I had qualified for one of the better postings. Mr. Pearson had me released from the army and I went to Canada House, working with him, Vincent Massey, Charles Ritchie, Hume Wrong, and this whole bunch of really incredible Canadians, every one of whom had a great influence on my life after that.

One of the things I recall most about Pearson was that he was first of all a minister's child and a true son of the manse. He had all the Christian virtues of humility, almost to the point of overdoing it, always playing down any question of status or personal importance. He loved to talk baseball and other commonplace things. He worked very hard and set a gruelling pace for the rest of us.

Even after he became foreign minister, and people were talking of him as the next prime minister, he would get very embarrassed and almost tongue-tied if someone brought the topic up. I think that although he knew it was probably going to happen, it worried him more than it excited him. He was an extremely good diplomat as proved by his winning the Nobel Peace Prize for the Suez Crisis. His good friend, Hume Wrong, used to say he was like a Houdini, who can get himself in the middle of a mess, and in the process of extracting himself he unties all the other knots. He was a great pragmatist, someone who could take a situation as he found it, see what the common ground was by private talks, and then try for alternative ways of bringing about agreement. He was a great diplomat and prime minister.

Fortune and good luck has played a great part in my life. How else do you explain the events that took our family from a sure death situation in the Russian Revolution to life in this great country?

Alice Frick

Twenty-Five-Hour Days

One of the most important factors in the shaping of present-day Canada was radio. The instant-communication aspects of the new medium which began to make an impact on people's lives in the 1920s were nothing short of miraculous. Suddenly, the impossible distances of a land like Canada didn't exist.

When CBC *producer Andrew Allan started producing fine drama on his acclaimed "Stage" series in the early 1940s, it seemed as if the entire country was tuned in. The actors and staff Allan gathered around him were as devoted to developing Canadian talent as he was, and they were as representative of the whole country as the plays they produced. They came from both coasts and the prairie provinces, and their backgrounds were varied. They were the sons and daughters of farmers and fishermen, miners and lumberjacks, doctors and lawyers, storekeepers, and businessmen from the cities.*

They flocked to Toronto, attracted by the excitement of broadcasting and the promise it held for effecting change in what was still an emerging country. Alice Frick was one of those young people. Fresh out of university, she came to the CBC *with a degree in English and an Alberta farm background.*

I had an older brother who built his own crystal sets at first, and then later, radios with actual tubes. I'd be so fascinated watching him putting them together with his soldering irons and wires. I guess those things planted the early seeds in my mind. Of course, there were other things that helped too. I was a reader, and in this I was fortunate in that, unlike most others in our community, our family were readers. We had a few books of our own, not many; but there were always magazines, as subscriptions were very cheap, and so we got all of them. Winter evenings were spent around the oil lamp, with everybody's head into a different magazine. I could actually read before I went to school, and because there was a scarcity of children's books, I was reading adult stories. When I was seven, I read my first novel, *The Thundering Herd* by Zane Grey, which was serialized in the *Ladies Home Journal.* I loved it! Although nobody in my family ever thought so, I suppose I must have been a bit unusual in this way. I realized this myself when I went to university.

There wasn't another girl within a fifty-mile radius of our home who went on to higher learning. Our neighbours couldn't figure out why I wanted to do that. They were very puzzled, and would ask me why I wanted to do a thing like that. It was unthinkable to them that a farm girl should be interested in going to university—especially a farm girl!

Thankfully my mother and father didn't feel that way. They thought that everybody, males or females, should get as good an education as could be afforded. It was in the middle of the awful thirties that I left the farm for the hallowed halls of learning so that I spent very little time on the farm after 1935. I worked in the summers to earn money, and went to school the rest of the time.

To help pay my tuition in the University of Alberta, I worked for the Extension Department, reading plays, helping to judge those that would go on to the different regional drama festivals, and then, hopefully, to the Dominion Drama Festival in Ottawa. I learned a lot from that, and this, combined with my early intense fascination with radio while growing up on the farm,was enough to get me the job.

I must say though, that radio in the early thirties wasn't all that great, except for a few programs in the evening, from the Canadian Radio Broadcasting Commission, the forerunner of the CBC.

We could pick up American stations much more easily than Canadian ones on cold winter nights. The American stations had powerful transmitters that just drowned out anything being broadcast locally. It wasn't until the CBC came into being in 1936 that we began to regularly hear anything Canadian of quality.

The only other thing I was hearing of any quality was the University of Alberta station, CKUA. They did plays on that station. All of this combined to make me want to get into radio when I graduated. I felt it was there that I could get to do all the things I wanted to do.

When the war started in 1939, there was a great push to extend the radio network all over the country through more CBC-owned stations, and privately-owned affiliates that would carry CBC programs. It was at this time, 1942, after I graduated, that I headed for Toronto, determined to get hired by the CBC. For a few months at first, I worked for the Toronto Board of Education, and then I was offered a script editorship at the CBC by Rupert Lucas, who was then supervisor of drama. It was then that I felt the eighty dollars I had borrowed for a bus ticket to Toronto had paid off.

About a year later, Rupert Lucas resigned to go to New York, and Andrew Allan came from Vancouver to replace him. He inherited me along with the job. When Andrew began the "Stage" series in 1944, excitement about live radio drama was already running fairly high because of what had been coming out of Vancouver, a series called "Baker's Dozen," which Fletcher Markle wrote and Andrew produced. It caused something of a stir among CBC people and listeners, and it even got a rave review in *Variety*, the American showbiz newspaper, and I believe it was due to Andrew's work on "Baker's Dozen" that he was given the big job in Toronto.

The drama department was really very small potatoes in the CBC scheme of things when "Stage" started in 1944. Everyone knew everyone else, and there was a great spirit of co-operation between those in drama and those in "talks." We did dramas from time to time for the schools broadcast department and there was a generally good liaison all around. Those other departments would take our recommendations for writers and things like that until they became experienced in these aspects of the business on their own.

As the "Stage" series progressed from one week to the next, it became almost like a repertory theatre. In fact, it was called elsewhere, rather pejoratively, a "clique." This was not true. There were a number of outstanding actors who were heard almost every week, but in fact, practically the whole Toronto acting fraternity was involved. In the ten years that the series was on the air, from 1944 to 1954, by actual count we used about 350 different actors. In Canada that would constitute an impossibly large "clique."

The actors who appeared most often were the ones who were thoroughly reliable, and the very best. It should be remembered that without actors of this quality, we couldn't have produced the series. The amount of time we had to prepare a broadcast live drama was almost impossibly short. When we finished putting a show on air on Sunday night, we didn't even have time to pat ourselves on the back, as we had to begin immediately preparing a new one for the next week. There was no such thing as having something recorded on hand, because there was no recording of any kind at that time.

The scripts would be prepared and the casting would be done on Mondays, and then, through the week, Lucio Agostini, the musical director, and Andrew would talk about the music. The actors would get their scripts and discuss their roles with Andrew, and it wouldn't be until Saturday morning that we would all gather in the studio for a first read-through and do the blocking out of the script. Everybody would discuss how it should be performed up until noon, when we'd break for lunch. Lucio would come in with a twenty-seven-piece orchestra after lunch and rehearse the new score and we'd put music cues together with the dialogue. This would all be practised over and over until all the timings were right, and then there'd be a rough run-through, and timing, always done with a blue pencil. If there were any cuts to be done, we would do them, and break about 5:30 or 6 p.m. on Saturday.

On 7:30 on Sunday night we'd all come back with the final script, which most times would have been cut overnight. Then the final dress rehearsal, where the script was timed in thirty-second intervals in red pencil. After a brief break we were on the air at nine o'clock, coast-to-coast, live.

In retrospect, it all seems impossible now, but it wasn't. That's the way it was done week in, and week out for ten years. Andrew often described those times as ten years of twenty-five-hour days. I think of them as eight-day weeks in addition. It's something that could never be repeated again. As the novelist A.P. Hartley wrote, "The past is a foreign country. They did things differently there."

Back in those early days, especially during the Depression and the years of the Second World War, CBC radio was the only secondary education that most Canadians could afford. Those of us who were fortunate enough to work on the "Stage" series with Andrew Allan realized that even while we were doing it. The letters just poured in from all across the country, and they told us that most listeners were excited and enthralled by what they were hearing. At that time we were treating topics that were more than a little sensitive to a few of the more puritanical audience, but the vast majority of those letters were laudatory. They made us feel that we were indeed working on something very important. We knew that we were pioneers in our field, just as much as our parents were in homesteading, and other fields of endeavour in Canada.

The thousands of letters were just a confirmation of what we believed in, but we also had further proof. One week we were startled to find from the ratings service that our "Stage" series was second in popularity only to Saturday Night Hockey.

People told us that they would rather miss their meals than miss a program, that they would be devastated if for some reason or other they couldn't be near a radio on Sunday nights when the program came on. Many of them told us they refused all social engagements on Sunday nights: that night was strictly for "Stage." You see, what made it truly exciting was that we were appealing to an audience that stretched right across the whole sphere — from labourers through the university-educated.

That ten-year period was the best time of my life. No question about that. I think things came apart at the seams in broadcasting after that, with the advent of television. Radio was beginning to be downgraded in favour of pictures, but the truth is that TV could not match the mental pictures that people drew for themselves while listening to radio. With radio one imagines one's own people, and radio stimulates the imagination, whereas pictures moving in front of you attract your attention, but don't give much opportunity to create for yourself. TV spoon-feeds everything you need to know and that leaves very little for the mind to do for itself.

Many refer to that period from 1944 to 1954 as "The Golden Age Of Radio," which maybe it was, although I think there were, in fact, many golden ages. For me, it was the golden age, because first of all, I think the "Stage" series had never been surpassed for quality. But there were other things too that kept people glued to their radios: the wonderful productions on Harry Boyle's "CBC Wednesday Night," and, "Jake and the Kid," with John Drainie and Billy Richards, and Frank Peddie as Old Man Gatenby. It was people like these and so many others who made the era golden — and especially Andrew Allan, who would not tolerate sloppiness or careless errors. He carried in his own head a complete picture of the way each performance had to go. He respected each work he produced. He respected the words and he respected his authors. Because he demanded excellence in himself, everyone around him rose to that, and they too became excellent, because they knew that for Andrew, "only the best is good enough."

Rev. Father René Fumoleau

The Dené

The original peoples of Canada were happy enough here when the first white men arrived. The newcomers, however, assumed that the natives were heathens and savages whereas they were anything but. They had a very efficient society and systems of governing themselves that rival some of our better governments today. They had their own gods and their own religions, systems of commerce and trading, and they often showed more humanity towards their fellows that do people in the so-called civilized societies of our present century.

Father René Fumoleau of the Roman Catholic Oblate order came to the Northwest Territories from France about thirty-five years ago to work with the natives and in that time he has developed close bonds with the Dené people.

When I came here to Fort Good Hope in 1953, I knew nothing of Canada, and even less of the natives I wanted to serve. If I've been successful in any way, it's because they have a lot of patience. When I talk to them now about those early days, I say, "I must have been so stupid," and they answer, "Yes, you were." And they laugh, "But you were young, and we had to give you a chance to learn by yourself just like any other young person." That is a characteristic that all Dené possess. They always give the other person a chance.

Their true name is the Dené, "people of the land" and the land on which they live is Denendeh, both of which are correct. After centuries they are only now claiming these names back in the same way that the Inuit are rejecting the Eskimo label put on them. In helping the Dené, I hope to be able to give back a small portion of what they've given me over the past three decades.

One of the problems was that white people who came among them were never here long enough to really understand them. They stayed for only short periods of time and their judgments were made too quickly. We think that our ways are always better, and it is that belief that created the colonial mentality and the colonial enterprise.

If you listen to the radio you will hear talk of eastern Canadians and western Canadians, but never of northern Canadians. When this part of the country is talked of at all, it is only as "northern resources." They never talk about the *people* of the North. I think many of the problems stem from that kind of ignorance. This has always been painful to the Dené, that they have been treated as non-existent with nothing to contribute. They don't want to separate from Canada. They want to become a true part of Confederation, where their values and traditions are accepted.

For me, this non-acceptance is the true original sin of Canada. At first, the English and French got together without even inviting the aborigines to play a part. In the Confederation discussions they weren't even asked to join the decision-making process about the future of their own land. Confederation will never be perfect until those wrongs are somehow put to right.

If we white people could gain from them their feeling for this land, how rich we'd be — that special feeling about the resources, for example, which they would like to share with everybody. Their reasoning is that the resources of the land should never be exploited for profit, that they are put there by God to serve the people. They feel that if God created the land for everybody, then everybody is of equal importance and every person should have a just share. Each individual is treated with much respect because every individual is unique.

Always, going back to the earliest days, what was important was the survival of the group, and this survival depended on the strengths of each individual. Because of this, each person was always given a great deal of freedom to become strong and independent on his own, so as to better serve the group. That's why in the Dené society there were no levels of importance as opposed to the white man's society, where you have great levels of wealth at the top, all the way down to grinding poverty at the bottom. In the real Dené way of life this could never happen unless it is imported from the south.

As a Catholic priest, I have no difficulty at all with the spirituality they embrace, because I find it very close to what the Gospel teaches. When Jesus spoke, he was talking with people of the land, and he spoke in a manner that they could understand. The values that he taught were simply human values, the same ones the Dené hold dear and those that should exist in any human society. They were always very close to nature, and from nature you learn that everyone is equal. Jesus taught by telling stories, something that the Dené have always used as a way of teaching. The only problem the Dené have with Christianity is the structure of the Church, the big buildings and such.

Early missionaries approached the natives with true dedication, but their problem was their ignorance of anthropology and the values of different cultures. We were all trained with that kind of colonial attitude, which existed hundreds of years ago, an attitude which doesn't recognize that other peoples have something of value to offer and that our way is not always the best.

The white man still feels like that in some respects. Big companies come up here with heavy equipment, smashing the landscape to build what they feel should be built. In most cases they think that what they do is going to be good for everyone, but the Dené are like all peoples; they don't necessarily want somebody doing what these others think is good for them. They want to make their own decisions of what is good and what is not. It's in their culture to share, and they don't want outsiders imposing "benefits" on them.

They want nothing more than respect and a degree of understanding and, as in all aboriginal societies in Canada, they feel they have something to share with us. We've given them our diseases and alcoholism, to be sure, but we have given some good things too, most important of which, I think, is the ability to communicate over long distances with one another. Teaching them to read and write is a good thing, but not if it carries the values of another society. Even helping them to exploit the resources is good to the point that it brings better and more human living conditions.

Television, which could be so good for them, carries the danger of cultural genocide by showing a way of life that they might assume is something to be strived for. I mean the values espoused by soap operas and shows of crime and violence. There is the danger that these shows might be thought of as some kind of a norm.

Some things are now changing for the better. Native languages are permitted in the schools and the Dené are being allowed to shape some of the educational programs. But even with these advances, the general goal of education seems to be to bring them into another culture and get them away from their true traditions, and assimilate them into our society. The school curriculum of the Northwest Territories is the same as that down south in the province of Alberta, and that doesn't fit.

That idea of assimilation was part of the official policy at the time of Confederation in 1867, and it is still there. It is all aimed towards making them forget their past. I don't think that we set out to exploit the natives. I think that we just ignored them and what they had to offer — and we still do. Theirs is a different way of life, with a different sense of time, a different way of relating to the country.

At one time, for example, they depended on dog teams. Now that has been replaced by a dependence on snowmobiles. That's fine to a certain degree, except that at one time they knew that in an emergency they could save themselves by eating the dogs. One can't eat a snowmobile. With a dog team one has time to appreciate the land and the beauty of it. On a snowmobile you don't, and of course a snowmobile costs a great deal more than a dog team does. In order to buy one a Dené has to get involved in the wage economy. With a dog team he doesn't. He can raise the dogs and feed them by fishing. It's a completely different lifestyle. The dogs put people into communion with nature. The snowmobile has the effect of wiping all of that out. Many still keep their dogs, although they have snowmobiles, but they are more or less just a reminder to them of their past culture, which is in danger of disappearing altogether in a couple of generations. That's just one instance of how everything we give them is not necessarily the best thing for them.

They hold on to some traditions like hunting for their own food, but the system of dependency brought up from the south is hard for many to resist. They know that welfare will keep them from starving.

They are coming to know too many of the southern ways where people are controlled by too many forces, too many institutions, too many regulations, and too many laws. All these things are coming to the north. It almost seems as though those in the south do not like to see people who are free and self-reliant, and want to make them slaves of the system as they are themselves. Is it jealousy on our part when we see a people who can manage for themselves and do things on their own? I sometimes think that this is why we have brought in so many social welfare programs for them. We want to bring them down to our level.

Over the past two decades many of the Dené have organized strong resistance to these things. They want the people to realize that the land is still there for them; it is still beautiful and they still have that relationship with it. They want southern people to realize that yes, we are here. Look at us as we are and please respect us.

The Dené are not asking to be left alone in isolation. They know there are good aspects in the southern way of life that can benefit them, but they also feel there are good things in their ways that could benefit the rest of Canadians. If it could only become a two-way system, there would be no problem. The key is that we have to learn to live together and be friends together. If someone like me could do that, someone who came here from a foreign land, then anybody can do it. I love these people, and it is my wish that when my time comes, I will die among them.

Ray Lowes

New Town, New Name

In the early part of this century, when Ray Lowes' father picked a spot in the middle of Saskatchewan to build his general store, there was nothing around him but space — no village, no houses, no town. In fact, that piece of prairie didn't even have a name. Nevertheless Will Lowes built his store there figuring, rightly as it turned out, that more people would come. He called his store "Will Lowes" after himself and, as his son Ray recounts, everyone who came after him thought it was just as good a name as any for their new town, which became known as Willowes.

He started the town simply by being the first one there, so I guess he deserved to have it called after him. Better than calling it "Gopher Hole" or something like that. A lot of the prairie communities got their names in that way. Settlers had more on their minds than worrying about things like that anyway. It was homestead country, and if you were going to survive, well, you just better get to work. It was just a little place. Population never got to be more than a hundred people. It had three grain elevators, two stores, and a livery stable, but not much else.

By today's standards there wasn't all that much for a young person to do, but I managed okay. I certainly developed an intimate relationship with the natural world for one thing. We kids rambled through the "coulees," which is what we in the west called these small valleys in areas of flat land. It was more like a shallow depression than a valley, but those of us who lived on prairies were happy to get any rise or fall in elevation that came along to relieve the flatness of the landscape.

It was wonderful country for kids. We would hike miles and miles and still be able to see our homes. We snared gophers and rabbits, and life was never boring. We'd go to the blacksmith's shop where farmers came to get new shoes for their horses and we'd be welcome to watch. It always fascinated us to watch him do that and to watch him put new rims on the wagons. The blacksmith was an enormously talented man who could make just about anything out of iron, it seemed to us. The pounding of his hammer on the anvil and the hiss of hot iron being plunged into water was like music to our ears. Whenever some kind of special tool or device was needed, people would come to the blacksmith and he never let them down.

Another pastime we had was going up to the elevators and watching them unload grain. Sometimes we'd sneak onto the little lifting elevator and go to the very top and jump down into the big bins of wheat. That could be more than a little scary, though. We'd go feet first and it wasn't until many years later that we came to learn how extremely dangerous it was, as you could be swallowed up and smothered by all of that loose wheat. Of course, that never even occurred to us at all. To us it was great fun and a big thrill.

In addition to having our small town named after him, my father was very involved in everything that went on. Besides owning the general store, he was justice of the peace, notary, and postmaster. His store handled hardware, flour, and feed, and part of it was a small restaurant. So there was plenty for us to do.

Aside from all this, there was a big community hall where we would have Sunday School and the women gave chicken suppers and concerts and that sort of thing. It may have been a town of just a hundred or so permanent residents, but it was a very busy place and a going concern.

The reason for this is that we were the hub of a very large area, and the farmers from all over came in to Willowes to do their shopping. They'd bring a load of wheat in to the elevator and they'd leave their wives off at the Lowes General Store, where they would trade their eggs and cream or whatever for groceries and supplies. After a couple of hours the farmer would come by the store to pick up his wife and off they'd go again back to the farm. There was a constant stream of farmers coming in on their wagons from miles around. We were open morning and night. People thought nothing at all of waking the merchant up even in the wee hours to do business. The storekeeper didn't mind either, as he knew that farmers had to do things like that whenever the time presented itself. They were subservient to their farms and the businessmen in town had to be subservient to the farming community.

Our entire family worked in the store — mother, father, and the children. We always had plenty to do. The eggs that the farmers brought in would have to be crated. Cream and cheese would be looked after. The farmers would take away with them the things that we had, and exchange them for what they had: big tubs of apple butter for example, that came on the train from Ontario. The Norwegian farmers would buy coffee from us by the bushel. A great deal of our trade was by barter. We'd take what they had for what we had, and we'd record the balance in our books. Most of our actual money came from shipping our surplus farm goods to the city.

What I remember of the general store mostly are the wonderful aromas and different smells of the various foods, and even the items of hardware. There were great coils of rope, barrels of tar, kerosene, and even the copper sulphate that the farmers bought for treating their wheat. Everything seemed to come in barrels. There'd be barrels of molasses and barrels of pickled meat, and great boxes of biscuits and crackers, sugar and candy, etc. All of these different aromas blended together to produce one wonderful and unforgettable smell — that of the general store.

Another thing that would come in were bags of shells from oysters and clams and other seafood. Just the shells. These were a source of calcium for the chickens who can't produce good eggs without it. At times, some greenhorn farmer who didn't know this would arrive at the store with a case full of gooey, broken eggs.

Zig Zag cigarette papers and loose tobacco was something that every farmer took home with him. Nobody bought what they referred to as "tailor-mades" in those days. A good man could extract a paper, fill it with tobacco and roll it into a cigarette with one hand while riding along on his horse. I saw that done many, many times. I never did it myself, as I never could cotton on to tobacco. The only time that my brother and I tried it was when we sneaked up on the roof of the house to try "a chew" as we'd seen the farmers do. We got so sick my father had to come to the roof and carry both of us down. That ended both our careers with tobacco.

I suppose that the practical joke is something that all small communities in the country go for. I remember one that worked very well. There was this fellow in town who tended to be a bit on the light-fingered side, so a bunch of the locals decided to play a trick on him. Somebody slipped the word to him that a number of gold nuggets had been found in a creek outside town, and that they were hidden in a small barn just down the street. In the meantime, someone else had taken a couple of lumps of hard clay and painted them gold and hid them in the barn. Well, of course, this man "found" one of the "nuggets" and took it home and hid it in his basement. Everybody in town was in on the joke, and when the poor victim appeared on the scene people would begin talking of the stolen gold nugget and how the town constable was conducting a house-to-house search for it. Anyway, eventually they found the "nugget" hidden in the poor fellow's basement. He was arrested, and immediately brought to trial—still not aware that the whole thing was a joke. They had witnesses and everything, and the proceedings were packed with townspeople. Finally, they sentenced him to jail and they didn't tell him until someone started leading him off to the cells.

Well, by this time the women began coming in with baskets of food and the men brought out their fiddles and guitars, and a party commenced. The "culprit" got as big a laugh from it all as anyone else, and that party went on for hours. It was a pretty elaborate trick to pull on someone, but in small prairie towns at the time happenings such as that weren't unusual at all, and it gave everybody something to talk about for months to come.

In those homesteading days one of the strangest practices was the paying of one-cent bounties for gopher tails. Those poor little animals were regarded as pests because they ate a certain amount of wheat, I suppose, but it was really the fault of the settlers that there were so many gophers around in the first place. When the settlers got there one of the first things they did was kill off all the coyotes, and as the coyote's natural food was gophers, there was nothing in the way of natural enemies to keep the little fellows from proliferating. As a result, the amount of wheat they consumed became considerable and the government decided to put a one-cent bounty on their tails. I myself became a gopher hunter, as did every school kid who lived on the prairies at the time. I snared them and trapped them, and pulled their tails off.

My friends and I carried a tin can in our pockets for the tails which would yield us a cent apiece. In Willowes the gopher was the enemy and it was our duty to destroy him. I wouldn't kill a gopher today for love or money, but I think as children we just adopt the morals of the communities we grow up in.

By the way, although none of us found out till years later, the prairie gopher was not a gopher at all. He was really a Richardson's ground squirrel. The true gopher is nocturnal and underground, and rarely comes up on the surface. Ground squirrels are running around all the time all over the place and are real cute. Some people who live on the prairies still call them gophers to this day, but they're not.

David Stephens

The Days of Sail in Nova Scotia

The smell of the sea and the great fishing schooners dominate the landscape and the thoughts of all those who call the south shore of Nova Scotia home. It was in the small town of Lunenburg back in 1921 that a new ship slipped into the water; a fishing schooner that was destined to live forever in the hearts of all who call the Maritimes their home. It was on March 26, 1921, when her hull was launched and it was less than a month later that the Bluenose *was ready to sail to glory and immortality.* Bluenose *was a fishing schooner, the best and the fastest ever built, as she was to prove many times over the next several years.*

Young David Stephens was fourteen on that fateful day, born to a seagoing family on nearby Tancock Island within sight of the launching. As were all other boys in the area, he had salt water in his veins and, like the Bluenose, *young David was destined for fame, too, as a builder of boats with sleek lines and great speed. While still very young, he moved closer to the town of Lunenburg to an area called The Second Peninsula, a long arm of land reaching out into Lunenburg waters where people didn't build boats but they sailed them.*

Most of the men were fishermen. They'd go away in the early spring on what they'd call a "frozen-bait" trip and be gone for six or seven weeks and then they'd go back on their "spring fishing trip" for the same length of time. After this, they'd come home and unload and leave again for a summer trip, when they'd be gone for two months. Altogether they would be gone close to six months and during this time the wives and children would be tending the farms. They were really farmer-fishermen with the fishing part being foremost. In the fall, when that summer's catch came in everyone would be busy washing and drying the fish.

I hauled a lot of the harvest from the Peninsula into town with an ox team and I remember it would take up to four hours to make that seven miles with the oxen. It was very slow going over those old paths that passed for roads back then.

It was all salt-fishing in those days of the early twenties, but that started to fade as the twenties faded away. Nobody was salting the catch any more and the demand was for fresh fish. It was a very different time when I was growing up. Instead of a car parked in the driveway, we had row boats which we'd use to row into town for provisions or whatever.

I believe we were the first family to go in for the bigger boats when we acquired a thirty-eight foot yacht and a thirty-foot motor boat and any travelling we did for seven or eight months of the year was done by boat. It was very seldom after that when we would go around by road with the ox team. Our main crop on the farm was cabbages, so we needed the big boat to take them all the way to market in Halifax, which was the big city.

Lunenburg was a small town, but when I first sailed into the harbour there as a young man I thought it was the prettiest sight I ever did see. Since that time I've sailed into many harbours but I never did see one that can come close to Lunenburg for beauty. There were always plenty of vessels there especially in the fall and winter months. Some would take salt cod back to the Caribbean, but most would just lay up in the harbour.

The shipbuilding industry flourished in Lunenburg at that time, building vessels as fast as was possible. The fishermen would only keep a boat for ten or twelve years and then they would order another and sell the old one to someone in Newfoundland where Lunenburg boats were in great demand because of the good quality of them. It was nothing at all to see one of these boats looking as good as new forty or fifty years later. I'm sorry to say, however, that that era is gone. The only ones still around outside the *Bluenose II* are in museums.

In those days the builders not only knew how to build a boat, but they really loved their jobs. Every one they built was given the care that would be given if they were building it for themselves, and in the years of the Depression, especially if a man didn't do his job properly, there was always someone willing and able to take his place. A job was a valuable thing to have and nobody took chances on losing his.

Of course, there was only the best of material put in those ships and there was the best of timberland around these parts. We had the finest type of hardwoods, oak and birch and so on, and the ship builders themselves were real artists — the best in the world. There's a few still, but very few, left. The old ones passed on, and the young ones went off to the city for the bright lights and eight-hour days. I'm afraid that very soon shipbuilding will become a lost art. That's why I still continue to do it just as a hobby, in hope that someone will take up where I leave off.

I'd find it very hard to stop altogether, though, as it just seems to be a part of me. When the fall comes I get as frisky as a young colt to get started on something. I go out in the shop to look around and it simply doesn't seem right not to see a partially built boat there, and I say to myself, "This will never do." Then I set out to change it. Last year it was in the middle of night when the urge came over me and I rushed to the shop and immediately began to glue some wood together for a half-model.

That's the first step, you see. You build a half-model first. That's like a full model except that it's split right down the middle and it serves you step-by-step as you build the real thing. Although we don't build them as large as we did in the old days of the International Schooner races when the *Bluenose* and the *Thibault* were in their prime, we do build them with the same thought in mind — quality and speed. We still have scaled-down versions of those races and I have to admit I'm very proud of the fact that my boat won the International in 1972, '73, '74, '77. It's not the big thing it was back in the twenties and thirties, but we do try to keep it alive in a small way. The boat I have in my shop now is my seventh since I supposedly retired. Right now I've just about got myself convinced to go for a big one the next time. In fact I've already got the half-model built for a forty-foot schooner. I'm only eighty now so I've got lots of time.

After the half-model is built in half-inch scale and I know what I want in a boat, I take the lines off her and put them on the floor and I'll draw a profile of the whole boat. Then I'll make a few patterns and head for the hardwood bush and cut some of the finest oak there is in this country. When I bought this farm almost sixty years ago they were just little seedlings. Now there's two- or three-hundred-board feet in every one of them. That lumber will go into the keel, the stem, the stern-post, the timbers and the ribs. I'll take delivery of the thousand feet of the best pine that I ordered a year before so it has the proper seasoning. I pick it myself so that there's hardly a knot. Then I'm all ready to begin.

One of the first things I'll do is melt some lead for the keel. This one will have approximately five thousand pounds which acts as ballast. We make a mould and melt the lead in wash tubs, pour it in and after it's cool we trim it off, make it fast to the wood keel and then set her up in position. Then on goes the stem, the stern post, and the frames. Then come the rest of the ribs and the planking which will all be copper-fastened.

The planking is all pine and we find that in these waters it's every bit as good as mahogany so long as you use copper rivets. The galvanized rivets will eat through the wood after a time and cause leaks, but the copper is good for forty or fifty years.

After she's all planked and rivetted we do the caulking and put wedges in the seams with waterproof glue. Then she's ready to be planed off, sanded and painted.

Inside the hull we install the steps, the toilet and accommodations, and in fact it's almost like finishing up the inside of a house and takes almost as much time. You only have so much space to fit all those things in so that takes a lot of planning to utilize all of it.

Next is the mast, and in latter years I've been making them hollow. I laminate them for greater strength, but when I use a mast from the woods I always go for black spruce which I think is one of the strongest woods in the world. Simply selecting the right tree in the woods is no small matter with me either. For one, that tree has to be straight and should have as few limbs as possible. When I find the one I want I have it taken to a mill to have it four-squared. This saves me a great deal of hand-hewing later. After the four-squaring, I can use a small electric hand saw to eight-square it and then for a fairly big mast, I sixteen-square it. After this, with a little muscle it's fairly easy to round it over and sand it down. Then she's ready for the sails and that's it.

Oh, I'll tell you there's nothing in this world that compares with a good boat and no thrill that matches watching the good ones in a race. Back in those great days of sail when *Bluenose*, *Thibault*, the *Henry Ford* and *Columbia* were the best in the world there was nothing that could even come close to it for thrills. The current competition for the America's Cup doesn't even hold a candle because that's all to do with technology and computers. Those old International Boat Races were all about good boats and real characters, fishermen who made their living from the sea. As a matter of fact the crews on the *Bluenose* and those others were mostly all captains of other ships. They all were seafaring men and they knew what boats and the sea were all about and I always say that any man who goes to sea must have a deep and abiding respect for it or his chances of making land again are slim.

You know, I believe that the *Bluenose* was such a national treasure that she should have been enshrined forever someplace in this country when her days were over. She was such a symbol of our national pride.

Instead, they allowed her to be sold into what I think of as the tramp business, hauling freight, and she died a horrible death on a reef off the coast of Haiti in 1946. When I heard that news I cried just as I would if I'd lost a member of the family. They left that noble ship just lying there with her back broken until she eventually slid to the bottom. Our national pride slid to the bottom with her. It was a national disgrace, the treatment we dished out to that noble lady.

Sandy Downie

Kapuskasing Is the Place for Me

From the beginning, this nation of immigrants has been built by people from other lands. Their reasons for coming to Canada have been varied — some have come to escape oppression or poverty, some for adventure, some in search of riches, and others simply to get a piece of land they can call their own.

Sandy Downie of Kapuskasing in northern Ontario came here for different reasons. Doctors in Scotland advised his parents to get their sickly three-year-old away from the city or he might not survive.

My parents tossed a coin to see whether they would move to Canada or Australia, so I guess Canada won out.

Father came over first and for a year the only work he could find was in the Toronto sewers. He didn't like that at all and anyway, he thought, it wasn't really what the doctor advised, taking a sickly child from one smoky city to another.

He heard about an offer of free land that the government was making to those who were willing to try farming in northern Ontario. Dad thought that this might be the answer, so he brought Mother and us children over from Scotland and away we went into the solid bush of the north. At that time — in 1910 — there was a great push on to develop northern farming country. We landed up there in a place called Frederick House, six miles from Cochrane and four miles back in the bush.

As I was only four at the time, I can't imagine how we ever made our way in through that bush to find our piece of land. There were no roads whatsoever, and Dad had to follow a blazed trail through a forest that even the sun couldn't penetrate. But we did get through and managed to settle in somehow or other.

There was no cleared land at all on our homestead lot. Every inch of it had a tree, and it was his first task to cut enough of them down to make a clearing for a house which he would have to build out of those same trees. That was an immense job because first of all there was only him and Mother. My brother and I were much too young to be of any help. You must remember, too, that my parents were city folks who didn't know a thing about forests. They hadn't even seen a forest before, and here they were, fresh out of Dunbar, Scotland, attempting to tame a forest.

Those virgin trees were huge, and the task of getting just one of them down could take an entire day. After that, the tree would have to be cut into log lengths before it could be moved. It took many logs to build a house, and in that first year, Dad also had to clear enough land around the house to make some kind of a garden in which to grow our food. This meant that the roots of those huge trees had to be burned out of the ground. There was no other way! The amazing thing is that they actually succeeded in doing all of this by themselves during that year and we were able to live in our log house that winter of 1910-11. One would think that that kind of work would kill a woman, but Mother would, in fact, outlive a great many, and didn't die until she was ninety-six.

Dad was as tough as they come, too. In addition to all the work he did there, he also worked on the roads that the government was driving through the bush — digging ditches, and things like that — and in the winter he'd go out and cut pulpwood. This was the only way he could make some money, and it certainly wasn't very much — twenty-nine dollars a month — but it was enough to get the essentials we needed.

There were no real towns or villages then — only a few families like ourselves scattered around in their small clearings. Maybe one of these people would have a post office and a few groceries for sale, but for all intents and purposes everyone was alone in the bush with no close neighbours. For most everything we needed Dad had to go ten miles into Cochrane and then carry it all home on his back. He'd come home with maybe a twenty-five-pound bag of flour, a twenty-five-pound bag of sugar, and a lot of other groceries — perhaps a hundred pounds altogether. There were no roads to take a horse and wagon on. What roads they were building were little short stretches here and there. This difficulty in getting food meant that we lived on a lot of wild game, especially rabbits.

Life may have been hard, but my brother and I never thought of it that way. We enjoyed playing. We got a kick out of cutting down some of the smaller trees and clearing out a little patch of land for Father and this became our play. We worked ourselves tired every day and got up the following morning and did it all over again. It never occurred to us that there were other children in the world who had things different. We didn't even see other children except once or twice. We'd have neighbours off and on, but they couldn't stand the life and would move away in no time at all.

It wasn't that the land was no good for farming. It was good land, but the task of clearing off that virgin wood was next to impossible. We were one of the few families there who stuck with it for any time at all. It's hard to believe, but eventually we had about twenty-five acres cleared just by chopping and chipping and working away. The reason we didn't have a horse was that there weren't any that far north away from the railroad tracks. And that's the way it was for us from 1910 to 1914 when the First World War broke out.

When the war came, Dad was in Cochrane for supplies and someone told him that men were needed at Kapuskasing where the government was going to bulid prisoner-of-war camps. At the time, Kapuskasing was only a tiny spot on the map, and there wasn't much to it except a small trading post serving a few trappers. Actually, its name wasn't Kapuskasing. It was called MacPherson, a place where the train would stop only if someone flagged it down. It was figured that this would be a good place for prisoners because of the great difficulty it presented for escape.

The only place to escape to was Toronto, and that was five hundred miles down the tracks through the woods. Anyway Dad saw it as his chance to get his family away from the drudgery of the homestead so he moved to MacPherson, and started work building these camps. We joined him there a year later, in 1915. That was the time they began building the Experimental Farm, with the help of the prisoners. They would clear the land, and Dad was with the crew constructing the buildings. The first prisoners weren't considered much of a risk because they were from Canada, but were considered some kind of a risk because of their previous nationality. It wasn't until they started to get captured German prisoners from overseas that the big barbed-wire fences were erected with guards all around. Actually, those fences weren't put up until some of those prisoners began causing trouble by trying to escape, etc. The only places that they could go anyway would be Cochrane, which was seventy miles away, or Hearst, which was sixty miles. They couldn't have been able to hide out in either of those small towns anyway, and there were guard houses every so many miles along the track.

As far as I know, not one prisoner made a successful escape. Not many wanted to try, as they were treated very well really. I believe there were about two hundred prisoners in the camp. They were in a big area which was fenced off as a compound, and they were fed as well as the guards. Dad told me that there were only a very few who were in any way troublesome. Most of them decided to accept their lot, and wait out the war.

In those four years, from 1914 to 1918, the worst thing that happened up there had nothing to do with war at all. That was the big 'flu epidemic of 1917 which swept the entire country. It killed thousands, including quite a few in northern Ontario, and also some of the war prisoners and their guards. It was a terrible strain of 'flu and if it struck you at night you might be dead the next day. We were lucky. My brother had it first, and then my mother got it, and then I got it. Luckily, my dad never caught it, and he was able to nurse the three of us and he kept us from dying. His friends said afterwards that it was the Scotch whisky that kept him from it, but it was no laughing matter at the time. Thousands died in that epidemic, in a time when there were no miracle drugs to stop it. The saddest thing of all was to see those bodies laid out on a railroad pushcart, and the relatives and friends following behind as the procession made its way to the cemetery on a hill just outside of town.

There was no road up there so the only way to it was the railroad tracks. The man who really saved a lot of lives was called Doc Foster. He wasn't a graduated doctor, but I believe he did have some medical training. He saved a great many lives and Father always gave him the credit for saving ours.

The 'flu died down eventually and the war ended in 1918. The prisoners were sent home and there was nobody left but the soldiers and the guards. The government decided to pick up again on its plan to settle the north and they offered every soldier a free house and a farm of his own if he'd stay on the land around MacPherson. The only problem was that most of those men had come from the cities in southern Ontario, and of course they didn't have a clue about farming. They were given nice homes and were helped to clear the lands, but it just didn't seem to work out. Gradually, all of them, with the exception of maybe four or five, drifted back to where they had come from, so that by 1920 MacPherson was back to where it was before the war. Just a little whistle-stop on the railroad.

However, 1920 proved to be a year that this town will never forget. A big tycoon from the United States, a man named J.C. Kimberly, came in here and liked what he saw. He thought it was the perfect place for a paper mill. Before we knew it, he was building this paper mill and the whole place was overrun with workers — building the mill, and building the town! The town was built right across the river from

MacPherson and it was this new part that Kimberly gave the name of Kapuskasing. He called his company Spruce Falls, and it was the biggest thing that had ever happened in this part of the north. Kimberly gave his workers the very best of everything including excellent housing and places of recreation, plus schools and churches. It was all planned to perfection and right to this day it's called "The Model Town Of The North." At first it was totally a company town, but in a while, others came in and built restaurants and stores and things like that, and as the years went by the company sold their real estate holdings to the people at a very reasonable rate. They gave the arena to the town for a dollar, and the curling club for a dollar also.

One of the biggest things to happen to Kapuskasing was when they got the road through from the outside. That happened between 1928 and '29. Before that came about, we had to cross some of those rivers with cable barges. We'd put our cars on those barges and then were pulled to the other side, and then continue by road until we came to another river and another barge. I can't begin to tell you how much of a difference the road meant to us who lived here. It opened up the whole world. But I'm telling you, if I had my choice of the world, I wouldn't want to live anywhere else than here. Kapuskasing is the place for me!

Paul Martin

Good Old-Fashioned Politics

Canada has produced some remarkable politicians—"men of the old school"—who not only acted as most of us feel politicians should act, but who also looked the way those of us of a certain age feel they should look. Paul Martin, the member for Windsor, Ontario, was one of those. He looked good in a Homburg, dark topcoat, dark suit, white shirt, quiet tie, and black polished shoes. He so epitomized the image of the old-time politician that he should have smoked cigars, even if he didn't. You couldn't help liking Paul Martin because he gave the impression, always, that he remembered you, was interested in you, and even liked you, even if you had to admit to yourself that you had never met before. With the exception of Prime Minister Mackenzie King, Paul Martin spent more years on Parliament Hill than any man—twenty-two of those thirty-nine years as a Cabinet Minister.

As a young lad I didn't know what politics was. My father was a workman in a steel equipment company. He was a Liberal, but he was also more of an athlete than a student. He was a reader and kept track through the *Ottawa Journal*, the accounts of what was going on in Parliament, notably the speeches of Sir Wilfrid Laurier which he read aloud to us.

I think maybe I got the bug at that time even though I was only about five or six years old. A few years after that the librarian in Pembroke, Ontario, a strong Conservative lady, Alma Beatty, took a liking to my father, who was fairly well-known around town due to his sporting activities. She told him that he should send that young son of his to the library more often as there were no books at our home.

So it was that I found myself in the Carnegie Library in Pembroke, which seemed as big as a cathedral to me, although in reality it was quite a small room. But it was such a nice room chock full of books.

Miss Beatty came over to welcome me and we walked around with her pointing out books and explaining what all the different sections contained. Then at one point she took down three volumes about a man of whom I had never heard. It was Gladstone, the great Liberal leader. "Some day, Paul" she said, "I want you to read these because I can see you've got politician written all over you." I don't know where she got that idea as the thought had never entered my head. Anyway I asked her why I had to wait until "some day" to read the books. Why couldn't I read them now? She said, "Well — why not? There are pictures there you might enjoy even if you won't understand what you're reading."

It was Lord Morley's *Life of Gladstone* and the frontispiece was a picture of the Commonwealth prime ministers and there was Laurier in there with them. As young as I was, I had already claimed Laurier as a hero — and it thrilled me to see him in this book with a world figure like Gladstone and those other prime ministers of the Commonwealth. It was a matter of Canadian pride, I suppose. From that moment on I wanted to go into politics.

My father's father was born in Ireland and he came to Quebec as an infant and later on married a pure French-Quebec woman, and although Father had this Irish background he and all the rest of us spoke French at home. Though the Martin name I carry is Irish, it always has been, as Duplessis once told me, "Mar-TAN" in the province of Quebec. I never forgot that and, you know, that has never hurt me in my political career.

I was first elected to political office in 1935, in Essex County in Ontario when R.B. Bennett's government was defeated in the middle of the Depression, and I never suffered a defeat in all of those years since then. I'm surprised that I won that first election, because I was a stranger to the people of Windsor, having only lived there about four years as a lawyer. I didn't really want to run at that time but my mentor, the Reverend Mr. Pollock, the minister at St. Andrew's Presbyterian Church, who was a great Liberal, thought that the moment had arrived for me to get my feet wet. He was right. I ran and I got in, although with a very small majority in contrast with the great majorities other Liberals were getting in that particular election; the reason being that R.B. had become a very unpopular prime minister, not because of himself, but because of the terrible economic conditions in the Depression. The only reason I became a Liberal in the first place was because that's how my parents voted. This was followed by my hero worship of Sir Wilfrid.

I actually saw Sir Wilfrid twice and he really was a wonderfully impressive figure. At the time of his death in 1919, I was at a small classical college in the Gatineau Hills of Quebec. I went to the head master and told him I wanted to go in to Ottawa to attend Sir Wilfrid's funeral. He said that that would be impossible as I had my studies to keep up with. I thought that this was unfair, so I ran away — took leave without permission — and I went. Because of the crowds I didn't get into the Basilica to hear the eulogy, but I remember that when it was over and they were all coming out, all of those statesmen. Sir Robert Borden: I can see him yet particularly, because he was the prime minister at the time. They were all dressed in tall silk hats and formal clothing.

I didn't recognize many of the figures, but the night before my aunt had taken me to the Victoria Museum, which was then the temporary buildings being used by Parliament. The House of Commons had been burnt — the Centre Block — and we had gone there to view the remains of Laurier. He was in full dress in a Windsor uniform looking very thin, but what was distinctive was his flowing hair, this wonderful hair that had always been his trademark. I felt very sad, of course, but I knew I was in a small way taking part in an historic occasion. This man was, after all, one of the greatest of Commonwealth Liberals.

Also, at university I studied John Stuart Mill and the works of other great Liberals.

I served in the Cabinets of four prime ministers: King, St. Laurent, Pearson, and Trudeau. They all were able men, each in his own manner.

King was a great political leader. I didn't agree with a lot of his attitudes, though. I was what was called a "Rooseveltian" in my first election. The country was full of unemployment and it seemed to me that Roosevelt was really doing something about it with his New Deal in the United States. I didn't think that *my* leader and the Liberal Party were doing enough. I went to see King during the election and I was told afterwards that he found me a very bold young man. But I must have had some influence on him, because he made three notable radio speeches in which some of my ideas were used. By the way that 1935 election was the first time that radio had been used in a political campaign. Those speeches were modelled somewhat after the Roosevelt programs in the famous "Fireside Chats," although King never had the capacity for a fireside chat that Roosevelt did. I don't think any man could have handled the situation in wartime more effectively than King did. He knew how to balance the two basic interests in the country, French Canada and English Canada, and he did that very dextrously.

I liked Louis St. Laurent for many different reasons. First of all, this man *looked* like a prime minister with his noble and regal appearance, but he was also the greatest manager of our national and international affairs of any of the four. He was one of the best lawyers this country has ever seen. He knew a lot about business — a director of the CPR, and all that sort of thing. Despite my great respect for him, we also had our differences.

He didn't approve of my health and welfare program. He didn't like health insurance and if it hadn't been for the fact that King had been committed to health insurance in 1919 at the convention when he was elected leader, I don't suppose I would have been able to convince King or the Cabinet as a whole that the time had come when we should move into that front. I feel rather proud of some of my accomplishments as minister of Health and Welfare for eleven years.

I think, though, that foreign affairs is where I came into my own. When I was at St. Michael's College in the University of Toronto I was imbued with the importance of trying to renounce war as an instrument of national policy. I learned to believe in the League of Nations, and ultimately the United Nations. King didn't believe in the United Nations at all and he didn't believe in the League. However, he did sign the charter of the United Nations in 1945 along with Mr. St. Laurent who did believe in the United Nations.

I went to the United Nations in London with St. Laurent in 1946. I chaired the delegation when the assembly met in New York for the first time that same year. I've been to eleven assemblies since long before I was External Affairs Minister with Pearson and with St. Laurent, and that was very much a part of my philosophy and my life.

Of those four prime ministers I worked with, I think the one who appeared to be unapproachable by the common man was Mackenzie King. He presented a rather chilly personality to most people, I believe. When I first went to Ottawa he had been a long time in office and I approached him with great diffidence. It took me a very long time to really feel that I was his colleague.

When I was a young member I hadn't made a speech in my first six months and I had told the electors that I would be very active on the floor of the House. I soon realized, however, what the inhibitions and restraints were, and I began to worry about not having made a speech or asked a question.

So one day I got up and did something that no Liberal private member ever did, and that was to ask my own leader, Prime Minister King, a question on foreign affairs. It wasn't a very penetrating one, but I could see that King wasn't too happy with this young backbencher who was invading a field where only prime ministers should roam. He looked at me with this cold expression and replied, "I will look into it." Well, I thought that I had killed my career chances with that one bold move, which Ross Gray the Liberal whip termed a "faux pas." So I was very surprised in the month of August, a few months later, when King called me on the phone. My nervous stenographer came in and said in a very shaky voice, "The Prime Minister of Canada is on the phone." He was inviting me to be a delegate to the second last assembly of the League of Nations under the chairmanship of the great Honourable Ernest Lapointe. There must have been something in the way of divine intervention, because I don't think there was anything else about my actions at that time that impressed him.

The next prime minister, Mr. St. Laurent, was just like a father—"Uncle Louis," as everybody referred to him, but never to his face. No one would ever presume to be that familiar with this very able man. St. Laurent believed that the federal government should never do anything that the provinces could do better, and he believed that the provinces should never do anything that the individual or the churches or the community could do better. He wasn't really a contemporary Liberal and he didn't profess to be. He looked on himself as a manager, president of the board of directors, and he looked after our affairs very well indeed.

His whole image was one of kindness and ability, but he was never the type of man one would slap on the back. I always called him "Mr. St. Laurent" or "Prime Minister." I got to know him very well when we spent those months at the end of the war in London at the first meetings of the United Nations. I can still see him when we both went to a party for the delegates to meet King George VI at Buckingham Palace. The man who seemed to be the most dignified of them all was St. Laurent as he bowed. I was very very proud of him.

We had great rows. I almost left the government over my disagreement with him on health insurance, but my colleagues backed me up, and St. Laurent realized that it would be politically unwise not to give in to my submission. As the party of reform, the Liberal Party wouldn't have been true to its principles if we hadn't done this thing.

He wasn't born an aristocrat but he certainly was one. His father was a little-storekeeper in the Eastern townships of Quebec. Young Louis was always the top student in his class. All of those around him at the time say that they always looked to him for leadership and, you know, he was the same way in government. There was nothing "uppity" about him at all. I recall going down one day to Bowles Lunch in Ottawa, where they had beans and toast for lunch for ten cents. I was surprised to see him there too. Although it was a nice clean place, it was also known as a place where drifters and beggars went. Uncle Louis was very much a man of the people who walked the streets of Ottawa every day without so much as an escort. People would say "hello" to him and he'd raise his hat and smile back in the most friendly of ways.

St. Laurent's greatest contribution was in the field of foreign affairs. He took our foreign policy as we stated it in San Francisco and made it a veritable program. He believed in the United Nations. He wanted to make it a strong force for peace in the world. St. Laurent was an idealist who believed in the law, who believed in the application of the law to country and states as well as to individuals. He gave Canada a great reputation in the world in the field of foreign affairs.

The trouble is that history won't remember him. St. Laurent didn't leave any papers or memoirs. I find that even now people can't recall him at all. Just as they don't remember Norman Rogers, the minister of Defence in King's wartime Cabinet. He was killed in an airplane crash; had he lived he would most certainly have succeeded King as the prime minister. Another great man was Jim Ilsley, King's minister of Finance during the war. Like Rogers, he was a strong, strong man, probably the greatest minister of Finance this country has ever seen. Both of these men, Rogers and Ilsley, were Nova Scotians. Good, good men. Neither of them left papers so nobody remembers them. For this reason I resolved not to be forgotten. My papers are pretty complete in the Archives and they are there for anyone to see.

Lester Pearson, who was called Mike by all of his friends, was a wonderful man who was liked by everyone, it seemed, regardless of their politics. He would have made a great Secretary-General of the United Nations. He wanted the job, but I knew he would never get it although his name was the one most bandied about in 1945. The Soviet Union would never have accepted one from the West. He tried again when Dag Hammarskjold was selected to succeed Trygve Lie. There again, I knew he wouldn't get it as the Soviet Union wouldn't support a NATO member. That was Pearson's real calling. He and I worked together and I think the Canadian foreign policy up to as late as 1968 was the fabrication of the ideas of St. Laurent, Pearson, and myself.

Pearson's greatest contribution was in the field of international affairs, too. He was an outstanding figure, a professional diplomat with a fantastic personality. I thought he was going to be a very strong leader, but I don't think he ever was. He couldn't win a majority government. Diefenbaker, who was not a great prime minister, but who was a master on the election platform, was able to deny Pearson his majority government. Even after Diefenbaker had lost three ministers from his Cabinet — Harkness, Hees, and Sevigny — Pearson wasn't able to get a majority government. I don't know that the fault is entirely his, but he has to take the blame.

Trudeau has always been a remarkable figure. He was prime minister even longer than Laurier. I ran against Trudeau when I thought I had a chance to be the Liberal leader, but at the time they wanted a young man. I was the old man — sixty-five at the time. The delegates forgot that St. Laurent became leader at the age of sixty-five and Churchill became prime minister at that age also. Trudeau met their demands more than anyone else, although I was away ahead of the others in the Gallup polls, up until Pearson's intervention in the campaign for the leadership. In any event I felt it was not my time. I said to Trudeau, "You're still going, but so am I."

I was disappointed with Pearson when he more or less "anointed" Trudeau, as Mike and I had been so very, very close. We had sat together in the House and our connections were very deep. I thought that he would want me to succeed him, but he felt as King felt — and I think wrongly for a Liberal — that the leadership should alternate between an English-speaking Canadian and one who was French-speaking. My view was that that was not a real principle. Mackenzie King had manufactured it to suit his wishes and he had no more business intervening in the election than did Pearson. Trudeau became the prime minister. That's about the only thing that ever came between us. When Trudeau accepted the leadership at the National Convention the only thing said about me at all was by Pearson. He didn't mention another soul. I have often felt that Mike must have had some remorse, because he knew me so well. But you know it was, in fact, the only real difference between us. When he ran for the leadership in 1958 with my help, I felt that that was something he couldn't possibly forget — but he did.

Frankly, it was very disappointing for me as I had those twin ambitions. One was to lead the Liberal Party and the other to be prime minister. Both of these were dashed on the rocks at that convention; but strange as it may seem, I didn't get too upset. I always knew that in some ways a Cabinet minister who is devoted to his task can do more than a prime minister. At the time that I ran against Pearson for the leadership, I knew from the outset that I didn't have a chance. He had won the Nobel Peace Prize and the principle of French-English alternation laid down by King was so firmly implanted, I knew I couldn't circumvent that, so I was prepared to lose. I knew that he would make the best prime minister of all of the other candidates other than myself.

Trudeau was a very hard man to know, but I did admire his mind. There were many things about him that I didn't like, but he was an able man. What he was able to do in arresting what I call the evils of the PQ is something that will endure to his everlasting benefit. He is the man who defeated those who wanted to destroy Canada's unity. He is the man who stood up and showed that it would be folly for Quebec to leave Canada and it may be that that was providential intervention. Maybe it required a man who came from Quebec, also someone

French who was *of* Quebec to handle those *in* Quebec who wanted to leave Canada and he did that job very well. I think that was his major contribution as prime minister.

Mackenzie King's contribution was that he held the country together in time of war by balancing the feud between those who wanted conscription and those who were opposed. He knew perfectly well how badly conscription had been handled in the First World War. He was able to keep conscription from the scene in the Second World War except at the very last. He was the best prime minister for wartime. Very few would have thought so as he wasn't warlike. He wasn't even in the local militia; but he knew how to manipulate people as a statesman in a country so varied as ours.

I suppose you could call me a successful politician. After all, thirty-nine years in the House of Commons and twenty-two years a Cabinet minister without ever losing an election has to be something of a record. I don't know why, except that I always truly liked people. But the truth is, and this may surprise you, I never liked politics. How about that from someone who is often called, among other things, "the politician's politician"? I really didn't like the game. I found electioneering tedious and difficult but I knew that I couldn't sit in government unless I was elected. On top of that my constituency was a hard one where the factory workers strongly supported the NDP. If I hadn't shown the interest in them and their problems I would not have been elected.

I'd have to see the constituents in my office, always catering to their whims and their problems. I found the daily and weekend travelling around the constituency, seeing the farmers, seeing the city folk, the factory workers, totally exhausting. Many times I would just crawl into an out-of-the-way ditch, and lie there trying to refresh myself. If I didn't go through that grind and just stayed at home, I would be disturbed. But after a while like it or not, it simply becomes second nature.

I remember one time when Trudeau came to my riding of Windsor as prime minister for the first time, contesting his first national election. I said to him, "I bet I can name more people in my constituency than you can in yours." "Oh," he said, "Well, I'm sure that this great reputation of yours that you know everybody in your constituency by their first names is greatly exaggerated." Well, I told him that he was probably right, but when we got to the top of Ouellet Avenue, which is our principal street, I said "Let's walk down this main street of ours and see how many I do know." We did and we stopped and talked with 108 people and I was able to call 101 of them by their first names.

But, you know, I have a little trick that I learned from Laurier. If you do meet someone and you can't come up with their name—just grab them by the arm and while looking them straight in the eye you say "And how is the old trouble?" They will almost always say "My gosh, Mr. Martin, do you remember my old troubles?" Of course I don't, but I just proceed on the basis that every man and every woman has trouble. It works every time. That's politics.

Mrs. Hugh Armstrong

Cobalt Was Six Years Old

The town of Cobalt in Northern Ontario was born in 1903 when a heavy showing of silver was discovered. Precious metal discoveries of any kind brought people in from everywhere, hoping to get some of the riches that this new country had to offer. In came the miners and the prospectors. In came the storekeepers, the entertainers, the gamblers, and the bootleggers. Before 1903, however, Cobalt was a wide open frontier town of muddy streets and board sidewalks, dance halls, silent movie theatres, and noisy casinos. It was a town for young people attracted by the adventure and excitement of it all, a town where memories were made to last a lifetime. I talked with Mrs. Hugh Armstrong when she was eighty and she remembered the day she stepped off the train in Cobalt in 1909.

When I came here there was nothing but mud, mud, everywhere, and the only thing that saved you at all from being swallowed up in it was this wooden sidewalk which was only two boards wide, so we had to walk very carefully. By the time I got here there was a lot of wooden houses built, but on the 2nd of July in 1909, we had the big fire which swept all of those houses away.

The whole of Lang Street, both sides, went up in flames. It was a terrible tragedy for such a new town, but the miraculous part of that is that nobody was killed. The fire started early in the morning in a restaurant kitchen, and very soon all these houses were going up, one by one, like little matchboxes. It cleaned up all those houses and stores all the way up to the bridge leading to the O'Brien mine. Then, for some reason, it stopped there. Both sides of the street simply stopped burning at the same time. I was eighteen years old, and I had to help carry all the stuff out up onto the hill at the place where I was working, for fear that that place would go up in flames too, but thankfully it didn't.

A funny thing about that fire was that all the houses that burned were occupied by French Catholic families, and where it stopped, the two houses on both sides of the street were Protestant families. Later on we would laugh about that and wonder whose side the good Lord was on.

Since the town was so young then, the fire wiped out quite a big section of what was there in 1909, although it didn't stop progress. The very next day people were out there putting up new buildings, and in the meantime living in tents or whatever they could get to live in. The merchants put up big tents, too, so they could carry on with their businesses.

I remember thinking at the time how strange it was to buying meat from a butcher in a tent. But, you know, it was just a frontier town then anyway, and pretty well anything could happen. Cobalt was only six years old, and the silver mines were attracting the best and the worst of people.

Everyone was busy and there was lots of work for everyone who wanted it. We had three big theatres — or was it four? They had silent movies and vaudeville shows and they did a rip-roaring business too. The Idle Hour was one of the theatres and it was all vaudeville. Travelling theatre companies would come in and put on plays and bring singers and musicians, and the people would flock to see them.

I loved it, but to tell you the truth none of us knew if the performances were good or bad. It didn't make any difference. We loved it anyway. Over a number of years every one of those theatres burned to the ground. They were built of wood and put up very quickly in the first place.

Nineteen-oh-nine was a big year for me: coming to a new town; working for the first time; seeing all the excitement, and best of all, meeting Hugh Armstrong, the man who would become my husband. You just can't imagine how exciting it was here at that time, with people crowding in from all over the world. They couldn't build shelters fast enough to accommodate them. We had twelve or fourteen thousand people here in 1909, and everyone seemed to have money to spend.

There were big boarding-houses for men who worked in the mines. Most of them had come to Cobalt to make a start and eventually a lot of them stayed on and built houses and raised families here.

My husband ran the sawmill that supplied the lumber which was needed to build all of those houses, and so we got to know just about everybody. I was sort of a practical nurse, and because doctors were always in short supply I was constantly called out to homes for one kind of an emergency or another. God only knows how many babies I helped bring into the world.

People helped one another. We had to, because there was no other way. We depended on our neighbours, and they depended on us. That's why I can truthfully say that just as I helped people into the world, I also helped them on their way out. When someone died, it was the neighbours who got the body ready for burial. All the undertaker had to do was to come to the house and put the body in a casket. Everything else would have been done by neighbours of the deceased.

Life was simpler back then, but I often think it was much more satisfying. Most of what you needed, you had to get for yourself. People built their own homes, made a lot of their own clothes, hunted and fished for a great deal of their own food, and just generally fended for themselves as best they could. There was an awful lot of satisfaction in that.

Robert Collins

Grasshopper, Grasshopper, Give Me Some Molasses

On the Prairies, nature took its cue from the economy during the Depression and the very act of staying alive became a nightmare. Money disappeared as readily as did moisture from the sky. The result was poverty heightened by wind and dust storms, drought, grasshopper plagues, and despair. The wind just blew away the soil, and what small crops did sprout, were chewed up by the insects. Robert Collins has vivid memories of his childhood during those years.

I did my growing up on a Saskatchewan homestead during those Depression years. There were four of us, a younger brother, my parents, and me.

It was a tough ten years with much of the blame lying with the farmers themselves, although they didn't realize what they were doing. It had to do with poor farming practices. The early pioneers of the prairies like my dad came straight out of England, not having a clue about farming, really. They just went right ahead and ploughed the land, cultivated it, and so on, without a plan of any kind. By the thirties, all of this land was drained of its nutrients, lying there barren, waiting for the wind and drought that caused those horrendous duststorms. There was no trash cover left on the land, something to tie it down and hold the moisture. The coincidence was that all of these natural horrors came with the Depression, and they seemed to rage on right through the thirties until the end of that decade, when the weather and prices for crops both improved at the same time.

The first storm I can remember came very early on, in May of 1930. My father locked the barn-door and took the windmill out of gear before running for the safety of the house. It was like night had come in the middle of the day. We had to light the lamps just to see each other. It lasted about an hour. When we went outside, it was a scene of desolation, with big ugly empty patches, where newly-sprouted crops had been an hour before. My parents' faces drained of colour, and they clearly did not understand what was happening any more than we children did. After that the dust storms came with increasing frequency, until they were almost routine.

The dust was everywhere. It seeped under the doors, and around the windows; people would keep wet towels around all doors and windows all the time. No matter what was done, that dust got inside, covering up even the pattern on the linoleum floors. On really bad days, our whole meal would have to be covered with a cloth while we were eating and we'd have to reach in under tea towels to feel for a slice of bread, or a dab of butter. Sometimes at school, the floor had to be cleaned with a shovel.

Only the hardiest of our grain stocks managed to withstand the force of the winds, but there was one weed, Russian thistle, that always seemed to flourish until it was fully ripened. When it was ready to do so, it would simply break away from its root, and roll with the wind along to the fences, which would gradually disappear under tons of these thistles and sand. With typical depression ingenuity, farmers found a use even for the thistle. It was dried out and used as bedding in the cattle barns, or used as cattle fodder when it was green.

The animals, when you think of it, were terribly hit by the Depression. My father used at least half of his small war pension buying fodder for them, and sometimes they got just a minimum diet of plain straw, soaked in molasses and water. But gradually their body resistance would go and they'd become infested with lice, and we would doctor them as best as we could ourselves. The horses, all of them greatly loved, would become so undernourished and weak that we would reluctantly have to shoot them. It was the kindest thing to do.

It was wise to be inside during a dust storm, but at times you'd be caught unawares, or the school would be shut down and the children would be sent home before it got bad. I remember one occasion when I was about seven or eight, my father, who had been forewarned by a phone call from the teacher, came to meet me. By the time we met, it had become really bad and we could hardly see at all. Meanwhile, my mother, was waiting back at the house. I guess she was terribly worried as the time stretched out, but when she finally saw us coming, there was I, skipping ahead of Dad, looking for the first crocuses that should have been poking their heads up at that time of year. I didn't have any of the worries that they had, even though this was one of those sand storms that turned day into night, with sand cutting into the face and eyes, and always the possibility of becoming lost.

The grasshopper plagues seemed to go hand-in-hand with the drought. It had something to do with lack of moisture encouraging the hatching of the eggs. At the very worst of times, plagues of grasshoppers would form a visible black cloud in the sky of a fine day. In the worst years, they would actually infest the fields and garden, and strip most of the growing things. They were all over the place.

When annoyed, a grasshopper will eject what we used to call "tobacco juice." It was its way of fending off enemies. We would pick them up and close our hands over them, and say, "Grasshopper, grasshopper, give me some molasses." To our delight, they always complied.

The good thing, and the only thing, about grasshoppers was that our chickens and hens liked them, which meant they always had something to eat. As I recall, it produced a certain flavour to eggs that wasn't particularly pleasant, but as long as the chickens were getting free food, we didn't complain. When those clouds of grasshoppers appeared on the horizon, we'd pray that they wouldn't descend on our fields, because they would just strip everything that wasn't already gone. They'd cover the walls of buildings and even the roads and railway tracks. The trains had a terrible time to get traction, because there would be so many of these things it would be like grease on the rails.

Grasshoppers were almost impossible to combat. Municipalities gave out this liquid poison that was mixed in a kind of mash and spread in the fields. It had a limited effect as there were so very many of them. It was a case of "grin and bear it," but there wasn't much grinning as I recall.

All of these things combined left people feeling totally helpless and hopeless, and as the Depression progressed, you'd see entire families just roaming across the land, looking for work that didn't exist. Our family stayed put on the homestead, but as young as I was, I could see the despair in my parents' eyes. There was this look of desperation when they would come in from the fields where what had looked like a promising crop had fallen prey to the drought or the grasshoppers or the hailstorms, another major problem in our area. These vicious storms could destroy anything that had managed to survive the other things in a half-hour. It was really a triple-whammy from nature. Everything came together, combined with the financial collapse of the economy.

I was six years old when it began and sixteen when it ended, so you might say these were all of my formative years. I was old enough throughout to witness my parents' despair and heartaches, but I was young enough to overcome it in my own way, so everything I remember isn't unpleasant. We were poor, but didn't know it, mainly because everybody we knew was in the same boat — down on their knees and down at the heels.

Our clothing was as plain as you could get, and there wasn't much of it. I did have one good suit, my Sunday suit, which lasted for three or four years. It was bought too big for me so that "I would grow into it." Too long in the sleeves and legs the first year, but by the fourth year my arms and legs would be sticking out all over the place. Our everyday clothing was just overalls, well-patched, and if we had anything on our feet, it was sneakers. In the really bad years, our clothes came in boxcars as charity donations from what we perceived as the "rich provinces" of the East, mainly Ontario. Church groups down there would send us these "poor barrels," which we no doubt needed and could use, but somehow resented, as I suppose most people do, who have to accept charity.

At the same time though, all of us "poor people" never really thought of ourselves as being poor. There was a tremendous unity because we had this difficulty in common. It more or less bound us together as a group. We didn't like it. We just made the best of it. Neighbours clung to each other and helped each other. There would be these "bees" where everyone would band together for any big jobs that had to be done.

In our family, as in most others, we made our own entertainment. We spent a lot of time reading together, we invented games, and there was a great deal of singing and telling of stories. All things that could be done without money.

We couldn't afford a radio for a good many of those 1930 years. Since there was no electricity, they required batteries, which needed recharging, and consequently they cost money that we couldn't afford. In 1939, my dad, who was an intense patriot, found the money to keep up on the war news. Then of course, we just revelled and luxuriated and rejoiced in what radio had to offer. Fibber McGee — Lux Radio Theatre — Orson Welles, and the early offerings of the CBC, including and perhaps especially for Father, the CBC news.

We felt very close to our farm, because as a homesteader after the First World War, my dad was the first person ever to turn the sod on that virgin land. It was "our land" from day one, and in fact there were still some parts of our acreage that had never been ploughed. In those parts, we often discovered little rings of stone where early Indians had built their teepees. For me that was incredibly romantic stuff.

The land was not good farmland. There were many rocks and it seemed that no matter how many you'd remove during the year, new ones would pop up like raisins in the spring. It was rolling land, and the only trees were those planted around the perimeter of their land by the farmers themselves.

In the night you would look out in the distance and see these little pinpoints of light where another family just like ours was surviving, families that we knew by name: our friends and our neighbours. There was a friendly feeling to just look out like that at night. It was so blissfully silent with maybe only coyotes howling off in the distance, frogs or crickets in season, and the occasional night bird. There was an awesome beauty to all of it night or day, and that "big sky" of the prairies where it seemed one could see forever. The sunsets were spectacular, even though science explains to us now that they were that way because of the dust in the air. It made the colours more vivid and rich. The stars, of course, were magnificent, because there were no city lights to drown out their brilliance.

Back in those days each family member had certain chores, right down to the youngest child. Many hands were needed to keep the "enterprise" going. My mother raised a lot of chickens to help supplement the income and my dad kept a few cows. We children fed the chickens, gathered the eggs, cleaned out the barns, learned to milk cows, and helped Mother with the huge garden she always managed to keep going in some form or other. We weeded and watered and all those other things, but we also had a lot of time for fun. With two boys in the family, games were something of a problem, but we managed somehow. One of us would be the batting side in a baseball game, and the other would be the fielding side.

We flooded little backyard patches in the winter to make our rinks where we skated and called ourselves hockey teams. I also liked school, which was about a mile and a half down the road. I liked it so much, because there were books there and I loved to read. In a way school became part of my recreation, although I couldn't admit that to my friends, who thought it was much better to be out catching gophers or working the land with their dads. I liked doing those, too, but I liked school better.

I must admit, though, that I loved staying home from school when the peak of the harvest came along. It was an enormous honour to be asked to help in this way. It made you feel needed and part of everything that was going on. It was the culmination of the entire year on those 320 acres that my father had broken himself over the years with nothing but one plough and six horses. It was back-breaking work for a man and horses.

Many farmers cracked under the strain of it all, and finally walked away from their farms. Others stayed long after they should have and they just withered away, but anyone who was there was marked for life by that period. I, for example, am a compulsive saver. I can't throw anything away — even bits of string, which I'm convinced will become valuable some day if kept long enough. Many, or maybe even most, of us who when through the Depression are like this. We know all too well what it's like to want something and not have the means to get it. On the other hand, we learned to value things once we did get them. I saved and worked for years to get my first bicycle, so that when I finally could buy it I looked after it like the rare jewel it was.

People on the prairies generally hated the idea of being on the receiving end of what charity there was. My father was a very proud man, and it hurt him to be getting those relief shipments of coal and bales of hay that he nevertheless needed so much. We never got food because we always managed to have enough for ourselves at least. Personally, I remember being excited about getting those clothing shipments from the East, because there were things in them I'd never before seen, such as T-shirts of a kind that you'd never get in Saskatchewan. I thought these things were pretty snazzy and even a bit of luxury. My father looked on these gifts as something of an indictment of him as a provider. He couldn't seem to digest the fact that this was no fault of his. In fact, he wouldn't even hear of my mother, who was a qualified teacher, going out occasionally to teach on a part-time basis. A woman working? Good heavens! That would mean that he was a man who couldn't support his family.

The Depression forged into me a lot of characteristics that will be with me all my days. I'm not a type who will take wild chances. I'll always go for the sure thing instead of taking a gamble. In terms of employment, I'll always stay with the familiar instead of moving on to something that looks more promising. I do think that the Depression helped in that one learned to be self-sustaining and self-contained, and you learned to be a survivor; partly because you learned to improvise — to make something out of nothing, or from very little.

I think the great tragedy of those years is that so many who saw the homesteads of the prairies as their great chance in life saw it all change from hope to despair because of circumstances they couldn't control. Then there were all of those young people who came to maturity while the Depression was still in full flower. There were no jobs for them and no chance for higher education. For them, the whole potential of their lifetime was never realized — all of that lost talent. For them the Depression was a lifelong tragedy.

The strange thing is that I look back with a great deal of fondness on those years. Today I love to hear rain and that goes back to the days of drought when rain was such a rare and welcome happening. It meant all the difference between success or failure in farming. Some prairie people of that time hate the sound of wind, even today. Not me. I like the sound, because it was such a part of our lives then. It brings back memories of the closeness we had in the very act of continuing our lives — in surviving.

Frank "King" Clancy

Sixty-Minute Men

The 1930s were the glory days of hockey in Canada as far as many are concerned. There were few teams and few players good enough to make those teams in the National Hockey League. They were the cream of the crop. A spot on the NHL was enough to guarantee near immortality for players like Charlie Conacher, the Cook brothers, or King Clancy, to name just a few.

King Clancy was one of the best, and one of my own heroes as a youngster. He was a great player of medium build who was a match for anyone. King was eighty-three when I met him in 1986. He may have been frail when I met him in old age, but his mind was sharp and he was working every day in his role as vice-president of the Toronto Maple Leafs. He was lively, enthusiastic, and entertaining at that time, two months before his death. The "King" was an easy man to like.

I first played hockey when I was fifteen with a team called St. Brigid's in Ottawa in the City League. At that particular time there were no junior leagues or anything of that sort. There was the school hockey team, and after you played in that and if you couldn't get into the city league, you couldn't play at all unless it was on one of those scrub teams with no league at all. But I played for two or three years with some really great players on that St. Brigid's club and afterwards when I turned professional, one of the guys, a fellow named Conway, from the same team also turned pro as a goalkeeper. It was a great education, playing for a team like that one. We had a schoolteacher for a coach and he was a fine man who would say, "This is a game for men, and even it you think you're only a boy you have to be a man."

Those were the days when almost everybody played on some scrub team or other. Every backyard had a rink in it, including mine. It wasn't very big, but it was there that I learned to shoot. One of my friends would put on pads, get in the net and let me shoot at him. I couldn't even break a pane of glass then, but with lots of practice I got to be able to pick the corner of a net pretty good.

The sports ability I had was inherited, I'm sure, from my father, who was a fine football player as well as being a great father. He would tell us that if we didn't intend to do our best then we shouldn't bother at all. "Above all," he said, "Have fun." That has always been my motto ever since I first stepped on the ice. If I didn't have fun, I didn't want to play and I can say honestly that it has been fun as a professional and as an amateur.

I was an amateur for only two years when I graduated to the pros with Ottawa. All the other players were older than me and all were fantastic players and wonderful people, who had time to spend with this seventeen-year-old kid who had joined them. The fact that those fellows were all so experienced helped me a lot as they were interested in passing on their knowledge of the game.

When I joined the NHL there were only four teams in it, Hamilton, Toronto, Montreal, and Ottawa. I believe we only played around twenty or twenty-four games in a season. There was also what was called the Coast League out west and the Prairie League. Now, in 1921 we went out there to play for the Stanley Cup. We had won in the East, so we played Vancouver two out of three and were fortunate enough to beat them; and then we played Edmonton, winners of the Prairie League, and we beat them and won the Stanley Cup.

What a thrill that whole thing was for me! It was my first time outside of Ontario or Quebec. They had such good players out there then that I felt we were very fortunate to win especially since they had good managers. Frank Patrick managed the Victoria team and Lester Patrick was managing Vancouver. Their boys Len and Muzzy Patrick — and in fact the whole Patrick family — could take credit as being the Fathers of Hockey out on the west coast. They built rinks and arenas all over that part of the country, including the Vancouver arena. That city was a hotbed of hockey at the time. That was my first Stanley Cup and for my contribution in winning it I got seven-hundred-and-eighty dollars. Of course, you must remember that they didn't throw dollars around then like they now do. My first year's salary for the Ottawa team was eight hundred dollars for the year. There weren't nearly as many games as there are now either. I think it was fourteen games plus playoffs and of course there weren't nearly as many players on a team. Due to this it was very, very hard to make it to the NHL. The ones who did make it were indeed the best in the land and were looked up to almost like gods. There weren't that many backups or substitutes, so some of those players never left the ice for the whole game. There were quite a few of those sixty-minute men and I must say I had more than a few of those sixty-minute games myself.

I remember all those guys as rough and tough players. They *had* to be once the game began. They knew how to hand it out and to take it too. I was amazed when I went out the first time with those Ottawa players who were a lot older than I was. They told me to watch myself because I would be playing against a lot of strangers who were not going to be easy on me. Well, I paid for it. They had not a shred of respect for my youth. They were rough but in quite a different way than it's rough today. The big thing then was the body check. High-sticking was something you'd hardly ever see. I can't remember ever getting hit by a high stick myself.

Of course, the rules made it much different. To start with the ice was surfaced only at the beginning of the game and never between periods. Before the end of a game you'd be skating in ruts. I remember one time when we were playing for the Stanley Cup in Toronto and there were ruts big enough to almost lose your skate in. My preference was always natural ice which was much faster and helped me skate a bit better.

In those days the goal judge would stand right on the ice behind the net, and if you didn't like him you always managed to run into him and knock him down. There were no lines on the ice — no blue line or centre line and even the crease around the net wasn't there. It really was quite a different game in many ways.

I think the game today is terrific. It's all speed. When I first began playing it was all position. You practically had to get a letter from the Pope and the twelve apostles it you went off your wing then. Today the players go any place they want. They don't play the positions the same way we did.

There used to be some very long games back in the early days too. I recall one game in Toronto that was 114 minutes and I never got off the ice once. It was like playing a couple of full games. At the finish of that game I weighed 132 pounds. When it began I think I was around 138 to 140 pounds.

Of course, I was really quite a small guy to be playing in the NHL. I never did weigh more than 150 pounds in my playing days. Today, most of the players seem to be big, six feet or more. A few of the guys were big, but not that many. Abel was big and so was Ching Johnson. Black Jack Stewart in Detroit was no midget and neither was Jimmy Orlando. Boston Eddy Shore, one of the greats, was big also. What a competitor! He was one of those guys who wouldn't even smile at you out on the ice, but when the game was over he was really a nice person.

A lot of the players were like that. They were murder on the ice when they played against you, but off the ice — total gentlemen. The only guy from an opposing team that I can remember smiling at me knocked me so hard into the boards that all my bones were rattling. He just skated by me when I was lying there and with a great big grin on his face he said, "What kinda perfume are you wearing tonight, Clancy?" I can't tell you here what I said back to him.

Gosh, I played a long time. Nine years with Ottawa and seven years with the Leafs. Connie Smythe got me to come to Toronto in the 1929-30 season. The Leafs had three lines then, four defencemen, and one goalkeeper. That was the full complement, fourteen in all. One guy that I remember well was "Happy" Day. He went on to become manager coach and just about everything else for the Leafs. He was terrific, but in my opinion he never got the credit he deserved — and that simply was because he didn't have the "colour" that they were looking for. He was a man who could do everything. He could teach how to play and he certainly taught me a lot. Also, at that time we had "The Kid Line" of Primeau, Conacher, and Jackson. We had Ace Bailey, Harold Cotton, and Andy Blair on another line, and we had Frank Finnegan. I don't remember them all, but I can tell you we had great teams here and fantastic players.

It's always difficult to put your finger on who was the best, especially now, since there've been so many changes in the rules and the style of play. I think Gretzky is a tremendous player, but before him there was Gordie Howe, Bobby Hull, Syl Apps, Charlie Conacher. I don't believe there ever has been a right-winger outside of Bill Cook who could hold a candle to Charlie Conacher. He could do it all. He played his position, he was rough, and he could shoot a puck very accurately. Every time he shot at the net it was a different kind of a shot — short side, far side on the ice, and all that sort of thing. He was a very good friend of mine and he protected me during games. I used to tell him that So-and-so was after me and he'd say, "I'll take care of him." And he would.

The rivalries between teams was fierce, and winning was all-important. Those players went so hard at each other during a game you'd wonder how they could even speak to one another after. But they did, and they were all really good friends — even those who were (or seemed to be) bitter enemies on the ice.

The smallest guy I ever played against was Aurel Joliet of the Montreal Canadiens. He was only the size of a minute, but was he *good.* He played with Billie Bushie and Howie Morenz on one line.

The greatest player of all time in my opinion has to be from among the ones who are playing today. Gretzky is great. Messier is great, and so too are some of those guys playing for Calgary. It's just too hard to name one from the whole roster of players I've seen over the years. I know we all say the game has changed so much that it's like comparing apples and oranges, but when I hear all this talk about change I think back to Mr. Moriarity, a teacher from my school who coached the hockey team. He would say, "Clancy, the idea is to put the puck in the net up at that end and keep it out of the net down here." When you think of it, that explains the whole game. Put it in there, and keep it out of here.

The roughest guy I can remember was Cleghorn with the Montreal Canadiens, followed closely by Newsy Lalonde. I recall coming out one night to take Frank Nihbor's place at centre ice and when I was passing Frank as I was going to take his position he said, "Watch him on the scratch." Now, I had never heard that expression before but I sure learned what it was that night. When I went to put my head down to try and help get the draw, I nearly had my nose taken off. Newsy Lalonde was the opposing player and as I was going for the puck, he was going for my nose.

Of course, you expected that kind of thing in what we felt was a game of give-and-take. You always waited for an opportunity to give just as good back to the guy as he gave you.

One night in Ottawa Rod Smiley who had come to play against us with the Toronto team gave me the worst whack that I'd ever got. He drove me up against the boards in the corner. I went down like a ton of bricks and it so happened that this was in the very corner where my father was sitting. All Dad could say was "Get up! Get up outa there!" When I got home I said, "Dad what do you do if you *can't* get up?" His reply was, "You get up anyway." I didn't forget that through all of my playing days and I still try to abide by that advice today.

I think that the man who did more for hockey in this country than anybody else never played the game. Foster Hewitt was a class individual, a credit to the game and a credit to his country. He was so good to the players and always so fair in the manner in which he called a game. He played a great part in making the game of hockey what it is today. We were very good friends.

I also think that Connie Smythe and Harold Ballard will go down as two more greats of the game too, although they weren't players either. Conn was a man of his word who never even asked me to sign a contract, and I didn't *need* one with him. Ballard is the same kind of man. They both spoke their minds, as indeed Harold still does. They had and have no fear of contradiction, as they believe in what they were and are saying. I was fortunate to have known both of them. Both of those men made it possible for me to spend my whole life in hockey the greatest game in the world.

Ena Edwards and Henry Lambert

An Outport Disaster

On the 18th of February, 1942, one of the worst disasters in United States naval history took place off the coast of Newfoundland. Two hundred and three sailors died and 187 survived, largely owing to the heroic efforts of the people of the outport communities of St. Lawrence and Lawn. The destroyer Truxton *and the supply ship* Pollux *were battered to pieces on the rocks during the worst storm in living memory for that part of the Newfoundland coast, which is no stranger to storms and disaster.*

Although this was a story of agony and death, it was also one of great humanity and courage. Two people who played a part, Ena Farrell Edwards and Henry Lambert, still live in the community of St. Lawrence.

ENA EDWARDS:

It wasn't until the morning of February 18, 1942, that we got word of the disaster. It was Ash Wednesday morning, and most of the people of St. Lawrence were on their way home from Mass, and there was a great sense of excitement everywhere. People were gathered in groups talking, and it wasn't hard to see that something was going on.

I asked someone, "What is it? What's happened?"

"There's a big warship ashore in Chamber's Cove," they said, "but we don't know much else about it."

And with that they all began rushing off in that direction. Within an hour there wasn't one male person left in town. All had gone to Chamber's Cove. Before long, most of the women were gone, too, except for a few like me who had to stay back.

In the store where I worked, all of the clerks and the manager had gone and I was the only one left behind to look after things, because the manager said to me before he left, "You stay here and keep the place open, because if it's as bad as they say, they're going to need the things we've got here."

How right he was. In the next three of four hours our supplies were exhausted. Every bit of tea and coffee went. All the stuff they needed for soups and sandwiches. The place was cleaned out as the rescue teams came back for more and more supplies, and of course they brought back all the news of how bad it was. How many sailors who had already been rescued, how many were still in the water, and so on. Also everybody in St. Lawrence knew of the need for clothing and blankets. All the stores were emptied of things like that, and in private homes people stripped the blankets off their beds and searched their houses for old overcoats and sweaters and anything else that could keep a body warm.

Finally, I could stand it no longer so I shut the store up — everything was gone anyway — and I went along to see the president of the local Patriotic Association which had been gathering up woollens for the war effort overseas. She gave me a big box of socks and sweaters that had been knitted for the soldiers, and my brother and I went in his truck with this stuff and we went from house to house, collecting whatever else we could. People would even pull their own things off their clothes lines to give to us. It was just marvellous. Our truck was soon loaded down with sweaters and long johns, overcoats and jackets of all kinds. These were all from families who wouldn't have more than one change of clothes, so what they were giving was really off their own backs.

By this time the survivors were arriving in town and the doors of every home were open to them. They were taken in, warmed up, clothed and fed, and, of course, scrubbed clean of that oil that covered their bodies. Every house had some of them. We had four at our place and some others had two or three or five, or however many they could handle. Most of these first survivors were in fairly good condition, and their morale was pretty high as they didn't have any inkling at that time of just how bad it really was or how many of their shipmates would die. We were able to get some music going because my brother and sister and myself all played piano, and my brother also played guitar and accordion.

We got other survivors over from the house next door, and we had a big sing-song going, with about twenty of us altogether. We just sat around the fireplace, and everything seemed so nice and normal, but at the same time, up at Chamber's Cove, the worst hell that you can immagine was going on. Henry Lambert, one of our neighbours, was one of the unsung heroes, and he can tell you about that.

HENRY LAMBERT:

I went to work in the mine at eight in the morning. We just got started to work underground when a fellow came down from the surface and said that there was a ship come ashore, and they wanted everybody back up on top. We all dropped tools and headed for the cage to take us up, and we immediately started running for Chamber's Cove. Before we got there we could smell the oil, so we knew it must be something big. It was a terrible day. The wind was howling and the waves were smashing in against the cliffs and we could feel the spray on our faces long before we got there.

We didn't know what to expect, really, but as we got closer we could see this big steel ship floundering out there on the rocks and the waters all around were covered with oil, and there were men in the water trying to make it to shore through all of that. The first thing we had to do was to get a rope down over those cliffs if we were going to be of any help at all. If was a straight drop down of something like a hundred feet, so getting down and getting back up with anybody we managed to pull out of that water was going to take a lot of teamwork.

We tied one end of the rope to a fence-post, and then I went down hand-over-hand to the rocks below. There was crude oil everywhere. All over the rocks and the beach and over the water from the shore out to the ship. It wasn't just a film of oil: it was about a foot and a half thick so you can imagine how impossible it was for a man to try and swim ashore in that, or for us on shore to walk on it. The men who were diving from the wreck into the sea only had a chance if they surfaced in a spot where there was no oil because as they would rise towards the surface, their heads couldn't break through this thick oil-skin, which was just like leather, and they simply drowned. We'd see these round humps in the oil slick where a man couldn't get through, and there was nothing we could do. The only ones we could get were those who were lucky enough to come up in a spot where the waves would crash through this oil.

We'd see a head pop through, and we'd go for that and get a rope around the body and pull him to shore. Sometimes they were dead by the time they popped through, and somethimes it wasn't even a body that popped out. It might be just a piece of wreckage from the ship, but we couldn't tell until we got to it. Anything that made it through that horrible oil we went for, as it *could* be a man and he *could* be alive! So we just pulled everything and anything out that might be a man. Even then, you couldn't be sure because they were so covered in this oily goo.

The ship wasn't that far off shore, but she was caught between two big rock clunkers and the wild sea kept rocking it back and forth, back and forth, breaking it up more all the time. We could see men diving off her sides, and some of us were trying to shoot lines out to her from shore, but they kept falling short and dropping into the water.

It was the wildest storm I ever saw in my entire lifetime. Some of those who dived off on the side facing the sea didn't get caught in the oil slick, but the waters were so wild that they didn't have a chance, and they got carried farther out and their bodies washed up about ten miles down the coast. There were about seventy-five of us on the rescue team, pulling men out and getting them back up the cliff. We were like a bunch of seagulls, racing around and grabbing at anything that moved.

I remember hearing one voice calling out from the water, and the boys tied a rope around me and I made for where I thought the voice came from. I had another lifeline rope with me, with a stick tied to the end of it. Then I saw what I thought was a man, so I swung the rope around my head a few times and threw it towards the figure in the water. It hit dead on, and it did turn out to be a man. He grabbed the rope and tied it around his waist and I started pulling him behind me towards shore through the oil slick. The weight was unbelievable! Like trying to pull a car uphill by yourself. At times I thought I wasn't going to make it, but when you're desperate something else seems to take over.

I was falling down, and going under myself, but I just kept pulling, and getting there inch by inch. On the way I bumped into another body, but I soon saw that he was already dead, so I kept going and finally, I had my man out and lying on the beach. Then I hauled him over to a place where the cliff was only twenty feet high. My fella was still alive, so I bundled him in such a way that he wouldn't get torn on the rocks, and began dragging him up the cliff until I reached the top. The snow was coming down thick and fast, and the wind was worse than ever by this time. I could hear nothing but the howling wind and I could see nothing but the snow, but soon some of the other volunteers came by and took over.

They had big bonfires going to thaw out the ones who were still alive and they had blankets and overcoats to put on them, and hot drinks and things like that. When I saw that my man was being looked after, I went to the site where the second ship was wrecked, and it was the same thing all over again. Some of it was so heartbreaking. Most of them were so young — just boys really — and they would just live long enough to be pulled from the water and then would die before we could get them thawed out. They seemed to die as soon as the heat from the bonfire would strike them.

I stayed there all day and all the following night, along with about three hundred other men from our two villages of St. Lawrence and Lawn. Not one of us gave up until we were sure there was nobody left alive at either wreck. I must say this, too: it may have been the men of the villages who pulled those survivors out of the water and up those cliffs, but it was the women of St. Lawrence and Lawn that kept them alive and nursed them back to health. It was a team effort from start to finish.

ENA EDWARDS:

It certainly was a team effort, and a desperate effort too, because those sailors were being pulled from water that was so cold that a human being couldn't last in it for more than a few minutes. And that terrible oil all over them — in their hair, in their eyes, and all over their bodies. That had to be got off as soon as possible. They had been cleaned up at the emergency station when they came out of the water, but that just took the big stuff off. When they came to our homes it took about another hour in the tub for each of them before they were clean. And even then you could see it in around their eyes.

One funny thing happened that I can remember so well. You know, most people around St. Lawrence had never seen a black man up to that time, and there were quite a few black sailors on those ships. Well, as the rescue operations proceeded, the men were responsible for getting them out of the water and the women took on the job of feeding them and cleaning them up. This one particular lady was really taking a long time getting this fellow clean. She said, "I just can't get the oil off this one. Look, I've been scrubbing for half an hour, and he's still black!" At this point the sailor said, "Please, lady, don't scrub me any more! This is as white as I get!" It was the first time she'd ever come in contact with a black man. The two of them had a great laugh over that afterwards.

As news of the disaster spread, naval ships from the United States base at Argentia came into the harbour, ready to take charge. There were helicopters flying all over the place, and there were Red Cross teams and so on. The whole town was alive with strangers. They immediately started to take the survivors away, but it was at this point that some of the townspeople began to object.

The U.S. Navy wanted to move the survivors back to the Navy hospital, but the townspeople who were caring for those who were very sick said: "No, these men can't be moved yet. They're too ill." So the

Navy had to back down and leave those men with the St. Lawrence people until their conditions improved. Even though we didn't have a resident doctor here at the time, we did have a couple of nurses, and a lot of women who had learned a great deal about caring for the sick, and they felt that those men would get better care from them than they would at a hospital. They were probably right, too.

Now there is something that's very important that I must tell you. I had received a small five-dollar camera from my mother as a Christmas gift less than two months before, and as the day of the disaster wore on, I made my mind up to go down with my camera to the site. I felt that this was something I should be getting on film.

The next morning, bright and early, I was there with several rolls of film, snapping everything I could. The ship on the rocks, and the ropes over the cliff, and the rescue site, and so on. The sailors were all out of the water by this time so I couldn't get any of them, but I got what I could. Over at Lawn Point I got pictures of the other ship, the *Pollux*, before she sank, and those were the only pictures that anybody managed to get. I took pictures of the funerals that took place every day in the town, and there wasn't an aspect of the disaster that I didn't get on film with my little Brownie. The strange thing about all of this is that those were the only pictures that anybody took, and when the story landed in newspapers all around the world, it was my pictures that were used to illustrate the story. Even in the *New York Times*! The *Montreal Standard* did the entire centrefold of their paper with my pictures. I can tell you I was some proud of that.

Funerals were a daily occurrence here for a while after that as other bodies were washed up on shore. Our parish priest would conduct a service at the graveside and a lot of the townspeople would show up to pay their respects. They were all interred in our cemetery here until the following summer when the U.S. Navy came and removed them for burial in the naval plot in Argentia, where they remained until the war was over. Then they were removed again and taken back to the States and buried in Arlington Cemetery.

There were more than two hundred young sailors who lost their lives in that disaster, and there were 187 survivors. We'll never forget it here, and in fact we do hold a memorial service on the 18th of February every year.

In 1954 the United States government, made us the gift of a twelve-bed hospital, the first one we ever had, in gratitude to our people. It still serves our community, and it also reminds us of our darkest but proudest day.

Dr. Robert Wilson

In the Footsteps of Banting and Best

The discovery of insulin in 1921 by two Toronto doctors, Frederick Banting and Charles Best, opened the doors to a new and longer life for millions of diabetes sufferers around the world. The first insulin for public use was manufactured at the Connaught Laboratories in Toronto, which had been in the business of developing vaccines for use in the field of killer diseases such as smallpox since 1914. Some of the leading researchers in the world of medicine have spent their working lives at Connaught, and their successes there have been impressive.

Dr. Robert Wilson of Vancouver came to Connaught from Vancouver in 1937, at a time when these Canadian laboratories were already world-famous, and he stayed until he retired more than forty years later.

When I first arrived on the scene, Connaught's work in insulin had spread their fame to every country in the world. The production of immunizing agents — diphtheria toxoid in particular at that time — was well-known because some of the pioneering studies on the effectiveness of diphtheria toxoid were done here in Toronto and the neighbouring areas of Hamilton and Brantford, areas that were some of the first in the world to successfully control diphtheria. These laboratories were started to control communicable diseases and particularly diphtheria, before the First World War in 1914.

The Connaught was about seven years old when Banting and Best discovered insulin in 1921, and it was their discovery of insulin that put these laboratories on the world map. Because of their international reputation, we were able to grab onto their coattails and keep on going. By this time, of course, Dr. Charles Best himself was a member of the Connaught staff, in charge of insulin production. Unfortunately [Sir Frederick] Banting died in 1942, but Dr. Best stayed on at the Toronto

University School of Hygiene. At that time you see, the School of Hygiene and Connaught Laboratories were partners. We shared the same building, the same director, and the same staff.

The work with insulin carried on because there was much to be done still to improve the quality of insulin, and that was being done by the Connaught staff too. What Banting and Best discovered was merely a substance that was in an extract of the pancreas. There were many other impurities other than the active insulin in this extract which caused distress on injection into a patient.

Our work was to find methods of refining the active ingredient, insulin, and it was eventually accomplished by a crystallization, which is a common method of refining any chemical. This method was discovered by a member of the Connaught staff.

The hope, of course, is that eventually needles can be done away with, and other methods of getting insulin to where it's needed can be utilized. Of course, we mustn't downgrade the needle, because it has done the job for millions of people over the years. There are many people over seventy years of age today who have been administering insulin to themselves since they were three or four years of age, and they remain well and active.

My own sister is one example. She developed diabetes when she was four. She's now seventy-two and she's been taking insulin with a needle since she was six. She's just been here to visit me from Vancouver. Prior to that, she went on a trip to Alaska, and she's going to Hawaii at Christmas to visit her daughter. The only effect it ever had on her is that she had to regulate her life around her diet and insulin — regularity of intake of food, and regularity of injections. A person with diabetes *has* to build their life around the fact they have this disease, and it's a lifelong commitment. Wherever they are, and whatever they do, they must remember always, those two things, diabetes and insulin. Aside from that, everything else is normal. They can still have a good and satisfying life.

In addition to any work I've done with insulin, my whole life's work has been in the area of vaccine, new vaccines for old diseases you might say. Diphtheria and polio vaccines are two examples and the deadly smallpox is another. Smallpox, I'm happy to say, is one that has been completely eradicated from the face of the earth. It literally claimed millions of lives before it was wiped out.

The last known case of naturally transmitted smallpox was in October of 1977 in Somalia. What a victory that was for those of us all over the world who were working on the eradication program. As one of my colleagues expressed it, "Everything since then has been an anticlimax." It's not often that a disease is completely eradicated from the world. That is the dream of all other medical researchers like myself.

Polio is another example. First, the vaccine to control it had to be found, and then the work just continued, to make that vaccine better and better, until we can now say polio is under control. Certainly in the industrialized countries, this aim has been achieved. There aren't many cases of polio in the industrialized world anymore. If they had two cases now they'd call it an epidemic, whereas before the polio vaccine there were literally millions of cases. That was another great medical miracle of this century. There have been others too.

Diphtheria is pretty well under control, at least in the industrialized nations, as are whooping cough, lockjaw, measles and tuberculosis. The thrust of the international community now is to get these diseases under control in the developing world as well. Control is the key word in all of this. Aside from smallpox there is no other disease that I know of that's been wiped out. Even with those under control, there has to be constant vigilance, and the research into better vaccines will always go on — I hope.

It's impossible to estimate the number of lives and the amount of crippling and suffering that have been saved by the men and women who work in medical laboratories like this one.

I guess one of the first major vaccines developed was the diphtheria toxoid, in the twenties and thirties. Dr. John Gerald Fitzgerald, the then director of the Connaught, was visiting the Pasteur Institute, Paris, France, in 1923, when a Dr. Gaston Ramon made a discovery he thought would be instrumental in being able to induce immunization to diphtheria. Dr. Fitzgerald immediately cabled the Connaught back in Canada to start work on this program immediately, which they did. Toronto and the surrounding areas put on a tremendous campaign with diphtheria toxoid inoculations. As a result, it was the first area in the world to really reduce diphtheria dramatically in a very short time.

Then, in the thirties, the whooping cough vaccine came along. After that, and just prior to the Second World War, another one of our staff members, again following Dr. Ramon's earlier discovery, worked on the tetanus toxoid for the deadly lockjaw disease. Now, because of this early start, we had the toxoid ready in time to vaccinate our armed services during the war. The result of that was that there was almost no tetanus in our wounded troops during the entire war. That was a vast contrast with all previous wars.

In the post-war era, a big advance was in the combining of the childhood vaccines for whooping cough and tetanus. That made us among the first in the world to do this. It did away with the need for a child to have up to as many as twelve different injections, and then when the polio vaccine came along, we combined the others with that. All of this made Connaught one of the major supporters of combined vaccines.

Another miracle during wartime was that of penicillin. We provided the Canadian government with that, which of course is a huge story of lives saved in itself. After the war, our role in the development of polio vaccine was very prominent. So, through the years there's been a steady procession of extremely important developments that emanated from this Canadian facility, which have had a vast impact on the world.

I am proud to have played a role in some of this. In looking back, it makes one feel that one's own life has helped to make a difference in the lives of others.

Hugh MacKay Ross

The Company of Gentlemen and Adventurers

Hugh MacKay Ross now lives in Winnipeg, but he spent most of his life in the northern reaches of Ontario as a fur trader with the Company of Adventurers and Gentlemen, the Hudson's Bay Company. Like many of the Bay personnel over its three hundred and eighteen years in Canada, Hugh MacKay Ross came from Scotland, where he was born, in 1912. He was an inexperienced greenhorn when he first came to Canada in 1930 as a lad of eighteen years. The wild and spectacular country north of Lake of the Woods in northern Ontario, still unknown to most Canadians, was the first he saw of this land of ours, and he saw it from an Ojibway canoe.

One wonders how and why Hugh MacKay Ross chose Canada, especially the North. Was it the adventure books he had read as a child, stories from the Boys' Own Annual*? Not at all. Nothing so romantic.*

I answered an ad in a magazine, because what I really wanted was a job, any job. I couldn't get work anywhere. I couldn't attend university because my family couldn't afford it, and when I saw this advertisement saying that the Hudson's Bay Company interviewed applicants twice a year I thought, "This is for me." I had had offers before this to go to Western Africa and the Malay States from old boys who had come back to my school, but I didn't want that as I couldn't bear the thought of snakes! I hated them, and I figured those countries were full of them.

So after the interview with the Hudson's Bay, I was given the opportunity of going to Canada. My brother was already with the army in India, and my sister was in Australia. My father had served in the Sudan in the Boer War in South Africa, so I thought it was time for one of us to try Canada.

I knew nothing at all about the country, except what I had read by R.N. Ballantyne. Every boy read Ballantyne in those days, and of course in reading the dime novels of the time, I knew all about "the noble red man" and that sort of thing, but my idea of the Hudson's Bay Company was Arctic—just *Arctic*! I don't really know why I thought that. Possibly I met Mr. McGibbon, a neighbour who had come home on holidays. He had been to Fort Chimo, and I remember that all I wanted to do was go to the Arctic after talking to him. That to me spelled adventure—carrying the British flag around the world, and doing work for the English. The Scots were always pretty good at that. First they did the fighting. You'll recall from those days how they always "sent the gunboat up the river"—to blow the natives all to hell? It was the stuff that dreams are made of, and I'm afraid that I was always a romatic.

I read anything I could get my hands on that smacked of adventure, and this chance to go to Canada was the answer to my dreams.

I felt there had to be more to life than being a solicitor's clerk or working in a bank. The Hudson's Bay Company, the Company of Adventurers and Gentlemen, seemed to be just the ticket. There was a certain appeal just in the name itself. And, in fact, once you become a Hudson's Bay man, you are always a Hudson's Bay man. The HBC rates higher than God with the men in the bush, even to this day. When it comes to breaking one or the other's laws, they think a lot before breaking any of the Company's regulations.

Well, when I landed in Canada, I was sent to North Bay, which was district office for that part of Northern Ontario. Then another chap and I were put on a train to get off at Hudson, Ontario. From there, a couple of days later, they put me on a smaller local train to get off at a place called Jones, a wayside station. That's where I was picked up by two Indians in a canoe and taken up to Grassy Narrows, my first Indian posting. Those noble red men must have had a great laugh later over this greenhorn in the double-breasted suit and brown pointy-toe shoes who was loaded down with books and violin, sitting in the middle of their canoe.

At Grassy Narrows, I met the man in charge, a grizzled old veteran with grey hair named Donald Murchison, garbed in brown corduroy, moleskins, tartan jacket, never a tie, and an old Hudson's Bay cap on his head. The first thing he said to me was in Gaelic, and I said, "I don't understand you." "Ah hah! You don't have the Gaelic do you? A hell of a fine Scotsman you are!" I could see I was off to a poor start. He was further incensed by the letter of introduction I handed him, which said, "This lad is here as an apprentice bookkeeper to learn the business, and he is not to be treated as a chore-boy."

This infuriated old Donald, but he went along with it, even though I would have preferred to be allowed to chop wood or drag water up from the lake to pass the time. But no—I was only allowed to do the books. Murchison gritted his teeth, and said, "It's a poor outfit that can't afford at least one gentleman, and I guess here in Grassy Narrows, you're it!"

Old Donald's wife was a native woman, and they talked Ojibway in the house all the time, except when they talked to me. Donald and I always ate at the table by the front window in the living room. His daughters waited on us, and they and the mother would eat in the kitchen separate from us, which is something I had never seen before.

They were really quite good to me, but I still got very homesick at the start. Very homesick. If I could have afforded to, I would have come right back home in the first six months. However, I had no option, and I'm glad that I didn't. In later years, I always told new boys that if they could get over the first six months, they'd have it made. Fortunately for me, while I was in the depths of my loneliness, an old Aberdeen man came up in the early spring to inspect the post. He talked to me like a Dutch uncle, and then said, "I know, lad. It's tough, but you'll get over it and you are leaning a lot about the business and you are picking up the Indian languages. Hang in till next summer, and I'll have you transferred to another post."

"Okay," I said, "I'll stay." I made it through the winter, and sure enough I was transferred to Minaki, north of Kenora, Ontario, in the Lake-of-the-Woods country. What a contrast that was! It was there that I truly became a Canadian. It was a contrast I needed because in the bush country of Grassy Narrows, I was cut off from the world. There was never a newspaper, except for the ones my mother sent me from Scotland with the home-town news. But I wasn't learning one thing about Canada. In that little settlement, I might as well have been on the moon.

At Minaki, I was to see another side of Canadian life. I met many young fellows and made friends with them, even though they called me "an oatmeal savage," and put me through the usual break-in period. But I lived and I learned to speak the way they did — to say twelve-gauge cartridges, not twelve-bore shells. I learned not to ask for a reel of cotton, but a spool of thread. Things like that.

For three months in the summer, Minaki really was the playground of the wealthy, but there was a core of locals who worked at the golf course and Minaki Lodge. There were railway men who lived there too, and so it was a good rounded community. At the Hudson's Bay, I worked hard from 5:30 in the morning till around nine at night, and sometimes later than that. Long hours to be sure, but in those days of the Depression, one didn't complain. You were lucky to have any job. I was getting twenty-five dollars a month and my board. The locals weren't nearly as fortunate. Their jobs were seasonal, and then they had to forage around for other things to do.

In winter they cut blocks of ice for the cottagers, or cut cordwood. That was an awful job. I can't imagine anything worse than walking two or three miles into the bush in winter, and cutting cordwood by hand with a bucksaw. At the end of the day they might have made two dollars. Those of us who worked for Hudson's Bay considered ourselves very lucky.

It's called "The Bay" now, but before 1950 that was a term that was never permitted by those who worked for the Company, even though everyone used it. We had to call ourselves "The Company of Adventurers" or "The Hudson's Bay Company."

There weren't a lot of settlers in northwestern Ontario at the time, but I got to know all the ones who were there. One fellow I remember, a commercial fisherman called Bud Hatch, would go up the English River and buy fish that the Indians caught. He would take them out in his boat and ship them to the markets in the States. He was a good man, who dealt fairly with the natives. That was the first time I saw sturgeon. I thought they were godawful huge things, at least five feet long. They were getting a dollar a pound for the caviar in them. Besides Bud up there, there would be a game warden or a Mounted policeman on patrol, or a native constable. And then, once a year, the treaty party would come in to pay the Indians their due. Then there was the Indian agent and the doctor along with the Anglican and Roman Catholic missionaries. The rest of the year you wouldn't see many other people other than the natives.

Canon Sanderson was a wonderful man, a full-blooded Cree from Kenora. He travelled thousands of miles a year in northwestern Ontario, looking after the needs of the natives. He saw to it that the old had warm clothing, and enough food before he began preaching religion. He'd come to the HBC store and give me an order for so-and-so and this-and-that. Then he'd sign it and send it in to the Department of Indian Affairs.

We'd also see the occasional American sportsman. They would fly into Red Lake and come from there over to our store at Grassy Narrows for their supplies. The Americans always wanted to go where no one had been before — to places where there wasn't a facility of any kind. I would hire an Indian guide for them, who provided his canoe, his tent, and the grub. I would set the price for all this, and the American would pay me. These fellows wanted to get a deer in wild country, so they could tell their friends how dangerous and tough it was.

Those Indian guides could find them a deer in two hours, but I would tell them "Take them up and down the river for a couple of days before you let them bag one. Otherwise they won't be happy, and neither will you, because you won't have made any money."

I had a great feeling for the natives. I just loved them. They reminded me of the broken clans of Scotland. The McPhees, the MacGregors, and so on. They struck me as being something like them — weather-beaten nomads with no man as their master, perfectly at home in the bush. An Indian will never starve or get lost in bush country. To me he is still noble, but not savage. There's been too much paternalism towards them between all the governments and the missions, however well-intentioned it might have been. You can't turn a semi-nomadic native into a white-man farmer or market gardener. That was the biggest mistake ever made, to even attempt to do that.

My gosh, they would take their kids away to residential schools, where they were not permitted to speak their native tongue. Just English. And when they came back to their homes at the age of sixteen or seventeen, some of them even married, they didn't even know how to set a snare for rabbits, or set a net for fish. The only good thing they did was to give the old age pension to them. Instead of being a drag on family resources, the old people were independent and could pay their way.

The family allowance was another thing. By the time that came in, there were schools right on the reservation, and in order to get the money the children had to attend these schools. This meant the mother had to stay at home with them, while father went off alone on his hunts. Before this, they all hunted together as a family unit.

The Indians are great family people in everything they do, so in effect, the family allowance broke up centuries of tradition in one stroke. The father would only get back home every three or four weeks. It spoiled the whole routine of their lives. It cut down on their earning ability, because they had to be on that reservation when they should have been making another circle of their trapline.

I like these people very much. I still have many friends among them, and I can converse with them in the Ojibway language. I also understand some Cree, although I hadn't had as much time with them and didn't learn it properly. The Cree are a very majestic type of Indian, tall and very formal.

The Indian languages are very beautiful, and the words spell out what they mean. For instance, the word for Grassy Narrows means a grassy area down near the river. It's a very sonorous language, and when the chief wants to make a speech, he can sound very convincing.

When I first met the Indians and heard them speak many years ago, I thought their language was some ungodly patois, grunted out by savages. It's not, and they're not, of course. They have no swear words in their language. When they feel they have to swear, they turn to English. They are a very gentle people, and if they feel that you like them, they will respond to you as much as you try to understand them. They'll do anything for you and are totally trustworthy in their own environment.

Unfortunately, when they're with white men they adopt all of the white man's ways, good and bad; but a native in his own element, in the bush, is proud, honest, and not scared to look anybody in the eye.

I've never looked upon myself as anything but a fur trader. I went into the North when there were no roads, no airplanes, no radio. In the summer you paddled. There were no outboards, and hardly any established communities. When my wife and I went to Grassy Narrows, we were the only two white people there, on an island in the middle of the lake with Indian reserve all around us. It was canoe in summer and dog team in winter, and, believe me, dog-team travelling is not the romantic thing that the movies would have you believe. They show it as people all wrapped up in furs, gliding across the snow with the Indian driver behind, cracking whip. That's a lot of bull.

In the North, a dog team is a working team, and nothing else. There are only four dogs, each of which can pull a hundred-pound load of freight, plus the driver's sleeping-bag, grub box, cooking pail, the dog food, and your axe. You never ride. You walk or trot behind, kind of a dog-trot which is neither a walk or a run. More than four dogs is useless, as they never all pull together. There's always one lazy dog who puts the rest all out of kilter. Four you can control. My response to those who say it must be so romantic is, "Looking up the south end of four dogs going north all day is not romantic!" Thirty miles in one day was about an average day for me, although I had days when I did forty or even more. The thing that must be remembered, though, is that I wasn't riding. I was dog-trotting all the way. Thirty or forty miles a day is about the best one can do in bush country, and you never think of how far you've gone, or how far there is yet to go. You simply put all that out of your mind and think beautiful thoughts.

Something I learned early on was not to go where there was no trail. The Indians who made those trails knew what they were doing, and they knew it was foolish to take chances. It was also drummed into me that you never take shortcuts. If the Indian trail goes to the side of the lake and in some cases over rocks, there's a reason for it. Maybe there's a spring under the water and the ice is weak. I learned to follow the footsteps of someone who had gone before.

The only time I ever got lost was when I got confused about directions that I'd been given. I came to a fork where two trails went off in different directions. The one I took just ran out, and by this time it was getting dark, and I was getting a bit nervous. Off in the distance, I saw a light and I headed my dog team for it. Inside this old house I found a group of Indians who were stopping off there on their way to Kenora to see their children for Christmas. They made a little space behind the stove for me, by what looked like a pile of luggage with a tarpaulin hauled over it. So I climbed into my sleeping-bag alongside this pile and went to sleep. In the morning, when everyone was preparing to get out on the trail, one of them came over and pulled the tarp off this pile of "luggage." Well, I got quite a start when the luggage turned out to be a dead body that they were taking along with them to be buried in the rites of the church. It really shook me to think that I'd been sleeping all night with a corpse. However, I got over it quickly, and in fact helped them load it on a toboggan and followed them out to where I got back on the trail again.

As a fur trader for the Hudson's Bay Company, there was much to learn. I knew nothing about it when I got there, so I had to start from the bottom. I found that the easiest part in dealing with the natives was arriving at prices for their furs. You see, it was done on kind of a barter system. I knew what every bag of flour or sugar and so on was worth, right down to the penny, because I handled all the invoices at the store. There were guidelines to follow as to the expected percentage of profit, so that part was easy. As far as the pelts were concerned, we had guidelines, too, for quality. There were samples which showed number ones, number twos, good seconds, poor seconds, thirds, fourths, and so on. After a while, it became second nature to know the value at a glance and I got so that I could practically just look at fur and could tell what part of the district it came from by the way it was dressed or stretched.

We kept records of each Indian: how much fur he brought in each year; how much debt he was allowed; whether he paid it; and so forth. Based on these notes, we also would prepare proposed amounts of credit that each trapper was allowed. Once we had all that, we were set to start trading goods for fur.

An Indian would come in and say, quite formally, "Are you going to give me debt?" You would reply, "Oh yes, we'll give you debt." "How much?" would be the next question, so you'd tell him. If you were going to give him fifty dollars, you'd say "forty." He might be happy, and maybe not, but it was all part of a game that had been played many times over the years. Both sides knew how to play it, and both sides knew the rules. Finally, he would accept the forty, but on my side, I would always know that he'd come back after the deal was made, for some merchandise that he'd "forgotten," something that would bring it up to the fifty dollars that both of us knew he would get in the first place.

Indians are not belligerent people. They love to talk. If you could stand and listen to half a dozen of them orating among themselves, and with the Hudson's Bay manager for an hour or so, you'd see what I mean. They get everything out of their systems in these sessions, and the manager will listen to what they have to say. He knows that if he's going to get along in his post, he'd better listen to what his customers like or don't like. That's something they've learned in the three hundred and eighteen years they've been here. In fact, the Indians have a name for the Company which means "Everybody working together."

For the fur trader who comes in and tries to make a fast buck off them they have another which means "the here today and gone tomorrow." They know the Hudson's Bay Company is going to always be there. That's the difference. Over the years I truly became as one with them. I knew their problems and I shared their joys and sorrows. I attended their weddings, and often conducted the services as they buried their dead.

In the forty-one years I was with them, I learned to love and respect the Indians, and when I left I did so with the knowledge that I was every bit as fair with them, as they always were with me.

Jeff Wyborn

Like Birds in the Air

Canada has its share of genuine heroes in all walks of life, and ranking up at the top of the list are the bush pilots, those intrepid young men in their flying machines who despite all the dangers were the ones who opened up our Northland. First were the boys out of the First World War, pilots with names like "Punch" Dickins and "Wop" May. They flew their small planes into the great unknown delivering the explorers, the prospectors, and supplies, knowing little of their destinations or what to expect when they got there. Maps and charts were few, and the weather was the greatest constant menace. The North was a new land and a land of mystery. They risked their lives to open it up.

Following on their tails came the young men who had chosen these originals as their heroes, young men of the twenties and the scarcity years of the Depression. These were youngsters who sold newspapers and scratched for pennies to pay for their flying lessons. Young men like Jeff Wyborn of South Porcupine in Northern Ontario. As a child, the sight and sound of a plane would drive young Jeff to distraction.

For the first six months that I worked at the airfield I got nothing at all, but I was so raring to go, I would have paid them. I was scratching for money for lessons all over the place. I'd go out delivering milk at five in the morning to earn enough to pay for streetcars and bus transportation that would drop me about four miles from where I was going. I'd walk the remainder of the way, but I was only seventeen and full of energy. I would hang around the air service at Bishop's Field where those great early pilots like Al Cheeseman, Duke Schiller, and Doc Oakes operated. They were the real pioneers of northern aviation in this part of Canada.

I had been airplane crazy from as far back as I can remember. When I could barely walk my mother says I would run to the window or outside whenever I heard one. All through school I spent more time tracing airplanes out of comic books and magazines than I did studying. I was constantly creating First World War air battles on sheets of paper, and I can't think of ever wanting to do anything else except fly. Maybe I should have had a broader outlook than that, but I don't know, even today after fifty years of flying, that I could have been happy doing anything else.

When I began flying back in 1937, it was exciting for anyone to get a ride in a plane, but for me, finally at the controls, it was an unbelievable thrill. Before I could fly I would get excited simply touching the wing of a plane. I'd be so thrilled about that that I would come home from the field and brag to my family and friends that I actually touched one — I really did!

Getting a license in those days was quite a bit different than it is now. Pilots were sent solo when their ability and know-how was judged by the instructor to be sufficient. Some went solo after just three hours; some took eight; some went solo after sixteen hours. I made it in about ten hours. All the instructor would say to you would be "Okay, Jeff, let's go up and do a couple more circuits." He would not mention that this was the day you were going solo. You'd do the usual couple of take-offs and landings, and then he might say, as he did to me, "I'm going to the washroom now. Away you go. Take off outa here." That was it. I was a pilot from that moment.

It was the end of all those years of just wanting to do it and of selling the newspapers and pop bottles, delivering milk, or doing anything to make a few more cents against the eight- or ten-dollar cost of a lesson. I don't believe anyone can really imagine the sense of exhilaration I felt. The nestling had finally gotten his wings, and the world was mine.

The airplane was still a novelty back in the late thirties and all kinds of people were attracted to learning to fly. I recall one middle-aged man who had done well enough to be given his chance at soloing. Well, he got up all right and was doing fine until it was time to bring her down. He didn't seem able to do it. He'd come down and make a pass, then give her the gun and go up again, time after time. He'd get to maybe ten or fifteen feet off the ground and he just couldn't manage to land! The instructor, O.J. Weaven, and I went up in another plane to help bring him down. O.J. had written out a sign on a small blackboard and I held it up as we flew alongside this fellow with instructions on the board telling him what to do to get down, and to follow us. Well, we had him right down to within ten feet of the runway and just when we thought we had him, up in the air he went again. We did the same thing five or six times and finally, thankfully, he brought it in safely. I don't know if that man ever took a plane up again.

Even though I had my license, I couldn't start flying and making money immediately. I had my engineer's license too by this time, and I earned my way mostly as an engineer and part-time pilot. This went on for a few years until I got on with Severn Enterprises and Austin Airways. I was based in Sioux Lookout flying supplies to various communities and in the summer, doing sturgeon hauls. When Indians were involved in this type of fishing, we would haul their catches out to Sioux Lookout and Hudson in northwestern Ontario. I picked up one sturgeon at a spot on Winisk Lake where it was netted and it weighed in at around two hundred pounds. This is pretty unbelievable for a fish in an inland water. It was like a big cow. Quite a load for a small plane. We would go into twenty or twenty-five different lakes just to pick up sturgeon. It was quite an industry. We'd bring in supplies and we'd pay them so much a pound for the fish.

By this time we had fairly good maps and usually knew where we were because all of our trips were done by what we called "contact flying." That's where you relate to your position through maps and the time element. Anyway, after flying over an area five or six times you became used to it and the rivers and lakes came to be as familiar as the highways down south. There are hundreds and hundreds of lakes up there, but you get to know them in the same way that you recognize faces. I would always position my map in such a manner that it would relate to the direction I was going in. In that way I could match the shape of a lake on a map to the real thing down below. In addition, you were also flying a compass course, and every fifteen minutes I'd check my position. It's nice to know where you are because if you do have to go down, you can say, "Well, I'm over Windigo Lake and have to land due to the weather." That was if you had a radio, of course.

I never had a crash in all those years except for one time when we were disabled by what was really a mishap rather than a crash. This was one of those times when a bad gust of wind pitched the plane in the wrong direction and this was followed by a stalled engine and a dive into the water. It was just a case of repairing the craft and flying out again. It wasn't serious at all.

One of the advantages of bush flying is that there is usually a lake or a river to land on when it's needed. You can always find shallow water, or, for that matter, a swamp to set the machine on. It doesn't matter, as long as you're down safely. Even if one has to go into the trees sometimes, you'll be okay if you're in a float-equipped plane. The floats will take the impact if you appraoach them at the proper speed and altitude and more or less stall the engine as you "mush" the plane into the trees.

Of course, there are always accidents where the pilots get killed. I believe they are mostly caused by weather-forced landings in places where the pilot is unfamiliar with the terrain. You know, you can be flying along in beautiful sunshine and suddenly it will change. Hurricane-strength winds will toss the plane around like a wood chip. You can get hailstorms, rainstorms and white-outs. Landmarks disappear and you don't know where you are, or how to get out of your situation. That's when you really feel alone but it's no time to panic either. You need all your wits together to keep from ending up against the side of a mountain or into a tree. I've lost some friends that way, and I've felt very upset, too, but that's part of the game.

Back then, we depended a lot on the Hudson's Bay Company, which had radio in all their outposts in places like Rupert's House, Old Factory, Great Whale, and so on — Albany, Attawapiskat, etc. All of the Hudson's Bay radios were on morse code and some of our pilots were trained in that, so we could get our weather from them. One Hudson's Bay manager at Moose Factory was more concerned about the pilots up there and looked after them more than anybody else. He would say, "Where is Rusty Blake? Where is George, or Jeff, or Hal?" He was never happy until he knew the whereabouts of everyone; and as far as we were concerned it was nice to know that there was someone on the ground who was so concerned. That's big country up there and it's not some place one would want to get lost.

There were so few people in the North at the time that all of us working there felt like a big family and nobody on the ground would be able to rest if there was an unaccounted-for plane. We had no facilities at all except our aircraft and some emergency equipment, plus a place to stay at Moose Factory in the Hudson Bay staff house. However, everybody in the North would invite you for a meal, or to stay over night. At the missions, people were always glad to see you, and when the plane landed the entire village would come down to meet you. It was real family. Everybody would be chitting and chatting, and looking for mail and/or parcels.

It was a big event in any of those northern communities when a plane came in. We'd bring in passengers and freight and then in the southbound trips we'd bring out furs and TB patients, who were Indians and Eskimos for the most part. Tuberculosis was rampant then, so we'd bring them out to hospitals.

We never flew at night. It was a VFR operation [visual flight rules] in those days, because we had no facilities to land after dark, although there were a few times when I got caught attempting to make it to an out-of-the-way settlement. You'd just hope and pray that there wouldn't be a rock in the water, or that some other plane wouldn't be anchored out where you couldn't see it. On those occasions your heart would pound hard, but we had great faith in the planes.

We flew the same ones for years and they became almost human to us. On long trips alone, we'd actually talk to them, and in a way they would seem to answer, with a little purr or a rattle, and sometimes a growl. They were like babies and we could recognize even the smallest abnormal sound — like a mother with her infant.

Sometimes we'd have to do seat-of-the-pants flying, but not too often. That phrase, by the way, originated in the First World War, and really means what it says — seat of the pants. If you make a bad manoeuvre and it's not quite right — say, when you're making a turn — the first place you'll feel it is in the seat of your pants, and lots of our training was done that way — learning to recognize the changes we could feel in the seat of the pants, and what those changes meant.

I have never in all those years lost my enthusiasm for the air. Whenever I'm down I can't wait to get back up again. It's a must! Some of us older fellows classify flying as a disease. It's something that one cannot explain. You have to fly to know what it's all about — the idea of controlling a machine in the free air.

I have felt and still feel more relaxed when I'm flying than I do anywhere else, because as a pilot you become part of that machine. You feel as if it's part human and that it knows exactly what you're going to do next. It's like a body within a body. It's one of those things that happen if you've flown long enough and flown the same aircraft for quite some time. In my case, after fifty years in the air, that's exactly how it is with me.

Muriel Braham Wells

Song of the Open Road

For many — perhaps most — people, age is something measured by the calendar, and one behaves during the various stages of life as one is expected to behave for that particular age. "Act your age" is a common and very old expression. For others, however, calendar age means nothing. For them, age is a state of mind and they do what they want — when they want.

So it is for Muriel Braham Wells of Grafton, Ontario. While she was raising her family she had a dream of getting herself an old fishing-boat from the Maritimes and venturing out on the wild Atlantic, the waves and spray lashing her face, and above all, feeling a sense of freedom. Well, when the time came she couldn't find the old fishing-boat of her dreams, but she did find an old maritime boatbuilder who fashioned the boat of her dreams and away she went.

I don't think that any of the things I've done are particularly startling or adventurous, but I do feel that people should always aim to do anything that is new to them as they proceed through life. I'm not trying to impress anyone or make a name for myself; I just get an idea in my head, and more or less give it a try to see what it's like.

Perhaps it's a spirit of adventure that came from my parents. I just don't know. I do know though, that it's not an attempt to hold back the calendar, as no matter how one tries, that's not possible. However, you can keep enjoying life for all of your life. My own parents must have had some of that, because they were part of that group who gave up the settled life in Eastern Canada in the early part of this century to make their way to the homestead country of western Canada. That must have been high adventure for them and those other pioneers who trekked across the western plains.

Muriel Braham Wells

I suppose I always had little dreams of doing various things, but the one that stayed with me long after my family had left the nest was one of owning an old, used fishing-boat, which I would buy from a fisherman in the Maritimes and which I would sail out of there up along the coast and finally up the St. Lawrence. When my kids were in their teens and still at home we'd sit around the kitchen table and discuss all the different aspects of such an undertaking, including how to get the smell of the fish out of such an old boat and how I could learn to be a sailor. It was a dream, really, rather than a plan, but it was a dream I never put out of my mind.

When all the children had gone off to build their own lives, I decided to go down to the Maritimes and see what I could find in the way of a boat. Well, I searched all over the fishing-villages of New Brunswick, and I'll never forget the shock and disappointment I felt. I had a nice little manageable boat in mind, but all of those boats were forty feet long, or longer. The kind one would need a crew to handle. I thought that surely there was something somewhere that would be just right for me as I went from village to village for a week. The weather that spring in New Brunswick was cold and miserable, and on Mother's Day I had made up my mind to go back home and put my dream on hold. I got in my car, ready to begin the long trip home when I spotted a man by the side of the road selling lobsters. I bought one from him, and as usual I told him of my wanting to buy a boat. He heard me out and said that there was an old man over in Buctouche who built boats and that I should go see him.

So that's how I met Arthur Jaillet, the boat-builder. He was such a nice man. He had very little English, but after we drove around for about two hours in my car, I got the story across to him and he said, "By God, missus, I'll build your boat!" I didn't have much money, but when I told him how much I did have, he didn't turn a hair. He went back to his house and he and his wife worked it all out in French, and they turned to me at last, and told me it would cost $650.00 for the hull. That was $50.00 less than I wanted to spend, so that was wonderful. I went away then, and the following year 1973, in June, he called me to tell me that my boat was ready and that I should come for it. Well, I was ready, so I got in touch with this fifteen-year-old boy who said he'd go down with me to help get it ready to sail home.

We went down and he helped put in the finishing touches, which included the engine. Two weeks later a big truck backed in, picked up *Le Bateau*, which I had christened it, and hauled it to the water. We hadn't even finished painting it. The young fellow and I got in; started the engine and began our thousand-mile trip along the coast and headed out for the St. Lawrence, with our final destination the port of Toronto. I had never handled anything bigger than a rowboat before that.

The fishermen down that way tried to dissuade me from making the trip. They said that I didn't know the water, that I was sure to hit a rock and sink, and all of this sort of thing. My friend Arthur the boatbuilder was fearful for me also, and wanted me to ship the boat to Ontario. He said, "Missus, you're going to drown pretty damn quick!" But taking the boat home by water was a big part of my dream, so nothing they could say would stop me. I felt I was ready as I had taken some navigation courses that winter, and thought their fears for my safety were groundless.

I must admit, though, that all the way up along the coast to Montreal, it was tough! I was very tense, because it was only then that I realized just how little I knew and how dangerous it could be. I really was just running the boat "by the seat of my pants." The navigation course I took was probably okay, but I found that I never stuck to any of the charts I drew. I simply went "by gosh and by golly," judging distances by eye and looking out for landmarks like lighthouses and other things like that.

The only times I really was frightened, though, was once crossing over the St. Lawrence and when crossing the Bay of Chaleur. The weather on those occasions was ghastly. The boat was pitching and wobbling and tossing around like a chip of wood. I had to hang onto the wheel all the time to keep from being washed overboard. When I needed anything I had to keep one hand on the wheel and reach for it. I couldn't even let go to go to the bathroom. The wind was roaring and the rain kept pelting down, and sometimes we couldn't see the tops of the waves. I discovered then that at times like those, you're just too busy to be too afraid.

The first thing I did when out trip was over and we'd reached Toronto, was to phone my friend, the boat-builder back in Buctouche, New Brunswick. "Arthur," I said: "I made it!"

"Oh my God, I'm so thankful missus! I can't wait to tell them fishermen they were wrong!"

That trip inspired me to try my hand at writing a poem about it, my first serious attempt at writing poetry.

Le Bateau
Before the memories begin to fade,
I'll tell you of a trip I made
Sailing along the ocean blue
Up the St. Lawrence and Seaway, too:

The Thousand Islands to port and starboard
Kingston, Belleville, Toronto Harbour —
I saw them all!

My little boat, called *Le Bateau*,
Fulfilled a dream I came to know;
A fishing craft of New Brunswick spruce,
Created there — to set me loose.
Shippegan, Gaspé, Rivière-du Loup,
Percé, Grand Breve, Cap-des-Rosiers too —
I saw them all!

'Twas twenty-three days from start to finish
When winds did rise and then diminish
The mighty St. Lawrence — long and straight
Where currents run at rapid rate,
Baie-des-Sable, Métis, Cape Ste. Anne,
Malbaie, L'Isle Verte and Matane,
I saw them all!

Buctouche, New Brunswick, I'll never forget
Where my boat was built by Arthur Jaillet;
But I sailed away on the ocean blue
Through Northumberland Strait by the Island Miscou,
Bonaventure, Rimouski, Trois Pistoles, Montreal —
On to Toronto, ports large and small —
I saw them all!

Later I had two other voyages: I returned alone to New Brunswick in 1976 and went alone from Buctouche to the Island of Anticosti and on to the North Shore of the St. Lawrence, up as far as Natashquan, above Havre-Saint-Pierre, and back to Buctouche in the summer of 1977.

My next adventure started in 1980 and was of a very different nature. On 5.4 acres of land in Grafton, Ontario, I started a nut farm called "The Crow's Nest." I learned about nuts and nut-tree growing through the organization called the Society of Ontario Nut Growers (SONG) and now I have the honour of being president. I don't pretend to know a lot about the art of grafting or the more technical skills in nut growing, but what I have learned I enjoy sharing by speaking at local horticultural societies.

Most people are the same as I was in 1980, knowing nothing about nut culture. I have hundreds of trees now, Carpathian Chinese chestnuts, butternut, and pecan. One special project is a group of three hundred heartnuts from which I hope to one day have a "superior" tree. Now, this is a satisfying project, and something I'll keep as an anchor in my life, but the open road has called me again.

I had a couple of cataract operations earlier this year, and it was while this was going on that I started thinking of the many areas of this great country I had never seen. So I hit on the idea of getting one of those camper trucks that you see, and just getting out there on the road, and going. The only plan I have is to be gone five months all by myself, heading east, and down into that lovely, rugged country of Newfoundland, going wherever there's some kind of a road that will take my truck. There's lots there that I want to see, and lots of people there that I want to meet. But you know, no matter where I go, I don't think I'll ever forget that lovely little town in New Brunswick that was really the catalyst for getting me started, and keeping me out of the rocking chair. This poem is for that town:

Buctouche, Buctouche, beautiful town
On the river,
Hiding behind your sandbar seven miles long.
Your old man built me a boat
Northumberland hull and strong
And sealed a bond of friendship
To carry me ever along.

Buctouche, Buctouche, beautiful town
On the river
Hiding behind your sandbar seven miles long
The bridge, the church, the main street
Are pictures I lovingly share
The Acadian people so friendly
Leave a feeling beyond compare.

Save a place for me at your dock
We'll return again and again.
To tie close to the bridge and the church
And be part of your town again.

Buctouche, Buctouche, beautiful town
On the river
Hiding behind your sandbar seven miles long.

This country is chock-full of beautiful little towns like Buctouche, and so many beautiful people too. It's a shame not to meet as many as I can. Next time I may head north and pick up a dog team!

Gordon James Duncan

Bringing the Law to the Peace River

Gordon James Duncan was born in 1884 in London, England, and it was his love of horses that led him first to the Mounted Police in South Africa where he fought in the Boer War. From there he made his way to Canada and joined the old North West Mounted Police. Then he graduated to the British Columbia Provincials as an inspector, and a posting to the Peace River in British Columbia.

I was twenty-one when I arrived in Canada. That was 1905, and I carried with me an honourable discharge from the Mounted Police of Natal in Zululand. It also gave me the option of rejoining the Natal force in six months if Canada didn't work out for me, but obviously it did as I didn't get back to Zululand until 1960 when I went for a visit. Actually, I knew I'd never get back within the six months because at that time transportation was very difficult. There was only one boat a month from Vancouver to Australia.

Anyway, I was very impressed with what I saw of Western Canada so I joined the North West Mounted Police, and made my mind up on the spot to stay.

I didn't exactly get into the NWMP immediately. For a while I worked on a horse ranch in Calgary and there was a bunch of mounted police stationed near this ranch. The sergeant was named MacLeod, and he was the son of the same MacLeod who was a founder of the NWMP, the same man that Fort MacLeod is named after. He had also been in the South Africa war with the Canadian Mounted Rifles. Anyway, I got acquainted with the young MacLeod, and he was more or less the one who talked me into joining the force. At this point I was still toying with the idea of going back, because I liked the climate of South Africa.

I had heard of Canada's North West Mounted Police before I came here, but up to that point I never had any thought of joining because

I really liked the South African force, and the only reason that I did leave was that I wanted to see more of the world. I had accumulated a little money because we were sent to some very remote areas in South Africa, where we had nowhere to spend our money. I took a six-month leave, which is what it was, more than a discharge, with the intention of making a round-the-world trip. I only got as far as Canada.

For a short time I was involved in the latter part of the Boer War, which was a very different kind of war from the First and Second World Wars of this century. There was not much mechanization, although they had long-range guns and things like that. It was a war that nobody, except a few leaders, wanted.

Although I was sort of impressed by Canada when I first landed at Quebec City in 1905, I didn't see much of it as I went across Canada by train to Vancouver. I was able to stop off for a day or so in different places like Montreal, Winnipeg, and Calgary, and it was the West that really impressed me.

At the time, Winnipeg was a lot bigger than Vancouver, which was, after all, only nineteen years old in 1905, just a beginning young town. Winnipeg, on the other hand, was a pretty up-to-date city. I don't remember seeing any automobiles at the time, but there were certainly plenty of horses. They did have streetcars on rails, and of course they had a big railroad station which brought people in from all over the world, most of whom would get their supplies in Winnipeg before setting out to start their homesteads. It was a very busy exciting city at that time, with the appearance of a frontier town in some parts. Other parts of the city were very settled and orderly, and looked as if they had been there forever.

A couple of years later I went back to Winnipeg as a member of the North West Mounted Police, accompanying the lieutenant governor of Saskatchewan, the Honourable Amédée Forget, who was the last governor of the Northwest Territories and the first governor of Saskatchewan, which had become a province in 1905. I was what they called his orderly. I got his mail and did chores like that, and I dealt mostly with his secretaries. Nothing very grand, but I was with him when he opened the first bridge over the Saskatchewan River on the way to Battleford. In Winnipeg we put up in the Royal Alexander Hotel which had just been built and was considered pretty grand.

That, too, was the trip where a fellow gave me my first ride in a steam car. The maker of the car was White. You don't see White cars any more, but we had a great time that day, driving all over the place. You know, I never saw one other car on the road that day. They still were a pretty rare thing then, and no matter where we went, people would stop dead in their tracks to stare at us. They had buses pulled by horses in Winnipeg, though, and a few electric trams.

My great love was horses, of course. When I was a boy in England the country was full of horses, and I would ride horseback quite a lot. Even then, I thought that if I could get a job where I could ride horses, then that's what I would do. As it turned out that's what I did, both in South Africa and in Canada.

I joined the force at the main headquarters in Regina. It was only a western force at the time, and there was nothing east of the Manitoba border. It had a complement of about five hundred men when I joined in 1905, and there was no doubt in anybody's mind that it was a good police force. It was also the *Royal* North West Mounted Police by this time, although most people still referred to it as the North West Mounted Police, or the North West Mounted.

My first job was guarding prisoners at Regina, where the guard room was used as a jail. We had quite a few prisoners, and so we had to use the attic of the building as a place to sleep. Actually, it was a good job for a single fellow like me as I could keep my horse in the livery stable and have my meals in the best hotel in town. That was quite a cut above life in the barracks. I did all the jobs a policeman can do in the four years I stayed with the force.

I left the RNWMP in 1909 to join the forestry service and then later joined another mounted force, the British Columbia Provincials. It was just a case of wanting to move on to something else. It was an excellent force, too, and then, just before the outbreak of the First World War, I was sent to the Peace River to become the first and only lawman that country had ever had. The only instructions my superiors gave me were "Do what needs to be done!" They sent me off with two pistols, a rifle, and a horse. That was it! Of course, I was a notary public, a coroner, and, very largely, a game warden.

The Peace River was full of people who were trapping, and that was practically all they existed on. It was very good country, and foxes were very valuable in those days. In addition, they were building the Grand Trunk Railway to Prince Rupert, and we had all those workers, in addition to some settlers who were taking up homesteads.

Of course, some of the railroad workers decided to stay there too, because it was all homestead land around there. With such a varied population, I could see there would be plenty for me to do. It was then that I thought about what Colin Campbell, the head man of the Provincials said when he gave me the job, "If anything goes wrong, just do what you'd do if you were still in the Mounted Police." I thought to myself, "Okay, if I do anything there that you don't like, I'll just say: that's the way we did it in the Mounted Police."

There wasn't even a place for me to start out or take over as the first lawman in the territory. One of my first jobs was to draw up a little plan for the kind of building I would need. Then I hired some homesteaders who knew how to use an axe and they built a log structure for me. That was my home and my office for the next six years.

I handled just about every kind of crime there was, including one murder. The fellow got off, though, because he said his victim had ambushed him and was going to shoot him. He said it was self-defence, and the jury believed him. Perhaps it *was* self-defence. There wasn't a lot of crime, but there was enough that a police presence was necessary.

Mostly the people were good, law-abiding citizens who were anxious to better themselves. In the so-called civilized parts of Canada, land was becoming scarce and expensive, so that the ordinary fellow had little chance of ever owning a piece of property. That's why they migrated to that wild country where land was available to anyone who was willing to work, and most of them were too busy to break the law.

Peace River country was the very best of land, something that was recognized as early as 1793, when Alexander Mackenzie went through there. His first camp was on the Smoky River, which runs right into the Peace, and in his writings he talks about what glorious country it was.

I feel pretty good about establishing the law up there, although that was the job I was sent to do. I believe I did a good job, because my superiors told me they didn't get any complaints. The way I tackled it was in getting around and finding out what they were like. I spent most of my time on horseback. In fact, I stayed on horseback most of my life and I was over eighty years old before I finally had to give it up.

Ray Munro

Those Daring Young Men

Adventure has always played a great part in the history of pioneering, whether it has been in opening up the land or in any other areas of endeavour. The thrill of discovery and the satisfaction of the chase towards goals ranks high among the reasons why individuals perform certain acts. It's the thrill of the new that most often motivates.

What Ray Munro of Oakville, Ontario, wanted to do was fly. His daring exploits as a fighter pilot in the Second World War are a matter of the offical record, and by his own calculations he should have been dead many times.

I took up flying during the latter years of the Depression at the old Barker Field in Toronto, and paid for those lessons by earning a nickel here and there. I wanted to fly so badly I'd do anything to achieve that dream.

By 1939 I had my private license but when war was declared and I went to enlist, I found I couldn't be taken as a pilot because pilots had to have a minimum of one year's university education. That was the requirement at the beginning of the war, but I felt there had to be some way around that. So what finally got me into the air force in 1940 was the fact that I had started my own little illegal airline. I was taking passengers up and charging them a few bucks for a trip.

One day I took a maiden-lady schoolteacher from Iowa on a flight from North Toronto over New Toronto. She wanted to see the place where she had grown up from the air, the school, the church, the old neighbourhood. Getting down over the Queen Elizabeth Highway which had just opened, my engine quit and a lot of smoke was pouring out and I knew the fire extinguisher was under her seat. I reached over to grab for it and instead I grabbed her ankle. She let me have it on the head with her purse and she kept hitting me. She thought I was getting fresh. She opened up a big gash on my forehead and the blood gushed out and blinded me in one eye. I managed to get the plane down and I landed on the highway in front of a big transport truck that was coming full speed right at me. I kicked the engine and it started just enough to get me out of the way and the truck roared by me a split second later.

Well, that started the biggest traffic jam ever seen up to that time, and I felt I was in big trouble! I managed to get the trouble with the plane fixed and I took off and landed safely a little later at Barker Field.

The next day the newspapers had a field day with some pretty imaginative headlines like "Pilot, 18, lands blazing plane" and "Credited with saving passenger's life at risk of his own". It was nonsense, of course, but that afternoon I got a call from the air force inviting me to drop down for a chat, and the next day I was a full-fledged pilot recruit in the RCAF.

That's when I understood why they wanted university-educated recruits, because in the classes that followed I couldn't even spell the trigonometry and calculus that they were teaching, let alone understand them. My education was sadly lacking as my father who was a peripatetic building contractor was constantly moving from place to place all over Canada and the United States. I swear there were some schools where I don't think I attended for longer than six minutes.

That kind of childhood gave me the feeling that you weren't living unless something new was happening all the time. You go or you stop. You live or you die, and everything you do has to be a challenge and a decision and the rewards make it all worthwhile. That's the way it was with me getting through that pilot's course. I had to get through it to get on with my life so I did it. I passed.

Before long I was overseas, flying Spitfires and loving every dangerous minute of it. In 1941 I crashed into the face of a mountain in Scotland because my plane had been sabotaged. I should have had another forty-five minutes of fuel, but it wasn't there and I lost altitude, couldn't do a thing about it, and watched in horror as the mountain came up to meet my plane head on. I survived, although just barely. I was horribly hurt, but my luck held up when a woodsman came along and cut me out of the wreckage and put me on a makeshift sled and dragged me over the hills to a hospital. They patched me up and eventually I was back flying again.

I recall one night when three of us, an RAF pilot, an Ottawa lad named Robillard, and myself, were sent up to intercept a twin-engined German fighter that was coming in. It was just a filthy, rainy, stormy night and in that horrible soup we couldn't spot the plane. It got away from us. Next day we learned that Hitler's deputy, Rudolf Hess, was in that plane.

Shortly after that Robillard and I were sent to what was considered the toughest spot in all of England where Douglas Bader, "the legless air ace" of the Battle of Britain had his wing, and where they had cannon-armed Spitfires. Our role was to fly at thirty-thousand feet and protect the bombers from incoming fighters. One night I had to go out on a lone convoy patrol. My job was to keep fighters and bombers away from the convoy. Generally it was a two-person job. Again it was terrible weather with rain and everything, so I had to go down to four hundred feet very near Cherbourg in France.

Out of the mist I spotted the conning tower of a German submarine and I flew in low and attacked it with cannons, but I did it so suddenly and I was at such a low angle that the cannon shells exploded on the other side of the sub. I missed. I just looped up in the air and came straight down at the sub and pressed the button of my guns. There was an enormous explosion and pieces of shrapnel were flying everywhere. There was a hole in the wing of my plane almost big enough to drop a horse through, and the wing was beginning to fold. My plane just kept rolling and rolling and I was attempting to keep it from crashing. Now, while all of this was going on I kept looking at that hole in my wing and it came to me that it wasn't the shrapnel that did it, and it wasn't shots from one of the enemy fighters in the area. One of my own cannon shells had exploded in the breech. It dawned on me that this is what had killed many of our pilots in previous unexplained missions where they only knew that an explosion had occurred and the planes didn't return.

Well, that knowledge might have saved somebody's life in the future, but at the moment my only thought was saving my own life. There were no seat dinghys in those days and radio silence prevailed, of course, and I was too low to parachute anyway. Besides you would be dead in sixty seconds after your plane hit the water, as the Spitfire will sink in that length of time.

What I did have was a "Mae West" which had to be blown up with a tube, and as I started to do that I discovered it was all full of little holes as if somebody had used it for a dartboard—which could have happened. So there were several reasons why I couldn't land except on land. In the meantime, my plane was corkscrewing through the air getting lower and lower all the time. I finally got it across the Channel, past the Isle of Wight and inland until I could see the little farmer's field we were using as an airfield. I had to crash-land, which meant that although I saved my life I had to spend a long time in hospital.

When I was released from there, Robillard and I were put on the North Sea patrol, protecting all of the convoys which were hugging the coast of England. Robillard got shot down over France. He was captured and escaped and he became the first French-Canadian in the war to be decorated. He is still referred to as "the Ace of Ottawa." He and I were the only two of a group of twenty-six fliers from early in the war who survived. We were the lucky ones.

We should have been dead many times as the war progressed, too, as we were always in one situation or another where it could just as easily have been us as the other guys.

It was luck in a way that we had the Spitfires and the Germans didn't. The Spitfire was a great little plane, agile and very fast for its time. To fly one was breathtaking. One didn't have to ham-hand it through the sky; it was a gentle thing. You could land and take off a Spitfire with your thumb and your forefinger if you trimmed it right and believed in it. At the same time, though, there were many aerobatics that you couldn't do with a Spitfire as it couldn't stand up to them. What you have to remember is that fighters were just gun platforms. They had to be fast and manoeuvreable, but they couldn't dive like a 109, the enemy fighter that we had to contend with. The 109 could outdive you and pull out, but the Spitfire could turn inside it and it was necessary for the Spitfire pilot to know what airplane he was coming up against: to survive you had to know what that airplane could do and where its weak spots were. So many fellows died because they just didn't know. That's why it was so important for the air force to capture an enemy aircraft intact so they could test it and learn what it could and couldn't do.

I don't glorify those days at all. I spend more time thinking of those who died in the prime of their lives. I think about those twenty-four early Spitfire buddies of mine who didn't come back and why two of us were spared. I think of my own brother whom I taught to fly and who was only a year and a half older, and who was a squadron leader while I was just a pilot. He didn't come back. My father was very badly crippled in the First World War. I had many relatives and friends who were killed. So rather than glorify it, I think that war is a terrible thing. No one should ever take pride in it. I don't deny however that is *was* one great adventure. I can relish the memory of that without relishing the memory of war.

By the same token, after the war, and when I'd turned to newspaper reporting and photography, I covered some of the greatest stories of the time. I covered things like the detonation of the atomic bomb, the founding of the United Nations, the Quebec Conference, and all of the big disasters of the time. I was there writing about them and capturing them on film. I was still flying through all of these happenings as staff pilot for these newspapers both in Toronto and on the west coast and I was permitted to do whatever stories I chose with no supervision whatsoever.

I never figured out whether I looked for danger or danger looked for me. It's probably a bit of both as from the time I was a tiny kid I figured that life was meant to be *lived*, that it is supposed to be an adventure. Give it your best shot and don't hurt anybody on the way through. I enjoy life and I always will, I hope, looking to the new day. It's sunrises I like, not sunsets. A sunset means it's all over. There's adventure promised in a sunrise.

Bill Houston

The Voice of the Pioneer

In January of this year, I received a letter from Bill Houston of Thunder Bay, Ontario. By happy coincidence he had met Hugh MacKay Ross, one of the pioneers in this book, and both the two men had discovered that Bill's father had come out to Canada on the same ship together in 1930, after which time Hugh Ross and Paddy Houston had lost touch with each other.

Bill Houston writes, "As a child, I simply took for granted the fact that my parents had lived all over the North in the 1930s and '40s and took little note that the phrase 'roughing it' is just a pioneer's way of saying 'pioneering.' And so, in an attempt to repay some of what I owe them, I have written this song. I am sending it to you as creator of 'Voice of the Pioneer' and I thought you should be the first to hear of a song by that title. I hope you enjoy it."

I enjoy it very much and would like to share it with you here.

Come, all you lads and rovers,
And listen to my song
Before my days are over
And my memories are gone,
'Twas in the spring of nineteen' nine
Not long before the war
In a land of strife and trouble
This Belfast boy was born;

Singin', sail away to Canada
For there's nothin' for you here;
Go join the boys who hearken to
The voice of the pioneer.

'Twas on the *Duchess of Bedford*
Of June, the nineteenth day
The year was nineteen-thirty
That we sailed from Liverpool way,
We were twenty-four and twenty more,
As green as green can be,
Each with a five-year contract
With the Hudson's Bay Company

"Come away to high adventure"—
The sound of the call was clear—
"Go dream the dreams that must be dreamed,"
Said the voice of the pioneer.

When we landed, none the worse for wear,
In the port of Montreal
We were handed sealed instructions
Telling what would soon befall.
Well, we all shook hands and bid farewell,
Except for a lingering few,
And boarded trains for parts unknown
In a land we barely knew.

But come, all you lads and rovers,
Whether you be far or near,
And listen very carefully
For it's this that you must hear:
Though the hardships, they were many,
They were taken with good cheer
And I'm glad I'm one who hearkened to
The voice of the pioneer.

Bill Houston
November 28, 1987